5/23/97

The VRML 2.0 Handbook

Building Moving Worlds on the Web

Jed Hartman
Josie Wernecke

Silicon Graphics, Inc.

D1410675

Addison-Wesley Publishing Company
Reading, Massachusetts   Menlo Park, California
New York   Don Mills, Ontario   Harlow, England
Amsterdam   Bonn   Sydney   Singapore   Tokyo   Madrid
San Juan   Paris   Seoul   Milan   Mexico City   Taipei

Silicon Graphics, the Silicon Graphics logo, and IRIS are registered trademarks and Inventor, Open Inventor, WebSpace, and Cosmo, are trademarks of Silicon Graphics, Inc. Java is a trademark of Sun Microsystems, Inc. Netscape Navigator and Netsite are trademarks of Netscape Communications Corporation. formZ is a trademark of autoInc. 3D Studio is a trademark of Autodesk, Inc., in the USE and/or other countries. Ez3d Modeler is a registered trademark of Radiance Software International. World Builder Foutain is a trademark of Caligari Corporation. UNIX is a registered trademark in the United States and other countries, licensed exclusively through X/Open Company, Ltd. Windows NT is a trademark of Microsoft Corporation. Gauntlet is a trademark of Trusted Information Systems, Inc. PostScript is a registered trademark of Adobe Systems Incorporated.

The authors and publisher have taken care in preparation of this book, but make no expressed or implied warranty of any kind and assume no responsibility for errors or omissions. No liability is assumed for incidental or consequential damages in connection with or arising out of the use of the information or programs contained herein.

Library of Congress Cataloging-in-Publication Data

Hartman, Jed.
    The VRML 2.0 handbook: building moving worlds on the web / Jed Hartman and Josie Wernecke.
       p.   cm.
    Includes index.
    ISBN 0-201-47944-3
     1. Computer Graphics. 2. VRML (Document markup language)
   3. Three-dimensional display systems. 4. World Wide Web
(Information retrieval system) I. Wernecke, Josie. II. Title.
T385.H3475 1996
006--dc20
                                     96-23156
                                         CIP

Sponsoring Editor: Kim Fryer
Project Manager: John Fuller
Cover Image: Delle Rae Maxwell
Cover Design: Jean Seal
Internal Art: Dany Galgani
Text Design: Electric Ink, Ltd., and Kay Maitz

Addison-Wesley books are available for bulk purchases by corporations, institutions, and other organizations. For more information please contact the Corporate, Government, and Special Sales Department at (800) 238-9682.

Find A-W Developers Press on the World-Wide Web at:
http://www.aw.com/devpress/

First Printing, August 1996

1 2 3 4 5 6 7 8 9–MA–0099989796

Through knowledge we behold the World's creation.

—Spenser

To my father, Peter, and my late mother, Marcy, the first and the best teachers of writing and computing I ever had.

—JH

To Steve—husband, friend, and cheering squad.

—JW

Contents

Figures

Examples

Foreword

In June, 1994, VRML was just a concept—three dimensional graphics on the Internet—and a four-letter acronym. Since then, VRML's rapid evolution has been surprising for several different reasons.

VRML is a two-year-old whirlwind that is still rapidly growing. This whirlwind is driven by several intangible properties of the VRML definition process that make VRML special.

The first is the open forum in which VRML was created. Encouraging a few thousand people to be involved in designing a new technology was a frightening concept. However, the immediate and interactive input from such a broad range of people, both creative and technical, was invaluable to the design process. VRML was created "out in the open," with the goal of building a standard that not only worked, but was accessible to everybody and not dominated or controlled by any one company or person. Because the process was open, thousands of would-be customers and developers got involved and provided information that no marketing study could ever match. The success of VRML is proof that the true power of the Internet is its ability to bring people with a shared interest together, allowing them to create things faster, better, and cheaper than ever before.

The second intangible property driving the tremendous growth of VRML is how accessible a technology it is. Technology can be put on a scale that ranges from "interesting but impractical pure research" to "boring but well-tested old technologies." There is a gap in the middle of this scale where very powerful technologies reside. VRML is advanced enough to capture the excitement and imagination of developers, and yet it is simple enough to be both practical and accessible. There has always been an unwritten rule that we only tackle problems that are truly understood and for which we can provide final solutions. Experimental extensions are encouraged, with the expectation that today's experimental extensions may be tomorrow's VRML standard.

Last is the vision shared by many people that VRML will be the next revolutionary user interface technology. The explosion of information, computers, and people all interacting with each other over the world-wide network requires a new user interface metaphor. The windows-based desktops of today were created to allow a single person to interact with a single computer; VRML allows the creation of virtual three-dimensional spaces in which other people can be included. Imagine a library that contains all of the world's information. Now imagine that this library is a building that has no doors and only one small window that can display one page of one book to one person at a time. This is the Internet today. The Internet of tomorrow will require standards that break out of this restrictive interface, allowing people to interact not only with a single web page, but with the ever-changing global information stream and with each other. VRML has been designed from the beginning to be the first step toward this vision.

It is an exciting time to be involved in VRML. The open process means that anybody can have a dramatic impact on its evolution. This book will teach you everything you need to know to be a VRML expert, ready to help define where VRML goes next. We would like to thank everyone involved so far for a great adventure, and we look forward to seeing your VRML creations on the Net!

GAVIN BELL

RIKK CAREY

Acknowledgments

Many people besides those listed as authors contributed to the creation of this book. Perhaps foremost among them were those who spearheaded the VRML 2.0 development effort—Rikk Carey, Gavin Bell, and Chris Marrin—and Delle Maxwell, who brought the Tenochtitlán model to life.

Our production editor, Laura Cooper, deserves high praise for the long hours she put in working on color plates, acquiring permission to use various images, keeping track of rapidly changing schedules, and coordinating with Addison-Wesley.

The Cosmo engineers at Silicon Graphics were immensely helpful throughout the writing process. Despite the intense pressure to get a product out the door, they somehow found time to review drafts, make dozens of helpful suggestions, and debug examples. Rob Myers provided enormous help with scripting; Rick Pasetto implemented everything we needed to test our examples in the Silicon Graphics Cosmo Player browser; the Cosmo managers, Helga Thorvaldsdöttir, Jackie Neider, and David Story, went to great lengths to provide us with engineering support. Sam Chen and Clay Graham provided reviews, enthusiasm, and numerous VRML examples. Dave "Ciemo" Ciemiewicz, Dave Immel, Chris Fouts, and Paul Strauss provided us with innumerable patient and clear answers to technical questions, as well as several detailed draft reviews.

Sumana Srinivasan and Aaron Siri stepped in to help with scripting examples when we needed them most.

Our editor, Cindy Kleinfeld, corrected our English; any remaining grammatical errors in the text are in spite of her careful reading. At Addison-Wesley, Keith Wollman provided steady guidance and a voice of calm amid the prevailing atmosphere of incessant panic.

Our managers (Linda Johnson, Maria Chambers, and Channing Hughes) allowed us free rein on a project that took far longer than anyone ever expected. Other writers at Silicon Graphics provided the moral support that kept us going.

Finally, we'd like to thank the VRML mailing list, and everyone else who helped make VRML 2.0 useful, efficient, and usable.

Individual acknowledgments from the individual authors:

I'd like to thank my friends, particularly my housemate Arthur Evans, for putting up with me and providing much-needed moral support through a year of delays, frustrations, and constant schedule changes. I'd also like to thank Josie for being such a great co-author; I would never have made it through this book on my own.

—JH

Deepest thanks to my family—Steve, Jeff, and Evan—for cheerfully tolerating my preoccupation with this project for almost a year. And special thanks to Jed, my co-author. Through luck of the draw, Jed's chapters included some of the thorniest issues, which he steadfastly pursued to the bitter end. It's been a rewarding journey.

—JW

About This Book

This handbook is intended to guide both experienced VRML authors and true neophytes through the process of creating a 3D world, fine-tuning its performance, and publishing it on the World Wide Web. It is designed for a broad audience that ranges from artistic content providers with little programming background to seasoned Internet hackers with modest graphical skills.

This book begins with a tutorial that leads you through the creation of a single, fully developed example world, the ceremonial center of the ancient Aztec city of Tenochtitlán, which just happens to include samples of almost all the objects in the VRML 2.0 specification. Since performance efficiency remains a key concern for the VRML author, general guidelines on using VRML objects are a primary focus of this handbook. The final chapters of the book are detailed alphabetical reference sections describing all VRML 2.0 syntax.

Chapter 2, "Getting Plugged Into the World Wide Web," offers general guidelines for selecting software and hardware and for getting started. Because VRML files are simple readable text files, you can create them with nothing more than a text editor or word processor and perhaps a few 3D clip-art libraries. Most people, however, will rely on authoring tools that help them create their own 3D models and flesh out the scene. These tools let you concentrate on the content of the scene without worrying about the details of VRML syntax. The most sophisticated authoring systems provide additional features tailored to VRML, such as editors for level of detail, behavior scripting, and textures, and tools for creating inlined objects.

In general, the more sophisticated your authoring tool, the less you'll need to know about VRML syntax and file structure. This handbook provides the behind-the-scenes details of how VRML works so that you can tweak the final output of your authoring system to optimize your files, or take advantage of some of VRML's "power" features such as prototyping, scripting, animation, and interpolators, which may not be supported in some authoring tools.

What This Book Contains

This book contains the following chapters:

- Chapter 1, "Introduction," describes possible applications for VRML and gives a short history of the development of the language as well as a summary of features added in the latest VRML release.

- Chapter 2, "Getting Plugged Into the World Wide Web," provides general guidelines for selecting software and hardware to view, create, and publish VRML files on the World Wide Web.

- Chapter 3, "Exploring and Building a World," describes some of the key VRML objects, including level-of-detail, anchor, inline, and viewpoint nodes. It describes the basic structure of a VRML file and important related concepts such as scope and inheritance. This is the first of six tutorial chapters based on the Aztec world.

- Chapter 4, "Building Objects," provides step-by-step instructions for creating one of the temples in the Aztec city. It introduces simple shape and appearance property objects.

- Chapter 5, "Lighting, Sound, and Complex Shapes," continues the tutorial, covering additional objects such as lights, sounds, elevation grids, and a simple extruded-shape node.

- Chapter 6, "Animation and User Interaction," explains how to route events from one node to another, and how to use this capability to animate objects in your world. It also describes the sensor and interpolator objects that keep animations moving.

- Chapter 7, "Scripting," demonstrates using simple programs called scripts to enhance animation and process user input. It provides example scripts in the JavaScript scripting language.

- Chapter 8, "Using Colors, Normals, and Textures," describes how to specify colors for individual polygon faces and vertices, how to specify surface normals, how to apply textures to objects, and how to specify background panoramas and colors for your scene.

- Chapter 9, "Publishing Your Work," provides general guidelines for publishing VRML files on the World Wide Web.

- Chapter 10, "Improving Performance," offers a detailed checklist for optimizing VRML files.

- Chapter 11, "Node Reference," and Chapter 12, "Field Reference," are alphabetical listings of all VRML nodes and fields, complete with default values, and detailed descriptions of how to use them. These chapters are derived directly from the VRML 2.0 Specification, whose primary authors are Gavin Bell, Rikk Carey, and Chris Marrin.

- Appendix A, "Obsolete Nodes," lists the VRML 2.0 equivalents of VRML 1.0 nodes that are now obsolete.

- Appendix B, "Java Notes and Examples," provides general information on using Java in scripts, and Java versions of the scripting examples from Chapter 7, "Scripting."

- The Glossary lists and defines common terms and concepts used in this book.

How to Use This Book

To download the examples found in this book, go to

`http://vrml.sgi.com/handbook/examples`

If you're new to VRML and the World Wide Web, you'll want to pay special attention to the following chapters:

- This chapter, which points you to additional sources of information

- Chapter 1, "Introduction"

- Chapter 2, "Getting Plugged Into the World Wide Web"

- Chapter 3, "Exploring and Building a World"

- Chapter 4, "Building Objects"

- Chapter 9, "Publishing Your Work"

- Chapter 11, "Node Reference"

- Chapter 12, "Field Reference"

These chapters lead you through the process of creating a simple world and publishing it on the Web.

To learn how to create more efficient VRML files, take a look at Chapter 10, "Improving Performance." When you're comfortable with the basics, move on to the more advanced node types described in Chapter 5, "Lighting, Sound, and Complex Shapes," Chapter 6, "Animation and User Interaction," Chapter 7, "Scripting," and Chapter 8, "Using Colors, Normals, and Textures." Some of the nodes described in Chapters 6 and 7 are actually very easy to use, while others, such as the Script node, require programming experience.

If you are an experienced programmer, are familiar with 3D graphics, and already know your way around the Web, you'll probably take the opposite path. Here's a recommendation:

- Skim Chapters 1 through 5. You can probably skip Chapter 2, "Getting Plugged Into the World Wide Web," since you're probably already up and running.

- Read Chapter 6, "Animation and User Interaction" and Chapter 7, "Scripting."

- Read and experiment with Chapter 8, "Using Colors, Normals, and Textures."

- Read Chapter 10, "Improving Performance," for tips on how to improve performance.

- Use Chapter 11, "Node Reference," and Chapter 12, "Field Reference," as general resources.

Conventions Used in This Book

Three icons are used to highlight information in the text.

 The Performance Tip icon indicates information about optimizing your VRML files. This icon shows a jaguar racing at top speed.

 The Artistic Tip icon indicates a tip or trick for using VRML nodes. This icon shows a vase with the face of the Aztec god, Tlaloc, carved on its sides.

 The Technical Tip icon indicates advanced technical information that can be skipped on the first reading. This icon shows the Aztec calendar.

Certain words receive special treatment or fonts. Node names are capitalized:

- WorldInfo node
- Anchor node

Italic type is used for filenames and field names, as well as for new terms or terms defined in the Glossary:

- *Tenochtitlan.wrl*, *History.html*
- *title* field, *name* field, *rotation* field
- the term *culling*, a *billboard*

VRML file format examples and URLs are in typewriter font:

- `http://vrml.sgi.com/handbook/tenochtitlan.wrl`

File format examples use boldface type to emphasize the focus of the discussion:

```
#VRML V2.0 utf8

Shape {
  appearance  NULL
  geometry    Cylinder { }
}
```

Related Reading

For a general introduction to computer graphics, see the following:

- *Computer Graphics Principles and Practice* by J.D. Foley, A. van Dam, S. Feiner, and J.F. Hughes (Addison-Wesley, 1990).
- *The Art of 3-D Computer Animation and Imaging* by Isaac Victor Kerlow (Van Nostrand Reinhold, 1996).

For general information on HTML publishing on the World Wide Web, consult the following sources:

- *Teach Yourself Web Publishing with HTML in a Week* by Laura Lemay (Sams Publishing, 1995).
- *HTML for Fun and Profit* by Mary E. S. Morris (SunSoft Press, 1995).
- *HTML Manual of Style* by Larry Aronson (Ziff-Davis Press, 1994).

Of course, the best place to learn about the Web is the Web itself. Places to start include the following:

- The VRML Repository, maintained by the San Diego Supercomputer Center. This site contains pointers to many other sources, including bibliographies, mailing lists, and newsgroups related to VRML.

  `http://www.sdsc.edu/vrml/`

- The VRML home page hosted by *Wired* magazine:

  `http://vrml.wired.com`

- The Silicon Graphics VRML Web site:

  `http://vrml.sgi.com`

- The VRML Architecture Group Web site: `http://vag.vrml.org`

About the Aztec Site

This examples from this book are taken from a single case study, a VRML re-creation of the ceremonial center of the ancient Aztec city of Tenochtitlán. The site is located at

`http://vrml.sgi.com/handbook`

Since most of the original structures have been destroyed, the model is based on educated conjectures, archaeological finds, the work of others, and a bit of artistic and architectural imagination. The original architectural model was created by Ignacio Marquina and is displayed at the National Museum of Anthropology in Mexico City. Marquina based his model on readings of sixteenth-century texts and on modern archaeological finds at the site in Mexico City. The original computer model, created by Bob Galbraith, was based on photographs of Marquina's physical model and on readings by Galbraith in modern texts. And finally, for the Tenochtitlán Web site, Delle Maxwell took Galbraith's AutoCAD model and reconstructed it in VRML, so that it is navigable in real time.

Color, texture, and more models were added and some minor inaccuracies were corrected. Animation, sounds, level-of-detail groups, references to supporting documents and pictures, narrative and background information were then incorporated. The original scale of the AutoCAD model of 1 unit equals 1 foot was retained. The walls measure 1440 feet (approximately 440 meters) on a side. This size was based on estimates given in a number of texts describing Tenochtitlán.

Credits

The quotation from a letter by Cortes in Figure 3-2 is reproduced with permission from *Five Letters of Cortes to the Emperor*, translated and with an introduction by J. Bayard Morris (W.W. Norton and Company, 1991).

The poem in Figure 3-5 is reproduced with permission from *Fifteen Poets of the Aztec World,* by Miguel León-Portilla (University of Oklahoma Press, 1992).

The Coyolxauhqui stone image in Figure 3-10 and the skull frieze used in the small temple are reproduced with permission from *Moctezuma's Mexico: Visions of the Aztec World*, by David Carrasco and Eduardo Matos Moctezuma (University Press of Colorado, 1992).

The Changing VRML World

As with everything on the Web, the VRML specification continues to evolve. At the time of publication, incremental releases are planned for the scripting language API and for multi-user support. For the current version of the VRML specification, go to the following location:

```
http://vag.vrml.org
```

This book is consistent with version 2.0 of the VRML specification.

Chapter 1

Introduction

The Virtual Reality Modeling Language (VRML) allows you to describe 3D objects and combine them into scenes and worlds. You can use VRML to create interactive simulations that incorporate animation, motion physics, and real-time, multi-user participation. The virtual landscapes you create can be distributed using the World Wide Web, displayed on another user's computer screen, and explored interactively by remote users. The VRML standard is defined by an advisory committee, the VRML Architecture Group (VAG), which continues to expand the language.

The uses of VRML are as varied as the 3D objects in our world today. Consider these possibilities:

- A family of four wants to purchase tickets to see the local ice hockey team play at the new arena. Tickets range from $20 to $40—but is the difference in price worth the cost? At the local ticket office or on your home computer, you can type in the seat location and view a simulated game from different seat locations. Then, you can decide for yourself if the seats are worth the extra expense.

- The frescoes in the Italian chapel have long been destroyed, but enough data remains to reconstruct the chapel in its earlier form. Using architectural models to create the building and image-scanning techniques to create the frescoes themselves, the chapel can be reassembled into a VRML file so that art history students can walk through the chapel corridors, look up at the ceiling frescoes, and see how the light through the windows hits the paintings at various times of the day. Additional information about the frescoes is provided by a guided audio tour and by interactive hot links on each fresco.

- The skid marks cross the road, the tree limbs overhead are broken at jagged angles, and the dirt along the roadside shows marks from heavy impact and tire treads. How did the accident occur and who's at fault? Road conditions, reported traveling speeds, and point of approach can be fed into a traffic simulation program at the Department of Motor Vehicles headquarters. Then using available data to see if the results corroborate the "facts" reported by both parties, analysts can re-create the accident and view it on the computer screen.

- A jewelry designer works with long-distance clients who want to be sure that the final creation meets with their initial expectations. Instead of sending a sketch of the planned design, the jeweler models a necklace using VRML authoring tools, then sends the design over the Web to the customer. Although he can't hold the real object in his hand, the client can examine the necklace from all angles, check the shape of the bezel, and determine the height of the stone set into the base. Any desired changes can be requested at the design stage, before costly materials and labor have been invested in the fabrication stage.

Applications for VRML range from the serious (medical imaging, molecular modeling, engineering and design, architecture), to the more entertaining (games, advertising of all varieties, virtual theme parks), to the mundane realities of everyday life (selecting and placing furniture in the living room, planning a weekend hike at a county park, repairing a carburetor).

VRML is not a programming language like C or Java, nor is it a "markup language" like HTML. It's a modeling language, which means you use it to describe 3D scenes. It's more complex than HTML, but less complex (except for the scripting capability described in Chapter 7) than a programming language.

3D Models versus 2D Images

VRML provides a highly efficient format for describing simple and complex 3D objects and worlds. It needs to be efficient, since VRML files are sent over slow telephone lines as well as faster ISDN and leased lines, and since the computers used to view the files range from low-end PCs to top-of-the-line supercomputers.

The power of VRML becomes apparent if you compare viewing a 2D image to exploring a VRML world. Suppose, for example, that you have six images of a certain area in San Francisco and a VRML file containing data describing the same general area. The images are flat rectangles showing a particular view of the city. All you can do with them is look at them. Each pixel in each image has a fixed, unchanging value.

With a VRML file, however, you can view the scene from an infinite number of viewpoints. The browser (the software that displays a VRML file) has navigation tools that allow you to travel through the scene, taking as many different paths as you desire, repeating your journey, or exploring new territory according to your whim. The VRML world can also contain animated images, sounds, and movies to further enrich the experience.

Sometimes, too, a 2D image just doesn't convey the same amount of information as a 3D model. For example, consider the diagram shown in the right portion of Plate 21, which illustrates how to assemble a desk.

The left portion of Plate 21 shows a 3D presentation of the same object. The added depth dimension makes it much easier to relate the illustration to the real-world desk pieces lying in the carton. What happens when it's time to put the desk together? With the animation features provided by VRML 2.0, you could create an application that would allow the user to click a part shown on the screen, then watch it snap together with the adjoining pieces. If the user didn't understand what was happening, he or she could click again to separate the pieces, then repeat the process until it made sense. To see how the pieces fit together at the back, the user could turn the part around and view it from the desired angle.

Cutting-Edge Technology

Whether the final goal is educational, commercial, or technical, most compelling VRML worlds have certain characteristics in common:

- A VRML world is immersive.

  The user enters this 3D world on the computer screen and explores it as he or she would explore part of the real world. Each person can chart a different course through this world.

- The user, not the computer, controls the experience.

  The local browser allows the user to explore the VRML world in any way he or she decides. The computer doesn't provide a fixed set of choices or prescribe which path to follow, although the VRML author can suggest recommendations. The possibilities are unlimited.

- A VRML world is interactive.

  Objects in the world can respond to one another and to external events caused by the user. The user can "reach in" to the scene and change elements in it.

- A VRML world blends 2D and 3D objects, animation, and multimedia effects into a single medium.

VRML is a powerful tool, but like all power tools, it must be used carefully and effectively. If you've already started to explore different VRML sites on the Web, you've probably been impressed with the beauty and creativity of the best sites, and disappointed in the content and painful slowness of others. Because VRML technology is relatively new, designers and programmers are just learning how to work with it. Authoring tools are still under development, so VRML authors have to rely on doing some things "by hand" until a well developed set of tools exists for all platforms. Chapter 10, "Improving Performance," addresses the issues of performance and efficiency, which are key concerns for effective use of this evolving language and technology.

A Brief Look at the Development of VRML

A major goal of 3D computer graphics has long been to create a realistic-looking world on a computer screen. As long ago as 1965, Ivan Sutherland suggested that the ultimate computer display would "make the picture...look real [and] sound real and the objects act real" (quoted from *Computer Graphics* V26 #3). Almost twenty years later, with researchers and programmers still striving for that realism, William Gibson's novel *Neuromancer* took the science fiction world by storm and incidentally refined the graphics target. From that point on, the goal was to create not just a realistic simulated environment, but "cyberspace"—a *shared* virtual-reality experience based on interaction between users over a network.

The first major combination of networking and graphics in the real world, however, involved only 2D images. The World Wide Web, the brainchild of Tim Berners-Lee, is essentially a graphical interface to the Internet. Launched in 1991, the Web immediately began to blossom into the major marketing phenomenon it is today. Coincidentally, 1991 also saw the publication of Neal Stephenson's novel *Snow Crash*, which has almost supplanted *Neuromancer* as a blueprint of the sought-after cyberspace of the future. The Web provided one of the three threads that interwove to form VRML—the foundation on which the language was built.

The second strand, though it didn't seem related at the time, appeared the following year, with the introduction of the Inventor™ graphics toolkit from Silicon Graphics. Inventor allows programmers to quickly develop interactive 3D graphics programs of all sorts, based on concepts of scene structure and object description. But Inventor, versatile as it is, has little in particular to do with networks. Inventor later was to provide the technical basis for VRML.

But the third strand was the one that brought everything together and sparked the creation of VRML. It came a year and a half after Inventor's release, at the first annual World Wide Web (WWW) conference in May 1994 in Geneva. Mark Pesce and Tony Parisi had been working for months on a virtual-reality interface to the Web. They brought their ideas to a scheduled Birds-of-a-Feather (BOF) session about virtual reality and found an enthusiastic audience.

The BOF group decided to develop a scene-description language that could be used in conjunction with the Web. The term *VRML*, coined at the BOF meeting, originally stood for "Virtual Reality Markup Language," analogous to the Web's HyperText Markup Language. The word "Markup" was later changed, for accuracy, to "Modeling."

Within a month, Pesce and Brian Behlendorf of *Wired* magazine had established a mailing list of people interested in developing a specification for VRML. During its first week of life, the list grew to include over a thousand members.

One of those members was Gavin Bell, an Inventor engineer at Silicon Graphics. He saw the enormous potential of using Inventor (which by now had evolved into a nonproprietary format called Open Inventor™) as a basis for the VRML specification. During one of the Inventor team's infamous weekly lunches, he told his manager, Rikk Carey, about VRML and about the need to settle quickly on a language for describing 3D scenes over the Web. By the end of lunch, Carey was converted to the cause.

Meanwhile, back on the mailing list, Mark Pesce had called for a draft specification for VRML to be prepared in only five months, in time to be presented that October at the second WWW conference. It was an ambitious schedule, but list participants were confident that a limited version of the language could be worked out in that time. There was general agreement that adapting an existing modeling language would be easier than creating an entirely new one. And so the search began.

Bell presented the Silicon Graphics proposal within a couple of weeks: a modified subset of the Open Inventor 3D Metafile format, with appropriate additions to handle networking. Silicon Graphics agreed to make this new file format publicly available and nonproprietary.

Debate flared on the list, evenhandedly moderated by Pesce and Behlendorf. Several other worthy proposals were contemplated and discussed, but the Silicon Graphics proposal won the vote, which meant that VRML would be based on the Open Inventor file format. At the WWW conference in October 1994, the VRML 1.0 draft specification was unveiled.

Paul Strauss, another Silicon Graphics engineer and the original architect of Open Inventor, began working on a public-domain parser for VRML, known as QvLib. This parser translates VRML files from their readable text format into a format understandable by a browser. QvLib was released in January 1995. The parser was ported to various platforms, and browsers began to spring up like mushrooms after a rain.

One of the first complete browsers available (that is, a browser that could interpret and display all of VRML) was the WebSpace™ Navigator from Silicon Graphics, written by David Mott and various other Inventor engineers. Template Graphics Software swiftly ported WebSpace from the Silicon Graphics platform to several other platforms, and all versions of WebSpace Navigator were made available at no cost.

In the fall of 1995, Silicon Graphics followed up with WebSpace Author, a Web authoring tool that provided the ability to interactively place objects in scenes, improve performance of scenes, and publish VRML files. At the same time, the VRML Architecture Group (VAG) met to discuss the next version of VRML.

During early 1996, the VRML community read and discussed a number of proposals for VRML 2.0, including the Moving Worlds proposal from Silicon Graphics, HoloWeb from Sun Microsystems, ActiveVRML from Microsoft, Out of This World from Apple, and others. Many members of the VRML community participated in revising and reshaping some of the proposals, particularly Moving Worlds, during the course of this review period. When the polls closed in February, Moving Worlds had received over 70 percent of the votes. In March 1996, the VAG decided to adopt that proposal as VRML 2.0, to be finalized by August 1996.

What's New in VRML 2.0?

The first version of VRML allowed you to create static 3D worlds. Objects in the world could be hyperlinked to other worlds, as well as to HTML documents.

If you've used VRML 1.0, you may want an overview of what's changed in VRML 2.0. With the second release of VRML, objects inside a world can move and can respond to both time-based and user-initiated events. With this release, for example, the desk application described earlier could add a feature that causes two pieces to snap into place whenever the user clicks on one of them. VRML 2.0 also allows you to incorporate multimedia objects such as sound and movies in your scenes.

New VRML 2.0 features can be grouped into four main areas:

- Enhanced static worlds
- Interaction
- Animation and behavior scripting
- Prototyping new VRML objects

If you're new to VRML, you can skim the following sections to get an idea of recent developments, or you can skip them entirely and move on to Chapter 2, "Getting Plugged Into the World Wide Web."

Enhanced Static Worlds

A number of new features in VRML 2.0 make the scene look and feel more lifelike. The *sound* node allows you to add chirping crickets, banging drums, or speech to your scene. The *elevation grid* node describes a rectangular grid of varying height that's useful and efficient for modeling terrain. The *extrusion* node is actually a simple modeling tool that lets you create extrusions, surfaces of revolution, and shapes formed by bending, twisting, and tapering different types of curves. The *background* node lets you describe a background panorama for your scene, such as mountains, plains, or some other distant landscape, as well as color gradations for the sky and ground. You can also create foggy atmospheres through use of the *fog* node. A new kind of texture node allows you to show movie clips within your scene. Combining this *movie texture* node with the *audio clip* node provides you with true multimedia resources: video and sound.

If you're already familiar with VRML 1.0, or with Inventor programming, you'll notice that the scene graph structure has been greatly simplified in VRML 2.0. A new *shape* node encapsulates both appearance and geometry, and appearance properties are no longer inherited within the file.

Interaction

The addition of behavior information to 3D objects in VRML files opens up vast new possibilities for creating realistic real-time global simulations for the World Wide Web. A *collision detection* node contains collision information so that, for example, you can no longer walk through walls in the scene. *Sensors* are nodes that wait for a particular event to occur and then do something in response to that event. For example, one kind of sensor can wait until the camera gets to a certain point in the scene and then trigger a change in part of the scene in response to the proximity of the user—perhaps by opening a door or turning on a light.

Animation and Behavior Scripting

Interpolators, another behavior feature added in 2.0, enable you to incorporate keyframe animation into your scene. You supply the object description at certain critical points, and then the interpolator performs the calculations for the in-between descriptions. For the opening door, you would need to describe the door only once and then give the door-closed and door-open positions. Using the interpolator, the door could open and close without additional information.

The *script* node is another key addition to the latest VRML release. You can think of this node as a custom black box that can contain its own scripts (routines written in a programming language such as Netscape's JavaScript or Sun Microsystems' Java™). The script can perform simple logic or complex analyses of user and environmental events in the scene and respond in some intelligent way. Scripts are especially useful for complex simulations. For example, you could create a football simulation in which you play the quarterback and control the plays, and the opposing cyberspace team responds appropriately to your movements and strategies.

Prototyping

VRML comes with a fixed set of objects, called *nodes*, which will cover most of your needs. But its creators have also planned ahead, knowing that you'll sometimes have to create your own objects, and you'll often want to assemble the same types of nodes in similar ways, with only small changes. The prototyping feature added to VRML 2.0 lets you create complex objects that you can reuse, changing certain characteristics of the objects when desired.

VRML File Information

Several features added in the second VRML release provide clues to browsers and allow you to store additional information with the file. The *navigation information* node describes the type of navigation style most appropriate to the VRML file—should users walk through the scene, fly through the scene, or examine it in their virtual hands? This object also lets you specify the speed with which the viewer moves through the scene and whether the browser should turn its headlight on. The *world information* node lets you specify a title for the file and other information that needs to travel with the file, such as facts about the author and copyright.

Chapter 2

Getting Plugged Into the World Wide Web

This chapter provides general guidelines for selecting and configuring the software and hardware necessary to create, view, and publish VRML worlds on the World Wide Web. Because of the wide variety of software packages available and the diversity of user needs, a detailed description of software installation and hardware configuration is beyond the scope of this book. The goal of this chapter is to provide you with a basic understanding of the options available so that you can select the appropriate solution for your purposes. Key concepts and terms relating to accessing documents on the World Wide Web are also introduced here. If you are already a seasoned Web surfer, you can probably skip this chapter entirely.

Locating Documents on the Web

Each document or file on the Web has a unique URL (Uniform Resource Locator) that consists of three parts:

- *protocol* used to retrieve the document (protocols are discussed further in the next section)

- *name of the computer* serving the document

- *path* specifying where the document is located on the server computer (or the program to run on the server that will return the document)

For example:

```
http://vrml.sgi.com/handbook/index.html
```

Note: URLs are case-sensitive. They are also subject to change. Check the *VRML 2.0 Handbook* home page (listed on the previous page) for updated URL information.

A VRML file contains the description of a 3D world that is meant to be navigated in real time. If it's small, you might call it a *scene*. If it seems large and immersive, you might call it a *world*. Technically, it can also be called a *document*, but that term seems less descriptive of the contents.

A VRML scene that you create and publish has its own URL. Within that scene, you can also use URLs to specify links or inline references to other files, textures, and scenes to include within your file. Chapter 3 discusses links (*anchor nodes* in VRML terms) and references (*inline nodes*) in more detail.

Browser and Server

There are two key elements in any Web transaction: a browser and a server. The action begins when the user requests a document (for example, by specifying a URL in the *location* field of a browser or by clicking an icon linked to a VRML world). A *browser* is a computer program that runs locally on the user's computer. This program sends user requests to the server and displays the documents sent by the server. Popular Web browsers include Mosaic by NCSA and Netscape Navigator™ by Netscape Communications Corporation.

A *Web server* is a computer program that handles requests for documents located on a particular host computer. The Web server locates the requested document and sends it over the network to the requesting client (usually a browser). There are several public-domain server programs, including *httpd*, available from NCSA (National Center for Supercomputing Applications) or from CERN (European Particle Physics Laboratory), and *Apache*, available at `http://www.apache.org`. Commercial server packages are also available from companies such as Netscape Communications (see `http://www.netscape.com`).

The browser communicates with the server using a particular communications protocol such as HTTP, FTP, or Gopher. HTTP (HyperText Transfer Protocol) is a popular protocol for transferring hypertext documents written in HTML (HyperText Markup Language), as well as VRML files, over the network.

Some browsers can display documents containing both HTML and VRML. Others are more specialized and can display only HTML documents. These browsers require an additional VRML mini-browser, sometimes referred to as a "plug-in," to render a 3D scene and view it in real time. (Chapter 10, "Improving Performance," gives you an idea of the sophisticated tasks some VRML browsers perform.) For a detailed list of Web browsers, visit this URL:

```
http://www.yahoo.com/Computers_and_Internet/Internet/
    World_Wide_Web/Browsers/
```

Viewing VRML Scenes

If you're new to the Web, you probably want to spend some time exploring, so the first thing to do is to set up your Internet connection. This section outlines some general considerations and points you to further sources of information. The type of Internet access and network connection you select depends on a number of factors, including your purpose for connecting to the Web (business or recreation; serving or browsing), whether you plan to publish a few or many documents on the Web, the size of your audience, and, of course, your budget.

Types of Internet Access

You can choose one of the following types of access to the Internet:

- Gateway service
- Dial-up direct connection
- Dedicated direct connection

Gateway Service

A gateway service is an Internet connection offered by a network service provider such as Prodigy, America OnLine, or CompuServe. When you dial the service provider, you are connected to one of its computers, which in turn connects to the Internet. In addition to the Internet connection, a gateway service provides a variety of other features, including real-time chat rooms, online newspapers, and advertising space. The network service provider charges a fee for its basic service, with possible additional charges levied for extra time online, disk space usage beyond a certain standard allotment, and other special services. Contact individual service providers for details on membership and prices.

Using a gateway service is generally an economical way for individual users to browse the Web, but it isn't suitable for serving content to the Web. Not all VRML browsers will work through a gateway service. You'll need to investigate the particulars with your service provider. Some gateway services provide a proprietary VRML browser.

Dial-Up Direct Connection

You can also obtain an Internet connection through an Internet service provider (ISP). Like a gateway service provider, an ISP charges a fee for its services, with additional fees for extra features or use. (The difference is that a gateway service provides a wide variety of services, one of which is an Internet connection. An ISP provides only the Internet connection.) The ISP provides a direct, dial-up connection to the Internet that uses either a standard telephone line or a special telephone line called an *ISDN line*.

Many service providers offer a complete software package that includes the necessary communications software to enable your computer to dial and connect to the ISP host computer. Be sure you obtain a direct Internet connection through the ISP, not just a shell account or a terminal emulator; otherwise, you will have access only to a text-based interface, which isn't suitable for VRML browsing.

Standard Telephone Line Connection

A standard telephone connection for direct Internet access requires a modem and software that uses a special protocol, either PPP (Point-to-Point Protocol) or SLIP (Serial Line Internet Protocol). The transmission rate of this setup is controlled by the modem speed, which is currently limited to 28.8Kb per second. This type of network connection is adequate for browsing the Web but not for connecting a Web server directly.

ISDN Connection

An ISDN connection requires a special telephone line. Check with your local telephone company to determine whether this service is offered in your area. This type of connection offers higher transmission speeds and a better quality connection than is offered by a standard telephone connection. (It also costs more.) You need special ISDN software and hardware (an ISDN modem and an NT1 network terminator) to use an ISDN connection. ISDN connections generally transmit data using PPP.

Dedicated Direct Connection

A dedicated direct connection requires a T1 line (another special kind of telephone line) or other high-bandwidth physical medium such as a T3 line. This type of connection is recommended for Web servers because it can offer full-time, uninterrupted service to the Internet. Most ISPs offer dedicated line access to the Internet for a flat rate. If your Web site has a large number of users or offers a large amount of data, you probably need a dedicated line connection. You could use ISDN to provide this connection, but it typically wouldn't be cost-effective for a round-the-clock connection.

This connection is typically the most expensive of the three options and offers the best transmission speeds. Dedicated lines run at speeds ranging from 56Kb per second to 1.5Mb per second for a full T1 line. In Europe, an E1 line runs at 2.048Mb per second.

Finding an Internet Service Provider (ISP)

You can obtain a list of service providers in your area through InterNIC. Its address and telephone number are

> Network Solutions
> ATTN: InterNIC Registration Services
> 505 Huntmar Park Drive
> Herndon, VA 22070
>
> Telephone: 703-742-4777

You may also be able to find a service provider by consulting the following:

- Your local telephone company

- Advertisements in a local computer magazine or newspaper

- A local computer store or computer user group

- A local university that is connected to the Internet

VRML Browsers

Once you're connected to the Internet, you'll have access to large amounts of information concerning any software or hardware purchase you're considering, including browsers. A popular VRML 2.0 browser is Cosmo™ Player, available from Silicon Graphics:

```
http://vrml.sgi.com
```

For a good descriptive list of other VRML browsers, many of which are available for free today, check the following URL:

```
http://www.sdsc.edu/vrml/software/browsers.html
```

If you require a separate VRML browser, you may be able to download one.

Creating VRML Scenes

To create your own VRML scenes, you'll probably want to purchase both modeling software and a VRML authoring tool. Again, the Web is a good source of information on current products:

```
http://www.sdsc.edu/vrml/software/modelers.html
```

You use *modeling software* to create the 3D models that make up your scene. Many conventional 3D modeling and animation applications, such as Alias|Wavefront Animator™, 3D Studio™, and form·Z™, can save their data as VRML files. In addition, a number of file converters allow you to convert data from existing 3D formats into VRML. You may also want to research the libraries of 3D clip-art models that you can incorporate directly into your scenes.

VRML *authoring packages* such as Cosmo Create 3D from Silicon Graphics, Ez3d® Modeler from Radiance Software International, and Fountain™ from Caligari Corporation can greatly speed up the task of creating attractive, efficient VRML files. The best packages provide special support for VRML files, including support for level-of-detail (LOD) nodes, anchor nodes, and inlines. Other important features to look for in an authoring package include tools for animation, scripting, wiring, prototyping, polygon reduction, and texture editing.

If you're just beginning to learn about VRML and want to experiment by creating simple scenes, the only essential tool you need is a text editor or word processor. VRML files can be either readable text files or binary files.

If you create the file in a word processor, be sure to save it as text so that the word processor doesn't add any extra formatting codes to the file. Chapter 4, "Building Objects," provides step-by-step instructions for creating a VRML file manually. Because this method is fairly slow and tedious, most users will compile scenes using available models and software authoring packages. The choice, however, is yours.

Publishing Your Work

If you want to publish material on the Web, you may want to use the server provided by your ISP. You can upload your documents to a specified location on the server, and the server will do the rest of the work. Depending on the coverage of your basic service, additional fees may be incurred for the disk space you use and the number of people accessing your documents. Using an ISP Web server frees you from the burden of setting up and maintaining your own Web server.

If you're part of a large organization that requires its own dedicated network server, you'll probably need to set up your own server. Chapter 9, "Publishing Your Work," presents issues to consider when setting up a server and points you to additional sources of information.

Chapter 3

Exploring and Building a World

Before examining VRML files in detail, this chapter begins with a brief tour through a virtual world—the ceremonial center of the ancient Aztec capital of Tenochtitlán, built on an island in the Valley of Mexico, where Mexico City now stands. You're going to view Tenochtitlán as it appeared when Hernán Cortés first saw it in 1519. Through the powers of virtual reality, the sprawling metropolis of Mexico City, with its smog and clogged city streets, fades away, and the massive stone pyramids and religious shrines of Tenochtitlán silently come into your view, enclosed by a long, imposing wall and bordered by the blue waters of Lake Texcoco.

Exploring the Aztec City

To begin the tour, enter this URL in the location field of your browser:

```
http://vrml.sgi.com/handbook
```

You are now standing at the West Gate of Tenochtitlán, on one of the three causeways that connect this island city to the mainland (Figure 3-1). The year is 1519.

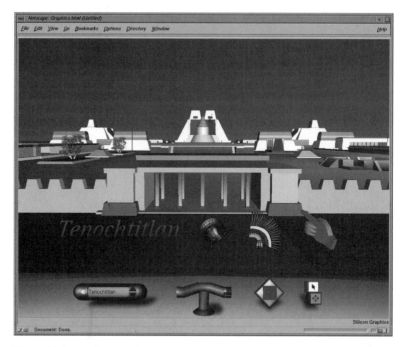

Figure 3-1   Entry view

For a brief description of how Cortés and the Spanish conquistadors responded to their first views of the city, click the mouse button on the conquistador helmet *marker*. The marker is *linked* to an HTML document, which appears on your screen, as shown in Figure 3-2. Clicking the word "Tenochtitlán" brings up background information on the city.

When you're sightseeing in a foreign city, your general approach may follow one of several patterns. You might be the type of intrepid traveler who likes to explore freely, without a definite plan or agenda. Or, at the opposite extreme, you might prefer to hire a tour guide or hop on a tour bus that takes you to the key spots of interest and presents pertinent background information along the way. Somewhere in the middle are the self-reliant souls who arm themselves with a map and a tour book and proceed on a self-guided tour. You have similar options as you navigate through the streets of Tenochtitlán.

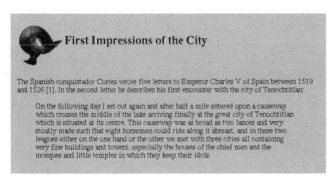

> **First Impressions of the City**
>
> The Spanish conquistador Cortes wrote five letters to Emperor Charles V of Spain between 1519 and 1526 [1]. In the second letter he describes his first encounter with the city of Tenochtitlan:
>
> On the following day I set out again and after half a mile entered upon a causeway which crosses the middle of the lake arriving finally at the great city of Tenochtitlan which is situated at its centre. This causeway was as broad as two lances and very stoutly made such that eight horsemen could ride along it abreast, and in these two leagues either on the one hand or the other we met with three cities all containing very fine buildings and towers, especially the houses of the chief men and the mosques and little temples in which they keep their idols.

Figure 3-2 How the conquistadors viewed the city in 1519

Do-It-Yourself Tour

You can navigate freely through the city using the tools provided by your browser. Click the markers provided to bring up HTML documents with additional information.

Map

If you'd like some structure, click the map icon (at the next viewpoint) to bring up a 2D map of the Tenochtitlán site. (You can also click "Map" in the Table of Contents frame.) You can identify the various buildings using the map and travel to the locations that interest you. (In some browsers, you can simply click a point of interest, and you'll automatically travel to that new position.)

Markers

You've already used the conquistador helmet marker to obtain additional information. You can also click the feathered headdress marker to read a description written from the Aztec point of view about what happened when Moctezuma, ruler of the Aztecs, and Cortés first met. The "i" marker, which appears later in the tour, is linked to additional information about archaeological research and excavation currently under way in Mexico City as well as further details about ancient Tenochtitlán. Browsers use a variety of methods to indicate "live" objects in the scene that contain links to other objects. In some browsers, the objects become highlighted when you move the cursor over them; in others, the cursor changes.

Guided Tour

If you prefer a guided tour, you have another option. A *viewpoint* is a preselected position for viewing a scene. Each vantage point has a name, and you can use a menu or other tool to cycle through the viewpoints.

One way to follow the *guided tour* that's built into the Tenochtitlán site is to click the pointing finger signpost when you're ready to travel to the next viewpoint. Some browsers, such as Silicon Graphics' Cosmo Player, also provide a menu that allows you to select a viewpoint.

On Your Way

The next few sections assume that you're following the guided tour. If you've decided to venture out on your own, you can just skim these paragraphs and turn to the section "Building a World" on page 34. Your ultimate destination is the Great Pyramid, or "el Templo Mayor" as Cortés referred to it, at the eastern end of the precinct. The tour ends at the top of the pyramid's grand staircase, where you can view its twin temples to the gods Tlaloc and Huitzilopochtli and learn more about the ancient Aztec rituals.

Click the guided tour signpost, which moves you closer to the West Gate (Figure 3-3). Click the guided tour signpost again to move inside the gate (Figure 3-4). Ahead of you are the walls of the ball court, or *tlachtli*, used by the upper class.

If you want to see the Tenochtitlán reconstruction in full detail, set your browser to display the highest image quality (if your browser provides such choices). Be aware, however, that this approach is slower than taking the tour with the browser set for lower image quality. Also, if your browser allows you to specify how much detail to display and whether to display textures, specify full detail with textures (unless you're in a hurry).

Your browser may provide controls for how fast you travel through the scene. In addition, if you can reduce the size of the browser window, the scene will redraw more quickly.

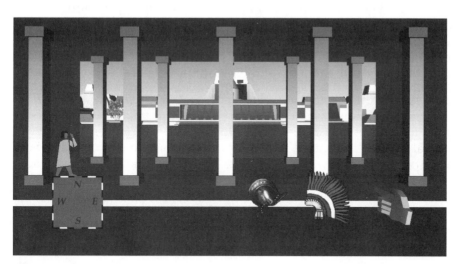

Figure 3-3   View from the West Gate

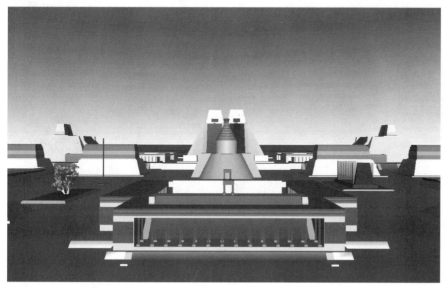

Figure 3-4   Inside the West Gate

The Eagle Lands

Click the guided tour signpost to move to the next stop, the spring (Figure 3-5). This ceremonial center was placed at Tenochtitlán ("place of the prickly pear cactus") because an eagle had landed on a cactus there, as predicted by the god Huitzilopochtli. Click one of the people seated near the cactus to activate the story of the founding of Tenochtitlán.

When you click the cactus, the eagle lands on it. In Chapter 6, "Animation and User Interaction," you'll learn more about how to animate objects using VRML script nodes, sensors, and routes. The eagle and cactus image is a special VRML object called a *billboard*—a flat image that always faces you no matter where your viewpoint is. The poem in the sky is connected to a *proximity sensor*. It appears when the user activates the sensor by moving to within a certain distance of it. The special effect of the blue water in the pond is achieved through the use of layers of *transparent* polygons covering the hole "dug" for the spring. A sound node produces the gurgling sounds of the spring waters.

Figure 3-5   Eagle landing at the spring

Temple of Quetzalcoatl

The next stop on your tour is the Temple of Quetzalcoatl, which stands out because of its round shape and conical roof. Click the guided tour signpost to travel to this temple (Figure 3-6).

Figure 3-6   Temple of Quetzalcoatl

If you click the sun icon, you'll see the path of the light rays on the spring equinox. On this date as the sun rises, the rays pass between the twin temples at the top of the Great Temple and shine directly on the shrine at the top of the Temple of Quetzalcoatl (Figure 3-7). A legend tells of how Moctezuma had the twin temples moved slightly so that this alignment would be more precise.

At the Base of the Temple

To move to the base of the staircase, click the guided tour signpost. You're now standing at the Table of Huitzilopochtli, facing the Great Temple (Figure 3-8). People gathered here while the priests at the top of the grand staircase prepared the human sacrifice for the Aztec gods.

Figure 3-7   Light rays activated by a touch sensor

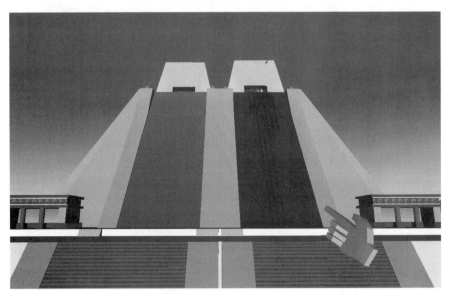

Figure 3-8   View from the base of the Great Temple

Click the "i" (for "information") marker to bring up an in-scene view of what the site looks like in present-day Mexico City, with the excavation of the Great Temple and the modern cathedral and city buildings (Figure 3-9). This new scene is a texture-mapped image that is applied to a VRML billboard object.

Level of Detail

The stairs of the Great Temple illustrate the level-of-detail technique, a useful VRML tool for achieving realistic 3D scenes. This technique also improves efficiency, because it allows you to omit unnecessary visual details for objects in the distance and to include realistic detailing for objects close to the viewer. When you were initially at the West Gate, the steps appeared as a flat gray polygon. Standing at the base of the staircase, you can now pick out the rise and tread of the individual steps. The section "Creating Levels of Detail for the Same Object" on page 51 describes this technique further.

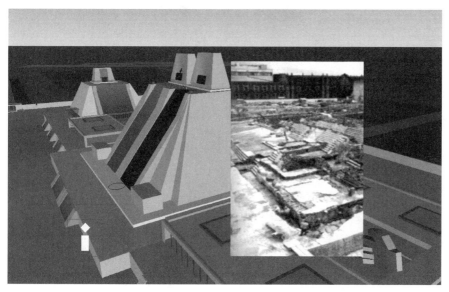

Figure 3-9   Billboard image showing excavation in present-day Mexico City

Texture Mapping to Add Details

If you're brave enough, you can travel to the top of the 130-foot staircase. There you'll have a panoramic view of all the buildings that make up this religious complex, with Mount Popocatepetl in the distance. Click the guided tour signpost to move halfway up the stairs (Figure 3-10).

In front of you is the Stone of Coyolxauhqui, nearly eleven feet in diameter, which was unearthed in 1978 by electrical workers digging in Mexico City. An image of this stone is *texture mapped* onto the scene. You can think of a texture map as a piece of wallpaper that's "pasted" onto another surface. For planar surfaces, the mapping is fairly intuitive. For curved surfaces, the way the texture is wrapped around the surface becomes more complicated. The sky, with its wispy clouds, is also created by a texture map that is part of the background description. Texture mapping and backgrounds are described in detail in Chapter 8, "Using Colors, Normals, and Textures."

Figure 3-10   Stone of Coyolxauhqui

Looking to the left, you'll see a small temple with two columns defining its entrance (Figure 3-11). Chapter 4, "Building Objects," provides a step-by-step description of how to construct the VRML version of this temple.

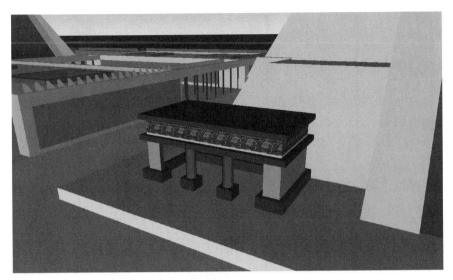

Figure 3-11   View of the small temple

View from the Top

Click the guided tour signpost to move to the top of the grand staircase. Click again to move in closer to the temples on the platform at the top (Figure 3-12). At the left, the Shrine of Tlaloc, the rain god, has a blue facade representing water. The horizontal beam above the doorway features the Aztec "goggle eyes" motif, a series of concentric circles. To the right, the Temple of Huitzilopochtli, god of war, is painted red and elaborately carved with a bow motif associated with Huitzilopochtli.

Click the circular arrow in the middle of the scene to activate a 360-degree view of the scene. The 2D map will help you identify each of the buildings in your view. Note that there's a fair amount of activity in this virtual world: flames and sparks rise from the braziers, boats sail around the lake, and a bird circles overhead. Each of these objects is animated by a custom script that describes how its placement changes over time. Figure 3-13 shows the view towards the west, as seen from this vantage point.

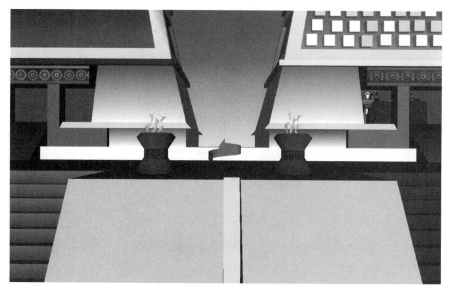

Figure 3-12   Shrine of Tlaloc and Temple of Huitzilopochtli

Figure 3-13   View from the top of the Great Temple staircase, facing west

Reusing Objects

Notice the symmetry between the two temples at the top of the staircase. Although the superficial decorations differ, the basic shape of the two temples is the same. In front of the temples, the four braziers used for burning sacrificial parts are also the same. When you begin creating VRML scenes, you'll want to capitalize on the economy of modeling an object once and then reusing it, with modifications, when it appears elsewhere in the scene. In the section "Using Multiple Instances of an Object," you'll see exactly how to reuse objects in a VRML file.

Exploring the Shrines

Click the guided tour signpost to explore the Shrine of Tlaloc. Clicking the *chacmool* (Figure 3-14), the reclining statue where offerings to the gods were made, brings up a related HTML page.

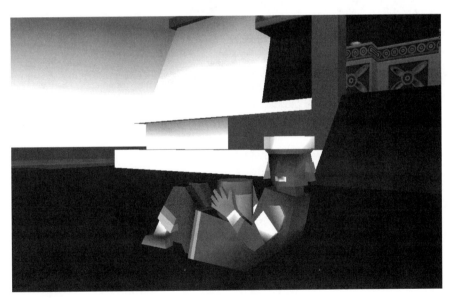

Figure 3-14   Chacmool at Shrine of Tlaloc

The next stop (Figure 3-15) shows a still life of a sacrifice in front of the Temple of Huitzilopochtli. In contrast to Tlaloc, who symbolized life—fertility, water, plants—this god represented sacrifice, war, and death. This scene uses texture mapping on simple square polygons. Click the small carved knife hovering in the scene to link to more information about Aztec rituals.

Figure 3-15   Sacrificial stone at Temple of Huitzilopochtli

Click the guided tour icon to move to the entrance of the Temple of Huitzilopochtli. Click again to enter the temple, where you'll hear the sound of beating drums played by two Aztec worshippers (Figure 3-16). Sacrifices to the gods glow at the foot of each statue. Here, you'll learn about the dramatic confrontation between Cortés and Moctezuma concerning the Aztec gods and sacrifices. Although your official tour ends here, feel free to spend some time clicking on the links to bring up additional information on the various stones and statues.

Traveling through Time

The guided tour you've followed led you along one possible spatial path through the Tenochtitlán scene. Using many of the same techniques, you could add another dimension by creating parallel versions of the model as it existed in different eras.

Figure 3-16 Animated drummers inside the Temple of Huitzilopochtli

For example, the Great Temple shown in this model is actually the outside shell of a series of pyramids built on top of one another—in fact, it's the seventh pyramid built over six earlier structures. You could add models for each of the earlier pyramids to this scene, correlate each model with a particular date, and allow the user to select a file corresponding to the era he or she wants to explore (the Aztec scene uses 2D HTML documents to convey this information).

The city also changed over time in other ways. Built on soft alluvial soil, it gradually sank. Additional study would be required to model these changes accurately and include them in the scene. And finally, Cortés and his men systematically destroyed many of these temples, using stones from them to build cathedrals that reflected their religious beliefs. The VRML tools at your fingertips thus allow you to create a scene that enables travel through time as well as space, providing endless possibilities for re-creating and experiencing scenes from the past as well as visualizing present and future worlds.

Building a World

Now it's time to go behind the scenes at Tenochtitlán to look at the VRML details that make the magic happen. The rest of this chapter describes the general outline of a VRML file, highlights some of the most important elements of the VRML file format, and introduces key concepts related to virtual reality modeling.

Creating Objects

A VRML file is essentially a collection of objects, arranged in a particular order. As in real life, an object often corresponds to something physical that has a particular shape, various surface properties (color, smoothness, shininess, and so on), and a position in 3D space. Other VRML objects include sounds, lights, and viewpoints, which also have positions in 3D space.

What Is a Node?

A *node* is the fundamental building block of a VRML file. Some nodes are objects—Cylinder, Cone, Box, SpotLight. Other nodes are used as containers to hold related nodes. A Shape node, for example, contains a geometry node and an appearance node. These nodes can, in turn, contain other nodes. In addition to nodes that have a visual effect, VRML defines a number of nodes that provide special features, such as hyperlinking, including objects defined in other files, and detecting collisions. Each node contains *fields*, which hold the data for the node.

In a VRML file, you can create objects that contain other objects. In the Aztec model, for example, each temple is composed of a number of separate objects. The Great Temple is made up of its sides, the staircases, two more temples on top, and various braziers and statues. The two smaller temples, in turn, are composed of a number of other objects. At the lowest level, these objects are all collections of various VRML nodes.

Creating a Simple Object

This section describes how to create a simple VRML file with one object, a purple cylinder. The file is short, but it contains all the basics:

- File header
- Shape node
- Geometry node
- Appearance node
- Grouping node

At this point, you're not expected to understand all the details of this example. This description is intended to give you the general structure of a VRML file. Full details on the shapes, transformations, and appearance properties introduced here are presented in Chapter 4, "Building Objects."

File Header

Every VRML file starts with the following header:

```
#VRML V2.0 utf8
```

The `utf8` specification refers to an ISO standard for text strings known as UTF-8 encoding. (See the description of the Text node in Chapter 11, "Node Reference.")

Shape Node

Next, you're going to add the object (the cylinder) to this file. Before you create the cylinder, though, you need to create a Shape node, which is the basic container node for a geometry object. Each piece of geometry is wrapped in a Shape node, which also includes a "slot" for nodes describing an object's appearance. You'll learn how to add appearance nodes such as colors, materials, and textures shortly.

```
#VRML V2.0 utf8

Shape {
  appearance Appearance {
    material Material { }
  }
  geometry    NULL
}
```

Geometry Node

VRML provides simple geometry nodes such as Sphere, Cylinder, Box, and Cone, as well as more complex geometry nodes such as IndexedFaceSet (see Chapter 4, "Building Objects"). The two temples halfway up the Great Temple are composed partly of simple cylinders and boxes. Most of the other buildings in the Tenochtitlán scene are composed of indexed face sets.

Here's how you create a default cylinder in VRML:

```
#VRML V2.0 utf8

Shape {
  appearance Appearance {
    material Material { }
  }
  geometry    Cylinder { }
}
```

Note: File format examples use boldface type to emphasize the focus of the discussion.

Each node contains a set of *fields* that specify various attributes of the node. A field has a predefined name and can contain a certain type of value, such as an integer or a floating point number. The fields of a node can be specified in any order. (For details on nodes and their fields, see Chapter 11, "Node Reference.")

When you create a node, its fields are automatically created and filled in with *default* values. Since the previous example didn't specify any values for the cylinder fields, it uses the VRML defaults. It has a radius of 1 and a height of 2. All of its parts are visible. It's in the default position with an upright axis centered on your screen. Because no material fields were specified, the default values for the Material node are used.

Note: If you don't include a Material node as shown in the previous examples, the object will be black, and you won't be able to see it. Including an empty Material node as shown here applies the default color (light gray) to the object.

You can specify new values for the fields in a node if you want to. For example, this cylinder has a radius of 3, a height of 6, and it has no top, like a drinking glass:

```
#VRML V2.0 utf8

Shape {
  appearance  Appearance {
    material  Material { }
  }
  geometry  Cylinder {
    radius   3
    height   6
    side     TRUE
    top      FALSE
    bottom   TRUE
  }
}
```

Figure 3-17 shows what this cylinder looks like.

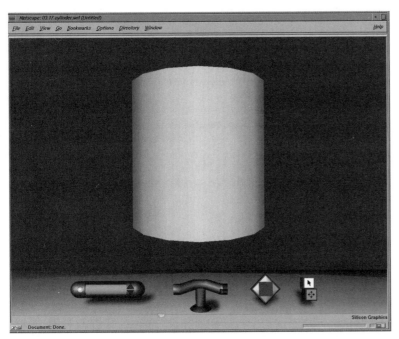

Figure 3-17   Simple cylinder

Note: In VRML, node names begin with capital letters. Field names begin with lowercase letters. The fields of a node are enclosed in curly braces.

Appearance Node

In addition to its geometry, an object also has certain surface properties, such as its color, the smoothness of its surface, how shiny it is, and so on. Nodes commonly used to specify an object's appearance are the Material and texturing nodes (ImageTexture, MovieTexture, and PixelTexture).

Here's an example of a Material node that specifies an object that is purple and shiny:

```
Material {
   diffuseColor   .5 0 .5
   shininess      .5
}
```

For simplicity, some fields are omitted from the example nodes. See Chapter 11 for the complete story on each node.

The *diffuseColor* field contains three values, for the *red*, *green*, and *blue* components of the color. In this system, often referred to as "RGB," a value of (0, 0, 0) specifies black (that is, no color), and a value of (1, 1, 1) specifies white. A value of (.5, 0, .5) thus specifies 50 percent red, no green, and 50 percent blue, which results in a medium purple color.

The *shininess* field takes a value between 0.0 and 1.0. Lower values produce soft, diffuse reflections, and higher values produce more focused, sharper highlights.

The Material node also allows you to specify other properties, such as the transparency of an object, the reflective quality of an object's highlights, and the amount of light emitted by a glowing object such as the sun or a light bulb.

The purple cylinder is now complete. Example 3-1 shows the VRML file.

Example 3-1   A purple cylinder

```
#VRML V2.0 utf8

Shape {
   appearance   Appearance {
      material   Material {
         diffuseColor   .5 0 .5
         shininess      .5
      }
   }
```

```
  geometry  Cylinder {
     radius  3
     height  6
     side    TRUE
     top     FALSE
     bottom  TRUE
  }
}
```

This example illustrates the rules for using certain nodes in a VRML file. Specifically, the Material node can be used only in the *material* field of the Appearance node. The Appearance node, in turn, can be used only in the *appearance* field of a Shape node. (For details, see Figure 11-2.)

Figure 3-18 shows the purple cylinder.

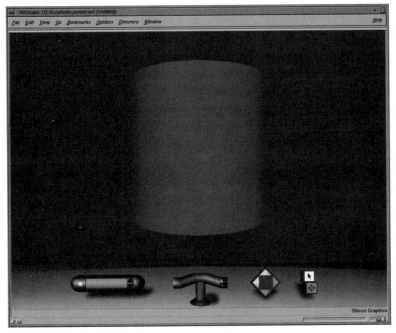

Figure 3-18   Purple cylinder

Scene Diagrams

It's often helpful to draw a diagram of your scene, especially when you begin to group nodes hierarchically, as described in the following section. This book uses a few simple conventions for scene diagrams, as shown in Figure 3-19, a diagram of the purple cylinder scene. Circles indicate nongrouping nodes. Shaded circles indicate grouping nodes. The scene diagram mimics the structure of the VRML file, with child nodes to the right of their parent nodes. Nodes that are children of the same parent node, such as the Appearance and Cylinder nodes in this example, are aligned vertically.

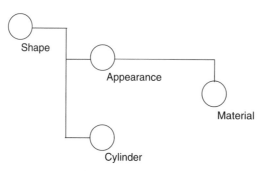

Figure 3-19   Scene diagram for purple cylinder scene

Grouping Nodes

In almost all cases, you'll create groups of objects, combining them into scenes and worlds. Grouping nodes in VRML are the Group, Transform, LOD, Switch, Anchor, Inline, and Collision nodes. For a summary, see Figure 11-1, which shows grouping nodes and nodes that can be added as children of grouping nodes. Some nodes, such as the Cylinder, IndexedFaceSet, Appearance, and Material nodes, have more limited use and cannot be used in the *children* field of a grouping node (see Figure 11-2).

For general grouping purposes, use the Group node. If you want to group objects together in space, use the Transform node, which allows you to position an object in 3D space by translating (moving) or rotating it. This node also allows you to scale the size of an object.

Note: It's common practice to separate the children of a grouping node with commas. Although this technique makes the file more readable, the commas are not part of the required VRML syntax and can be omitted.

Here's an example of how to move the purple cylinder in the scene. Figure 3-20 shows the corresponding scene diagram, with a shaded circle for the Transform grouping node.

Example 3-2   Translating the purple cylinder

```
#VRML V2.0 utf8

Transform {
  translation  -2.4 2 3
  children [
    Shape {
      appearance  Appearance {
        material  Material {
          diffuseColor  .5 0 .5
          shininess     .5
        }
      }
      geometry  Cylinder {
        radius  3
        height  6
        side    TRUE
        top     FALSE
        bottom  TRUE
      }
    }
  ]
} # end of Transform grouping
```

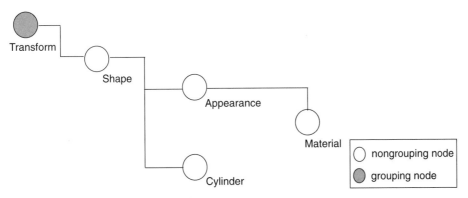

Figure 3-20   Scene diagram for translated purple cylinder scene

The *translation* field takes three values, which specify where to move the object along the x, y, and z axes. The VRML convention is that the +y axis points up, the +x axis points to the right, and the +z axis points out of the screen toward you, as shown in Figure 3-21. (This is what's known as a *right-handed* coordinate system.) A translation of (–2.4, 2, 3) moves the object

−2.4 units in the x direction (that is, to the left), +2 units in the y direction, and +3 units in the z direction.

Chapter 4 describes other fields of the Transform node, such as *rotation* and *scale*, in further detail.

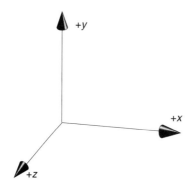

Figure 3-21   VRML coordinate system

Comments

Comments in a VRML file begin with a number sign (#) anywhere on a line and continue to the end of the line. In the following line

```
diffuseColor   .5 0 .5 # purple
```

the browser ignores the comment # `purple`.

Using External Files: Inline Nodes

Frequently, you'll want to incorporate models created by other sources into your scenes. Typically, the best way to use these models is to keep them in their own files and just include a reference to the file in your scene description. You can think of the Inline node as a shorthand method of adding a copy of the original file to your scene. The Inline node allows you to reference external sources by specifying their URLs, like this:

Example 3-3   Using an Inline node

```
Inline {
  url   "tlalocStatue.wrl"
}
```

Inline nodes also allow you to break up your own files into manageable chunks. If you do not specify the protocol (for example, `http://`), the browser assumes the file's path is relative to the URL of the current document.

Remember, external references require an extra round trip to the server to fetch the data, which increases download time. For models with a small amount of data, it's usually best to paste the data directly into the main scene file.

While they are fetching Inline nodes, many browsers display a simple box as a placeholder for the inlined objects. When the complete file has been downloaded, the inlined objects pop into place and the box disappears.

Using Multiple Instances of an Object

If you're going to reuse the same node multiple times in a scene, it's best to *name* the node the first time you describe it and then just refer to the node by name each time you want to reuse it. Aside from making the VRML file shorter and easier to read, this technique decreases the time it takes to download your scene and increases overall performance. Make it a general practice to reuse nodes whenever possible.

Creating a node and then referring to it by name in multiple places is called *creating multiple instances* of a node, or simply *instancing*. If you change the original named node, all instances of that node will change as well.

As noted earlier, sometimes you'll have the same geometry repeated in a scene, but with different colors and textures. In such cases, you can name the geometry the first time and reuse it, but include different material and texture nodes to change the appearance.

Use DEF (short for "define") to define a name for a node. For example, to define the texture map used for the beam over the entry to the Temple of Huitzilopochtli so that you can use it in multiple places, you define a name for the ImageTexture node the first time you describe it in your file.

Example 3-4   Defining a node

```
Appearance {
  texture  DEF BOWS ImageTexture { url  "http: ... " }
  #Names the texture map "BOWS"
}
```

For subsequent uses of the object, follow this example.

Example 3-5   Reusing a node

```
Appearance {
  texture  USE BOWS # Use Huitzilopochtli bows texture map
}
```

This Appearance node contains an *instance* of the original ImageTexture node shown above.

Here's an example of how the Aztec scene reuses the braziers at the top of the Great Temple. (Examples from the Aztec scene were generated by the Cosmo Create 3D authoring tool.)

Example 3-6   Multiple instances of the brazier objects

```
DEF BothBraziers Transform {
  children [
    DEF Brazier Group {
      children  Inline {
        url  "TMBrazierTlaloc.wrl"
        bboxCenter  799.5 127.01 -1187.5
        bboxSize    124 5 5
      }
    },
    Transform {
      children     USE Brazier
      translation  54.5 0 0
    }
  ]
  translation  0 -1.43 0
}
```

Linking to Other Objects

One of the most versatile VRML nodes is the Anchor node. This node provides hyperlinks to other scenes, to HTML pages, and even to sound and movie files located anywhere on the Web. (These features are analogous to the links/anchors features in HTML.) If you specify a VRML file, that world replaces the current VRML world. If you specify a sound or movie file, the browser decides how to "play" the file.

Specify the file to link to in the *url* field of this node. The file can be specified as a URL or as the path to a local file. In the *children* field, specify the object or objects the user will click to activate the hyperlink. If you want to describe the link to the user, fill in the *description* field. This description is displayed by the browser when the user moves the mouse over the child objects.

Here's an example of the Anchor node used in the Aztec example to bring up introductory information on Tenochtitlán. In the scene, the word "Tenochtitlán" ("TitleText.wrl") highlights when the user moves the cursor over it (or the cursor itself changes to indicate the link). If the user clicks this word, the HTML document appears.

Example 3-7   Using an Anchor node

```
DEF Title Anchor {
  url   "Tenochtitlan.html"
  description "The Aztec City of Tenochtitlan"
  children [
    Inline {
      url "TitleText.wrl"
      bboxSize    5.8 .75 0
      bboxCenter  0   .37 0
    }
  ]
}
```

If you want to link a number of "hot" objects to the same file, simply include them as children of the anchor node. Clicking on any one of the Anchor node's children automatically activates the link. The child can be an inline node or an object with geometry, properties, and position that you describe explicitly in your VRML file.

Example 3-8   Anchor node with multiple children

```
DEF Title Anchor {
  url  "Tenochtitlan.html"
  description  "The Aztec City of Tenochtitlan"
  children [
    Inline {
      url  "TitleText.wrl"
      bboxSize    5.8 .75 0
      bboxCenter  0   .37 0
    }
    Transform {
      children  Shape {
        geometry  Box { size  1 1 1 }
      }
    translation  0 1 0
    }
  ]
}
```

Combining Objects into Worlds

As you add objects to your world, you'll often want to group objects
together. If the objects are located in the same position in the scene, or if
the objects move together as a group, they need to be in the same Transform
group. Here is a simple file that contains two grouping nodes.

Example 3-9   Grouping objects

```
#VRML V2.0 utf8

Viewpoint { position 0 5 10 }

Transform {
  translation  0 5 0
  rotation     1 0 0 .8
  children  [
    Inline {
      url        "brazier.wrl"
      bboxCenter 0    0    0
      bboxSize   3.14 3.13 3.12
    },
```

```
Transform {
  translation  0 1.5 0
  children  [
    Inline {
      url            "coals.wrl"
      bboxCenter   -.15 -.09 .135
      bboxSize      .84  .46 .61
    }
  ]
  }
 ]
}
```

For readability, the child nodes are indented so that you can easily identify the hierarchy of parent nodes (to the left) and child nodes (indented to the right of their parents). This white space is ignored by the computer; in fact, some authoring systems strip it out before publishing a file to reduce file size. But it's important to preserve the white space when humans need to read the file.

Figure 3-22 shows the scene diagram for the brazier file.

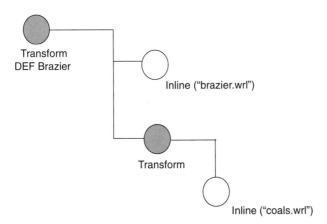

Figure 3-22   Scene diagram for a group hierarchy

Figure 3-23 shows this scene.

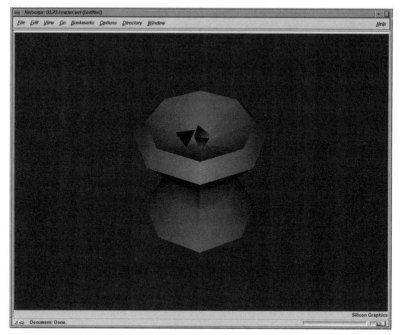

Figure 3-23   Brazier with coals, affected by a translation and a rotation

Scope

A Transform node affects all nodes inside it. If a Transform node contains another Transform node, they are said to be *nested*. When you nest Transform nodes, the parent (container) nodes affect their children, as follows. The basic rule is that transformation values set within the opening and closing braces of a Transform node affect everything *inside* the braces. Once you're outside the Transform's braces, the effects of its transformations are canceled.

Figure 3-24 shows a VRML file with Transforms depicted as a set of nested boxes. Transformation values set within a given box affect only the nodes inside that box.

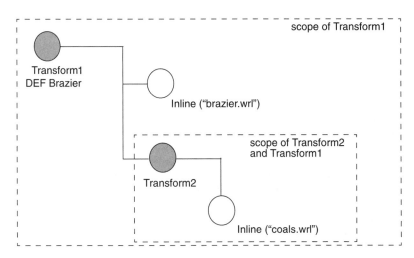

Figure 3-24   Scope of Transform nodes

Accumulating Transformation Values

When Transform nodes contain other Transforms, their settings have a *cumulative* effect. In Figure 3-24, the coals are affected by both Transform1 and Transform2. The brazier is affected only by Transform1.

Order of transformation is important too. To see the effects of nested transformations, you first apply the transformations of the object's own Transform node. This transformation puts you in the object's *local coordinate system*. Next, you apply the transformations, if any, of the parent node (that is, the node one level to the left in the file). If that node has a parent node, you apply its transformations too. Continue working back through the file until you're at the last parent Transform (all the way at the left margin). The final set of accumulated transformations, starting with the object's own transformation and including all of its parent transformations, puts you in the *world coordinate system* for this object. For the coals in the previous example, the world coordinate system is created by applying Transform2 and then applying Transform1.

Be aware that Transform nodes at the *same* level (using our analogy, these would be *siblings*) do not affect each other. (Sibling Transforms form stacked, not nested boxes.)

Looking at the Scene

A Viewpoint node describes a potential *position* and *orientation* for viewing the scene. Creating a viewpoint is like identifying a designated photo spot, so users can view the scene at a particular location and from a certain direction. You can also specify the *field of view* to indicate how much of the scene is visible. A small field of view, like a telephoto lens, focuses on a small part of the scene. A larger field of view, like a wide-angle lens, focuses on a large part of the scene.

The default viewpoint position is (0 0 10). You may need to modify this position to view your objects properly (as in Example 3-9). This default position works well for small objects located at the origin.

The field of view for a Viewpoint node is specified in radians. One radian is about 57 degrees. 2π radians equals 360 degrees.

A viewpoint's position and orientation are affected by a local transformation and by its parent transformations.

Example 3-10   Using a Viewpoint node

```
DEF CamTest Group {
  children [
    DEF Cameras Group {
      children [
        DEF TheGate Viewpoint {
          position    797.8 3.52 -60.14
          orientation  -.07 1.    0      .04
          description "TheGate"
        }
      ]
    },
  ]
}
```

Defining Multiple Viewpoints

Since you're the creator of the scene, you'll probably want to guide the user to the best vantage points for viewing it. You can define multiple Viewpoint nodes, each with different positions, orientations, and fields of view. Use the Viewpoint node *description* field to name each viewpoint—for example "View from Quetzalcoatl Temple" or "Entering the West Gate." Some browsers create a menu that includes these named viewpoints to allow the user to jump quickly from one viewpoint to the next.

To allow your world to be viewed easily on systems with limited resources, it's recommended that you include a number of preselected camera viewpoints in your scene. That way, the user doesn't need to navigate through the scene manually.

Shortcut Using the Anchor Node

When an Anchor node specifies a URL, it can include a viewpoint name preceded by a # sign to indicate a specific viewpoint from which to look at the scene when it is first loaded. The viewpoint needs to be defined within the referenced file using DEF. This example brings up a VRML scene viewed from the "WestGate" viewpoint (defined in that file).

Example 3-11   Specifying a viewpoint inside an Anchor link

```
Anchor { url  "Tenochtitlan.wrl.gz#WestGate"
```

Guided Tour

In the Silicon Graphics Cosmo Player browser shown in the figures in this chapter, when the user selects a new viewpoint from the Viewpoints menu, the viewer animates from the current viewpoint to the next, moving the user smoothly along a path through the scene. In the Tenochtitlán world, similar movement is achieved using the pointing hand icons, which activate Script nodes. Each Script node contains a small program that describes the path for moving the user from one viewpoint to the next. Chapter 6, "Animation and User Interaction," provides an example of animating between viewpoints.

Creating Levels of Detail for the Same Object

As you move closer to an object in the real world, you can perceive more of its visual details. The Aztec model simulates this effect. For example, standing at the West Gate and looking at the Great Temple, the grand staircases appear as two flat polygons. By the time you are at the base of the pyramid, though, you can make out each of the individual steps. Similarly, from a distance, the statues in front of the shrines at the top of the temple appear as simple block shapes. You can't discern their exact shape until you move closer.

This effect is achieved through the LOD (level of detail) node. The LOD node has children that all describe the same object in the scene, with varying levels of complexity (Figure 3-25).

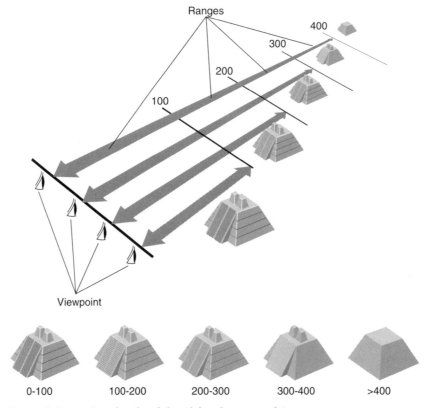

Figure 3-25   Five levels of detail for the same object

The children are arranged according to how much detail they contain, from the most detailed representation of the object to the least detailed. This node improves the efficiency of your VRML file, making it easier to travel through the scene, because the browser doesn't become bogged down trying to render details that would not be perceived by the user.

Here's an example of an LOD node that describes the chacmool in front of the left temple at the top of the Great Temple.

Example 3-12   Using an LOD node for a complex object

```
Group {
  children DEF ChacmoolStatue Group {
    children LOD {
      center 763.88 122.81 -1196.75
      range  [ 60, 200 ]
      levels [
        Transform {
          children Inline {  # first level is a detailed statue
            url
            "Chacmool.wrl"
            bboxCenter 0    0    0
            bboxSize   4.29 2.53 1.16
          }
          translation  764.06 124.07 -1196.75
        }
        '
        Transform {
          children Shape {    # second level is just a box
            appearance Appearance {
              material Material {
                diffuseColor      .25 .31 .31
              }
            }
            geometry Box {
              size   4.29 2.53 1.16
            }
          }
          translation  763.88 124.07 -1196.75
        }
        '
        Group {
          children       [ ]  # last level is an empty group
        }
      ]
    }
  }
}
```

The *center* field contains the *x, y, z* coordinates for the center of the object under consideration. This position is ultimately affected by any Transform nodes above it in the file. The browser calculates the distance from the transformed center point to the viewpoint. Then it looks at the *range* field, which specifies a distance for each of the LOD children. If the distance is less than the first value in the range array, then the first child is drawn. If the distance is between the first and second values in the range array, the second child is drawn, and so on.

 See also Chapter 10, "Improving Performance," which shows how to use the LOD node with the Inline node to increase rendering speed.

Interacting with the Scene

Some of the nodes in the scene provide special effects that allow the user to interact with the scene in different ways. A class of nodes called *sensors* reacts to user events in some prescribed way. For example, clicking on a TouchSensor could turn on a light, or a ProximitySensor could sense when the user arrives near a certain spot and play a sound. Often, a sensor is "wired" to a Script node that runs a program when the sensor sends it a message.

In addition to their fields, most nodes contain *events*. An event is an indication that something has happened—for instance, that another field's value has changed, that the user has clicked the mouse, or that a certain amount of time has elapsed. There are two kinds of events: incoming events (labeled "eventIn") and outgoing events (labeled "eventOut"). The wiring that connects the eventOut of one node to the eventIn of another node is called a *route*, shown in Figure 3-26. When a field receives an event, its value changes to the value of the corresponding event. When a field sends an event, the event's value is set to equal the value of the field that is broadcasting the event.

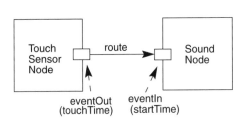

Figure 3-26   Routing an outgoing event to an incoming event

The Aztec world uses a variety of sensor and script nodes to respond to user events and to animate objects—for example, the flames start to rise from the fire when the user clicks on the brazier and stop when the user clicks a second time. The drummers inside the Temple of Huitzilopochtli at the top of the Great Temple start to play when a proximity sensor activates a script. Chapter 6, "Animation and User Interaction," examines each of these elements in more detail.

Starting from Scratch

Looking at the complex Tenochtitlán world, it might be difficult to visualize starting with a basic idea and expanding it into a vast collection of models, textures, scripts, and wired routes between nodes. Here's a suggestion of how to begin planning a world. Basic steps to follow include:

1. Start with a basic concept and develop a "story board" that describes the key features and behaviors that make up your world.

2. Build the objects and assemble them to form your world.

3. Add animation and scripts.

4. Refine the models, textures, animations, and viewpoints. Add extra features such as HTML pages, vertex colors, and materials. Test constantly to ensure that rendering performance is at an acceptable frame rate.

Develop a Story Board

Before you begin modeling objects, develop a basic plan, perhaps in the form of simple annotated drawings to illustrate your ideas. You'll need to answer a number of questions, such as:

*   What is the purpose of your VRML world?

*   What kind of audience will be visiting this world?

*   Is there any story associated with the world?

*   What path will the visitors take through the world?

*   What objects will it contain?

*   Do you need links to other worlds or to related HTML pages, and what will their content be?

- How will the user interact with the world? Interaction might be through realistic devices such as doorbells, light switches, and elevators, or it might be through imaginary devices created as part of the world (magic signs, talking icons, and so on).

- How will you use special effects such as sounds and movies?

At this point, you might also decide on a general style for the world. It may need to be somewhat realistic, as the Aztec world portrayed in this book, or it may be completely fantastic, as are some of the worlds illustrated in the color plates section of this book.

As with any large job, breaking the task into smaller pieces helps make it more manageable (and helps you meet any pesky deadlines). Prioritize the pieces according to their relation to your overall purpose in creating the world.

Build Objects

List the objects that will make up your world. Analyze which objects, textures, and materials can be reused. Use simple colors for the objects at first; refinements can be made later as time allows. Before you build the models, decide which ones will be animated so that you can create an appropriate transformation hierarchy as you build their components.

Add Animation and Scripts

Once you have the basic objects created, you can add interpolators and write scripts to add behavior to the objects. At this point, you'll want to define a series of viewpoints in your scene which can form the basis for an animated path through it.

Add sensors and interpolators to respond to user actions.

Refine and Test

As you refine the objects and add textures and materials, be sure to test the world and gauge its rendering performance. An important step is to create LOD and Inline nodes to facilitate browser optimizations. Refine the different models in the LOD levels until the changes between levels are almost imperceptible.

Moving On

This chapter has provided a brief tour of the Aztec world and an overview of how to create objects and assemble them into scenes. In the next chapter, you'll take a closer look at all of the nodes used to build the small temple located at the base of the Great Temple.

Building Objects

This chapter looks in more detail at one particular building in the Aztec city: the small temple at the left of the base of the steps up to the Great Temple. (The temple on the right of the steps is identical, and in fact was created using the DEF/USE technique described in "Using Multiple Instances of an Object" on page 43.) The temple was created by combining a few relatively simple pieces; in this chapter you learn how to construct a temple just like it. You may want to open the file

`http://vrml.sgi.com/handbook/examples/temple.complete.wrl`

in your VRML browser and examine the finished temple before you proceed. It should look like Figure 4-1.

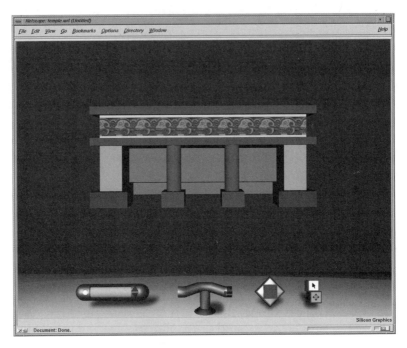

Figure 4-1   The completed temple

If you were going to build a VRML Aztec temple from scratch, you'd probably use a modeling program to design each shape, then combine the resulting models into a VRML world using a VRML authoring tool. Since this chapter is a tutorial, though, you can create the example temple described here by typing text into a text file, except for certain pieces that are too big to be listed in detail. If you'd rather not type everything in, you can download the VRML file for each step of the construction from

```
http://vrml.sgi.com/handbook/examples
```

Note that the temple this chapter focuses on is only one piece of a complete VRML world. Creating a full world requires integrating many such pieces—buildings, objects, creatures, sounds, motion, lighting, and so on. It's best to create these items as individual files, then combine them (using inlines) into a complete world.

Starting Your Temple

First, using your favorite text editor, create a new VRML file containing nothing but the header and an empty grouping node:

```
#VRML V2.0 utf8
Group {
}
```

Then save the new file with a descriptive name like *temple.wrl* and open it in your VRML browser to verify that it really is a valid VRML file. (Since the scene is empty, the browser should read in the file and then display a blank scene.) If the browser complains about the file, check your spelling and capitalization carefully—note especially that the "V" in "V2.0" must be capitalized.

Now go back to the file and add some information about your new world, in a WorldInfo node. Put the world information at the top of the file, before your Group node—you could make it a child of the Group node if you prefer, but since it provides global information about the scene, it's appropriate to put it at the top of the file. A WorldInfo node provides a *title* for the world, which the browser can display in its title bar or elsewhere. It also contains an *info* field; *info* strings are ignored by the browser just like comments. Comments, however, can get stripped out of a VRML file during transmission; using a WorldInfo node ensures that important information remains part of the file.

Example 4-1   Using a WorldInfo node

```
#VRML V2.0 utf8
WorldInfo {
  title   "Temple"
  info    "VRML model of an Aztec temple."
}
Group {
}
```

Note: *info* is a *multiple-valued* field (of type MFString), so it can contain more than one string. If you want to include more strings in *info*, be sure to surround the list of strings with a pair of square brackets. (For information on field types, see Chapter 12, "Field Reference.")

If there are multiple WorldInfo nodes in a file, only the first one matters; all the rest are ignored. Thus, you can include a WorldInfo node in every VRML file, even if the file is intended to be brought in as an inline in a larger scene; only the first WorldInfo node in the top-level scene is used.

You can supply other information about how you want the scene to be viewed by using a NavigationInfo node. Both kinds of information nodes can appear at the top level of a VRML file or as a child of any grouping node. If you don't specify any navigation information, the file behaves as though it contains a default-valued NavigationInfo node, which is the way that you probably want most files to behave most of the time. For information on changing navigation information, see Chapter 11.

Now the basic structure of the file is in place. Before you can start building the temple, though, you need to understand more about VRML transformations and shapes.

Transformations

The Transform node contains several fields that define a *transformation*, which consists of a translation, a rotation about a given point, and scaling around a given point. By using a transform, you can move objects anywhere in a VRML world, turned to any orientation, and stretched by any amount in each direction.

Translation and the Standard Unit of Distance

In Chapter 3 you learned how to use the *translation* field to move a transform's children by specified amounts in the *x*, *y*, and *z* directions. Those amounts, like all distances in VRML, are measured in meters. To a certain extent it doesn't matter what units you use in your own files as long as you're consistent, but if you want to have any sort of connection to other people's worlds or objects it's a good idea to build everything using the standard units.

Note: The Aztec world model was built using data that gave distances in feet; rather than change all the measurements in the file, this book provides examples from that world measured in feet.

Rotation

A *rotation* field rotates the transform's children around a specified axis, by a specified number of radians. The field's value consists of four numbers. The first three numbers define a location in 3D space; the axis of rotation is the line going from the origin to that location. The final number in the field indicates how many radians to rotate around that axis. For example, to make the chacmool lie on its side, you could rotate it by 1.57 radians (or around 90 degrees) about the *x* axis.

Example 4-2   Rotating an object

```
Transform {
  rotation  1 0 0  1.57
  children [
    Inline { url  "chacmool.wrl" }
  ]
}
```

The rotation axis doesn't have to be one unit long; you could specify

```
rotation  50 0 0  1.57
```

in the preceding example if you wanted to, since all that's really important is the direction the vector points in. But it's usually more convenient to give a unit-length vector.

A positive rotation value rotates counterclockwise if you're looking along the rotation axis toward the origin, while a negative rotation value rotates clockwise. You can remember this by using the right-hand rule. Hold your right hand out on front of you, palm up, with your thumb pointing to the right. Now curl the rest of your fingers over toward you as if making a fist, leaving your thumb pointing to the right. If your thumb points from the origin along the axis of rotation, your fingers curl in the direction of positive rotation. Figure 4-2 shows the right-hand rule in action on all three coordinate axes; it works as well for any arbitrary axis of rotation.

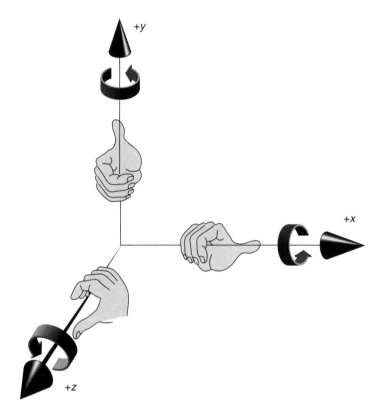

Figure 4-2   The right-hand rule

If you want to rotate around more than one coordinate axis, you have to either use multiple nested transforms or figure out what single axis to rotate around to get the same effect. You can't specify more than one rotation in a single transform.

Note: Be careful when rotating objects not located at the origin. As such an object rotates around an axis, it may also move through space. If you want it to rotate in place, you must first translate it to the origin, then rotate it, and finally translate it back to its original position. See "Order of Transformations" on page 66 for details.

Scaling

Scaling stretches or shrinks the transform's children. You specify a *scale* field as three numbers—the amounts to scale by in the x, y, and z directions, respectively. Scaling by 1 in any direction leaves the extent of the object in that direction unchanged, so scaling by (1, 1, 1) has no effect. Scaling by 0 in any direction makes an object infinitely thin in that direction, and is a bad idea.

Note: Be careful when scaling objects not located at the origin. Scaling is usually performed relative to the origin, not relative to the center of the object. See "More About Scaling and Object Size" on page 73 for details.

Combining Transformations

The Transform node has a couple of advanced fields with which you can do more complicated transformations; these are covered in the reference section titled "Transform" on page 361. For ordinary transformations, though, you can treat the fields of a Transform node just like a combination of a simple translation, a simple rotation, and a simple scale.

Here's a sample Transform node, with arbitrary values filled in for each basic field, and the chacmool model specified as the child:

Example 4-3   Combining transformations

```
Transform {
  translation  2    2.5 0
  rotation     0    0   1    1.57
  scale        1.7 1    0.7
  children [
    Inline { url  "chacmool.wrl" }
  ]
}
```

If you leave out a field, that field's default value is used. For default values, see "Transform" on page 361.

The example above results in the chacmool being scaled about the origin (by a different amount along each axis), rotated 90 degrees around the z axis, and then translated away from the origin. Figure 4-3 shows the original chacmool sitting at the origin and a copy of the chacmool after being scaled, rotated, and translated using the example values above.

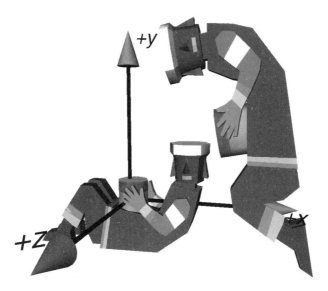

Figure 4-3   The chacmool transformed

Order of Transformations

When you combine transformations, keep these facts in mind:

- The order of a series of transformations makes a difference—a rotation followed by a translation doesn't have the same result as the translation followed by the rotation. Figure 4-4 and Figure 4-5 illustrate the difference.

- The most recent parent transform is applied first, then that node's parent transform, and so on, as described in "Accumulating Transformation Values" on page 49.

- The order in which a series of transformations is performed within a single transform is fixed—it's always scale, then rotation, then translation. If you want to apply transformations in a different order, you need multiple nested transforms.

The best way to develop a feel for the way combined transformations behave is to put a couple of nested transforms in a file and try varying the field values slightly and viewing the results.

If your shapes show up in the wrong place, or are rotated incorrectly, try using a separate Transform node for each part of the transformation (translation, rotation, scale), and then try varying the order in which the transforms are nested. It's easy to get the order of transformations wrong if you're not used to how they work.

Figure 4-4 shows what happens to a chacmool when it's first rotated, then translated:

Example 4-4   Rotation followed by translation

```
Transform {
  translation  6 5.3 0
  rotation     0 1  0  1.8
  children  [
    Inline { url  "chacmool.wrl" }
  ]
}
```

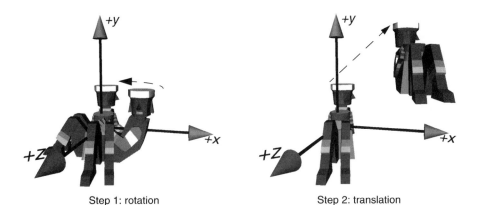

Step 1: rotation   Step 2: translation

Figure 4-4   Rotation, then translation

Figure 4-5 shows what happens to a chacmool when it's first translated, then rotated:

Example 4-5   Translation followed by rotation

```
Transform {
  rotation  0 1 0  1.8
  children  [
    Transform {
      translation  6 5.3 0
      children  [
        Inline { url  "chacmool.wrl" }
      ]
    }
  ]
}
```

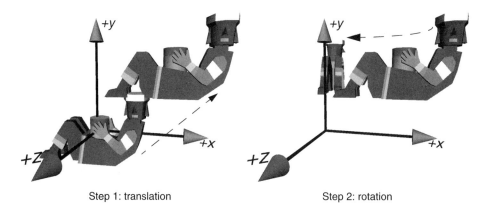

Step 1: translation   Step 2: rotation

Figure 4-5   Translation, then rotation

Geometry

Shape nodes, as described in Chapter 3, form the building blocks from which VRML worlds are created. Recall that each Shape node consists of two parts: the shape's *geometry* and its *appearance*. This section explains how to use geometry other than the purple cylinder of Chapter 3. For now, ignore the appearance part and focus on the geometry. Later, you'll learn how to apply colors and other aspects of appearance to the geometry you've created.

The geometry for some objects is given as a list of vertices plus information on how to connect those points to form the object's flat polygonal faces. Such geometry is called *vertex-based*; see "Irregular Geometry" on page 76 for information about vertex-based geometry. Other objects' geometries are given as simple mathematical definitions for certain types of predefined solids. VRML browsers know how to draw such objects without your having to list every polygon that makes them up.

Simple Geometry Nodes

There are four simple, compact types of geometry nodes that all VRML browsers understand without having to be told in detail how to draw them: boxes, cylinders, spheres, and cones.

Box Nodes

One of the simplest geometry nodes is the box. The default Box node is a cube two meters on a side, centered on the origin. A Box node's *size* field contains three numbers, indicating the length of the box along each of the three axes. Figure 4-6 shows an image of the default Box node, combined with a set of coordinate axes so that you can see that it's centered at the origin.

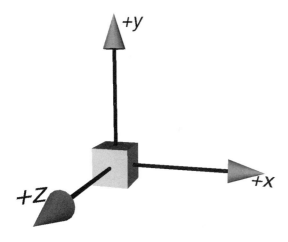

Figure 4-6   The box, with coordinate axes

A box can be a good building block. To build an Aztec temple, for instance, start with the simplest piece of it: build the rectangular blocks that the pillars rest on. To create the first of these blocks, go back to your temple file and edit it so it looks like Example 4-6 (the new lines to be added are in boldface).

Example 4-6   Using a Box node

```
#VRML V2.0 utf8
WorldInfo {
  title   "Temple"
  info    "VRML model of an Aztec temple."
}
Group {
  children [
    Transform {
      translation  -5 1.25 -1.875
      children [
        DEF COLUMN_BASE Shape {
          appearance  Appearance { material  Material { } }
          geometry  Box { size  3.75 2.5 3.75 }
        }
      ]
    }
  ]
}
```

The new transform is a child of the Group node. The transform's *translation* field moves the transform's child to the location where it's to be drawn. Nothing new so far.

The transform's child is a Shape node. The "DEF COLUMN_BASE" gives this shape a name, as described in "Reusing Objects" on page 31. The shape specifies a minimal *appearance* with an empty Material node to ensure that the shape is visible, as mentioned in the section titled "Geometry Node" on page 36. The shape's geometry is defined by a Box node. The *size* field indicates the extents of the box along the x, y, and z axes, in that order. The result is a slightly squashed cube—it has a square horizontal cross-section, as you can tell by the fact that the first and third (x and z) values in *size* are the same, but it isn't quite as tall as it is wide. This block is centered at the point indicated by the transform's *translation* field. It has the default color for a VRML shape, an unappealing gray. Go ahead and load this new file in your browser and take a look at your squashed cube.

Now you can add another transform right below the first one.

Example 4-7   Placing a box in two different places

```
#VRML V2.0 utf8
WorldInfo {
  title  "Temple"
  info   "VRML model of an Aztec temple."
}
Group {
  children [
    Transform {
      translation  -5 1.25 -1.875
      children [
        DEF COLUMN_BASE Shape {
          appearance  Appearance { material  Material { } }
          geometry  Box { size  3.75 2.5 3.75 }
        }
      ]
    }
    Transform {
      translation  5 1.25 -1.875
      children [
        USE COLUMN_BASE
      ]
    }
  ]
}
```

All you're doing here is putting the column base shape in two different places by putting it under two different transforms, as shown in Figure 4-7.

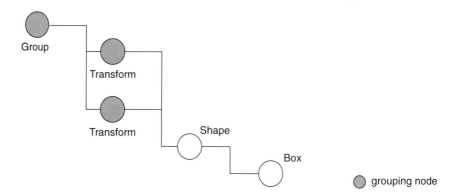

Figure 4-7 Scene diagram for column bases

Since you cleverly used DEF and gave the base a name at its first occurrence, it's easy to draw the base again elsewhere with USE. Of course, the USE has to come after the DEF in the file; you can't refer to a named object before you define the name.

Figure 4-8 shows what the column bases look like right now. Box nodes, like all VRML geometry, can be assigned a variety of appearances—they can be blue or fuchsia, shiny or dull. For information about assigning such appearances to your box, see "Appearances" on page 87. In designing your own world you might alternatively give each object a color as you create it, but in this case you're going to create the entire temple and then go back and color it in.

Figure 4-8 Gray bases without columns

More About Scaling and Object Size

Another way to create a column base is to use a *scale* value with a default Box node, instead of specifying the box's dimensions within the Box node itself:

```
Transform {
  scale  1.89 1.25 1.89
  children  [
    Shape {
      appearance  Appearance { material  Material { } }
      geometry  Box { }
    }
  ]
}
```

This approach is a little tricky, though, because the simple geometry nodes (such as the Box node) extend by default from −1 to +1 along all three axes. Therefore, the default *size* of a Box node is 2 meters in each direction, while the default *scale* in a Transform node is 1. So if you want to end up with a cube that's 3 units on a side, you can either use a *scale* value of "1.5 1.5 1.5," or a Box node with a *size* of "3 3 3." In other words, for simple geometry nodes, the *scale* value along a given axis should be half of what you want the total length of the geometry (along that axis) to be. Notice that the *scale* field in the preceding example uses numbers equal to half the length of the sides of the temple's column bases.

For any geometry that isn't centered on the origin, scaling gets more complicated; be sure to remember that scaling takes place relative to the origin (or to some other particular point if you use the *center* field of the Transform node). That is, if an object extends from −3 to +2 along the *x* axis and you scale it by a factor of 3 in the *x* direction, the new object extends from −9 to +6—multiplying every *x* coordinate by the scale factor. Not only that, but if an object extends from +1 to +2 in the *x* direction, scaling it by a factor of 3 in the *x* direction will make it go from +3 to +6; in that situation, the new object's extent doesn't overlap spatially with where the old object was at all.

> For ease of construction, model each object around the origin and then use a transform to move it to the right spot.

Cylinder Nodes

Now that you've got something for the columns to rest on, you may as well add the columns themselves. These columns are made from a cylinder, another of the simple geometry nodes in VRML. If this were a Greek or Roman scene, you could create detailed Ionic, Doric, or Corinthian columns using Extrusion or IndexedFaceSet nodes (described later in this book), but such items aren't even from the same continent as the Aztec temple you're building; the architectural styles would clash horribly. So keep the columns simple for now.

To create the columns, use much the same procedure as with the column bases, but use a Cylinder node instead of a box:

Example 4-8   Using a Cylinder node

```
Transform {
  translation  -5 6.25 -1.875
  children  [
    DEF COLUMN Shape {
      appearance  Appearance { material  Material { } }
      geometry  Cylinder {
        radius  1.25
        height  7.5
        top     FALSE
        bottom  FALSE
      }
    }
  ]
}
Transform {
  translation  5 6.25 -1.875
  children  [
    USE COLUMN
  ]
}
```

A Cylinder node's fields are somewhat different from those of a Box node. A cylinder is defined by the *radius* of its circular base and by its *height*. A Cylinder node consists of two circular disks—a top and a bottom—as well as the cylindrical side piece that connects them; the node includes three Boolean fields (*side*, *top*, and *bottom*), each of which tells the browser whether or not to draw the corresponding part of the object. (A *Boolean* field is a field that can take the value TRUE or FALSE.) The default is to draw all three parts of the object; in the preceding example, you're requesting that the top and bottom (the circular caps) not be drawn, because the caps won't be visible anyway in the finished temple.

> Drawing geometry that the user can't possibly ever see serves only to slow down rendering. VRML creates the illusion of solid objects, but all you need to draw to create that illusion are the visible surfaces of those objects.

Load your scene into your browser. It should look something like Figure 4-9.

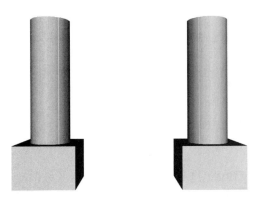

Figure 4-9　　Gray columns on gray bases

> It's best to place adjacent objects (such as the column and the base) in such a way that the surfaces exactly match up (for instance, the top of the column base is at $y = 2.5$, as is the bottom of the column). Some rendering systems can draw nonintersecting objects faster than intersecting ones; if you separate the objects a little, you may end up with a visible gap between them.

Now place another stretched-out box on top of the columns, to form the ceiling of the temple:

```
DEF LOWER_CEILING Transform {
  translation  0 10.625 -10
  children [
    Shape {
      appearance  Appearance { material  Material { } }
      geometry  Box { size  37.5 1.25 20 }
    }
  ]
}
```

Since much of the upper surface of this piece is going to be hidden from view, it would improve rendering speed to specify the visible surface of the piece as an IndexedFaceSet node (which will be described shortly). However, for the purposes of this example, ease of modeling won out over performance. Note that if you model the ceiling as an indexed face set, you can make each face a different color (as described in "Specifying Colors Per Face" in Chapter 8); a box must use a single color for all its faces.

Cone Nodes and Sphere Nodes

There are two other simple geometry nodes, the Cone and the Sphere. Both of them have syntax much like the box and cylinder. This particular Aztec temple contains nothing resembling either a cone or a sphere, so if you want details about syntax for these nodes, see "Cone" and "Sphere" in Chapter 11.

Irregular Geometry

The simple compact geometry nodes can be surprisingly versatile, but there comes a time when you need a shape that you can't make from them—not everything in the real world can be modeled using boxes and cylinders, or even cones and spheres. That's when the vertex-based geometry nodes come in handy.

Coordinates

Every piece of vertex-based geometry must include a list of the vertices to be used. The Coordinate node allows you to list a set of coordinates in 3D space that you can use as part of vertex-based geometry. The Coordinate node contains one field—*point*—consisting of multiple floating point triples, each of which defines a point in 3D space. Here's an example of a very simple Coordinate node, to give you an idea what such nodes look like.

Example 4-9   Using a Coordinate node

```
Coordinate {
  point [ -1 -1 0,    # point 0
           1 -1 0,    # point 1
           1  1 0,    # point 2
          -1  1 0 ]   # point 3
}
```

That example node defines a set of four points in the xy plane (since the z value of each point is 0); if you connect those points using a vertex-based geometry node, the result is a flat square. Note that the Coordinate node can't be used by itself; it can occur only inside a vertex-based geometry node.

As indicated by the comments in the example, you can think of each point in the Coordinate node as having a reference number, or *index*; the initial point in the Coordinate node is point number 0, the next is point number 1, and so on. Figure 4-10 shows a square drawn by connecting the points given in the above Coordinate node; the points are labeled by their indices into the Coordinate node.

3   2

0   1

Figure 4-10   A polygon with numbered vertices

Note that the vertices are numbered in counterclockwise order. This ordering isn't required, but it comes in handy when it's time to list the vertices to define the polygon.

IndexedFaceSet Nodes

Models in 3D graphics don't generally have smooth surfaces, as objects in the real world do; 3D models are usually rendered as a set of small flat polygons. Most curved surfaces, for instance, are approximated by a large number of small triangles or quadrilaterals. Figure 4-11 shows a curved surface and a close-up of its breakdown into flat rectangular faces.

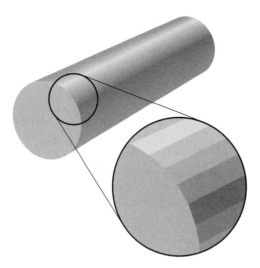

Figure 4-11   A model showing its faces

Each of those polygons can be described by listing its vertices; each vertex is a point in 3D space, as listed in a Coordinate node. To draw a polygon, you need to specify which vertices to connect, and in what order, using an IndexedFaceSet node. An indexed face set consists of a list of vertices (in the form of a Coordinate node in the *coord* field) and a list of polygons (in the *coordIndex* field). Each polygon is specified as a series of indices into the Coordinate node. When drawing an indexed face set, the browser draws each polygon by connecting the points in the given order, connecting the last vertex back to the first one, and then filling in the resulting shape.

For each face, list the vertices by starting at any vertex and continuing counterclockwise around the polygon when looking at the front of the polygon. It's possible to use a clockwise ordering, as long as all the polygons in the node go in the same direction and you specify the indexed face set's *ccw* field as FALSE, but clockwise ordering is not recommended.

To indicate that you've reached the end of one polygon and that it's time to start the next, use the number −1 instead of a vertex number.

Note that each polygon must be *planar*; that is, all of its vertices must lie in the same plane. Results are unpredictable (and probably ugly) if you try to draw a nonplanar polygon. The easiest way to avoid this problem is to use only triangles instead of more complex polygons; any triangle is guaranteed to be planar, since, in general, three points define a plane.

Most of the Aztec temple model is made up of indexed face sets; in fact, most models are made entirely of indexed face sets. The simplest indexed face set in the temple is the middle layer of the roof, the layer above the ceiling that you already added.

For this roof layer, use an indexed face set to create a wall out of four rectangles. Like the columns, the middle layer of the roof has no top or bottom—but users won't be able to tell that, because they'd never be able to see the top or bottom anyway.

Note: In general it's best to use triangles instead of rectangles, but when you're certain that rectangular faces are planar you can use rectangles to keep the node simple.

Start with a shape (which is a child of the top-level grouping node in your file), then use an indexed face set to list the coordinates to use and to indicate the order in which to use them:

Example 4-10   Using an IndexedFaceSet node

```
DEF UPPER_WHITE_BAND Shape {
  geometry  IndexedFaceSet {
    coord  Coordinate {
      point [  17.5 11.25  -1.25,   17.5 15      -1.25,
              -17.5 15      -1.25, -17.5 11.25  -1.25,
               17.5 15     -18.75,  17.5 11.25 -18.75,
              -17.5 11.25 -18.75, -17.5 15      -18.75 ]
    }
    coordIndex [ 0, 1, 2, 3, -1,
                 4, 1, 0, 5, -1,
                 6, 7, 4, 5, -1,
                 2, 7, 6, 3, -1 ]
  }
}
```

Each line in the *point* field of the Coordinate node describes two vertices, and each line in the indexed face set's *coordIndex* field describes a single polygon. (Of course, that's just for readability; for each of those listings, you can put all the numbers on a single line if you prefer. The comma marks the separation between vertices in the Coordinate node; and in the *coordIndex* field, the –1 marks the end of one polygon and the beginning of the next.) The first face is to be drawn by connecting points 0, 1, 2, and 3 (that is, the first four vertices listed in the *point* field of the Coordinate node) in order, then connecting point 3 back to point 0, and then coloring in the resulting rectangle. And so on with the other three rectangles, until you have four rectangles standing on edge on top of the lower roof piece.

Your temple-so-far should look something like Figure 4-12.

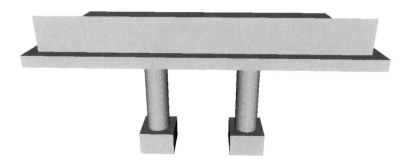

Figure 4-12   Columns and roof pieces

Note that you can't see the faces that face away from you, though you can see them if you walk around the model to look at the fronts of those faces. This is because the indexed face set left the *solid* field at its default value of TRUE. The *solid* field indicates whether the geometry you're defining is a solid object—that is, an object that has no holes in its outer surface. When there are no holes in the surface, the user can never see the inside, so there's no need to draw the inside surface. Thus, there are fewer polygons to draw, resulting in faster rendering. The field is TRUE by default, because more often than not indexed face sets are used to define solids. In this particular case the object isn't actually solid, but once you put a roof on it the user won't be able to see inside it, so it can be treated like a solid object.

Of course, if you're building an object that the user can see the inside of, you need to set *solid* to FALSE so that the backs of polygons facing away from the user are drawn.

Note: The IndexedFaceSet node has other fields besides *coord* and *coordIndex*; they're the subjects of more advanced sections in Chapter 8. For now you can ignore them.

The rest of the temple also consists of indexed face sets (except for the upper roof piece, which is another stretched-out box). However, the remainder of the indexed face sets are significantly larger than the one shown above, requiring a total of several dozen vertices and triangles. Rather than typing in the entire temple file by hand from a full listing, download the full (gray) temple from

```
http://vrml.sgi.com/handbook/examples/temple.gray.wrl
```

and take a look at the file listing. Once you understand its structure, continue on.

IndexedLineSet Nodes

An IndexedLineSet is essentially the same as an indexed face set, except that instead of filling in polygons, the browser simply displays line segments between the given points. This node type is useful for wireframe models or displaying the outlines of solid objects, and it renders quickly. One use for the node is illustrated in the full Tenochtitlán world, near the temple of Quetzalcoatl: the light rays that appear as you near the temple's door are implemented as an indexed line set. A slightly simplified version of the light rays is shown in Example 4-11.

Example 4-11   Using an IndexedLineSet node

```
#VRML V2.0 utf8

Transform {
  rotation  1 0  0  -1.37  # tilted down at an angle
  scale     8 80 8
  children  [
    Shape {
      appearance  Appearance {
        material  Material {
          diffuseColor   1 0.8 0  # bright yellow,
          emissiveColor  1 0.8 0  # to look like sunlight
          shininess      1
        }
      }
      geometry  IndexedLineSet {
        coord  Coordinate {
          point  [ 0    -1 -1,    0    1  0,
                   0.4 -1 -0.9,  0.7 -1 -0.7,
                   0.9 -1 -0.4,  1    -1  0,
                   0.9 -1  0.4,  0.7 -1  0.7,
                   0.4 -1  0.9,  0    -1  1,
```

```
                        -0.4 -1  0.9, -0.7 -1  0.7,
                        -0.9 -1  0.4, -1    -1  0,
                        -0.9 -1 -0.4, -0.7 -1 -0.7,
                        -0.4 -1 -0.9
                    ]
            }
            coordIndex  [ 0, 1, -1,  2, 1, -1,  3, 1, -1,  4, 1, -1,
                          5, 1, -1,  6, 1, -1,  7, 1, -1,  8, 1, -1,
                          9, 1, -1, 10, 1, -1, 11, 1, -1, 12, 1, -1,
                         13, 1, -1, 14, 1, -1, 15, 1, -1, 16, 1, -1,
                        ]
        }
      }
    ]
}
```

PointSet Nodes

A PointSet displays a one-pixel point corresponding to each vertex listed in the Coordinate node inside the point set. This node can be very useful for items like airport lights or stars; in the Tenochtitlán scene, it's used for the animated sparks that fly up when a user lights a brazier.

Text (Flat)

It's often useful to add 2D text to a scene—information on signs, labels for objects, and so on. There are two nodes you need to know about in order to put text in your scenes: Text and FontStyle.

The Text node allows you to specify any number of strings to be displayed and a *length* (measured in the local coordinate system) in which to display each string. (Each string is displayed as a separate line of text.) If the string is too long to fit in that space, it's squeezed together; if it's too short, it's stretched to fit.

The Text node also contains a *fontStyle* field, which in turn contains a FontStyle node. (FontStyle is a separate node so that you can define a style with DEF, and then USE it for text anywhere in your world.) The FontStyle node, described in "FontStyle" on page 84, defines a style of text to use for the containing Text node; you can specify any of three different kinds of typefaces (serif, sans-serif, or monospace/fixed-width) as well as whether the text should be roman, bold, or italic, how it should be justified, and whether it's to be displayed horizontally or vertically. As you might guess from the fact that you can display text vertically, text strings are not limited

Chapter 4: Building Objects

to English; they can include any character in the UTF-8 character encoding standard. (ASCII is a subset of UTF-8, so you can use English strings just the way you'd expect.)

Here's a simplified version of the sign at the front gate of the Tenochtitlán model:

Example 4-12   Using a Text node

```
#VRML V2.0 utf8
Viewpoint { position  28 2 50 }
Shape {
  geometry Text {
    string "Tenochtitlan"
  }
}
```

Figure 4-13 shows how this example Text node looks.

Figure 4-13   Default text

The sign in the Aztec model is actually an indexed face set, not text, because a more sophisticated coloring mechanism is available for indexed face sets than for text; but for most textual purposes, it's much better to use a Text node.

Note: VRML doesn't have any special support for extruded 3D-looking text, but many modelers can extrude ordinary text into a 3D look; then it's simply a matter of including the extruded text as an ordinary polygonal object in your VRML scene. However, text created by a modeler is composed of indexed face sets; the many vertices and polygons that make up each letter must be specified individually. The Text node provides a way to place text in your scene without the file size and performance problems that modeled text is likely to create.

FontStyle

The FontStyle node, which appears only inside a Text node, describes how the text should look. (It may seem that it's therefore analogous to Appearance, but it's not; it's more like the Coordinate node, a sub-node within a piece of geometry. You can apply an Appearance node to text just as you can to any other geometry.) There are two main aspects to this description: choosing a font, and orientation and placement of the text.

Font Specification

Three fields in the FontStyle node allow you to specify what sort of font to use:

- *size* indicates how tall the characters should be. It's also used, with the Text node's *spacing* field, to determine how far apart two consecutive lines of text should be.

- *family* specifies whether to use a proportional-spaced font with serifs (specify `"SERIF"`), one without serifs (`"SANS"`), or a fixed-width font, in which all characters are the same width (`"TYPEWRITER"`).

- *style* indicates whether to make the text ordinary plain roman (upright) text, italic, bold, or bold and italic.

You can't specify exactly which font you want to use; there are too many different kinds of fonts on different systems. The browser chooses a font that matches the given parameters from the fonts available on the user's system, in much the same way that HTML browsers choose fonts. Thus, text doesn't always look exactly the same from browser to browser, but it always has the right general look. Here are some examples of different font specifications:

Example 4-13 Specifying fonts

```
#VRML V2.0 utf8

Viewpoint { position  10 3 18 }

Transform {
  translation  0 3.5 0
  children [
    Shape {
      geometry Text {
        string  "Italic serif font"
        fontStyle  FontStyle {
          size     2.5
          family  "SERIF"
          style   "ITALIC"
        }
      }
    }
  ]
}

Transform {
  translation 0 1.5 0
  children  [
    Shape {
      geometry Text {
        string  "Bold sans-serif font"
        fontStyle  FontStyle {
          size    2
          family  "SANS"
          style   "BOLD"
        }
      }
    }
  ]
}
```

```
Shape {
  geometry  Text {
    string  "Roman typewriter font"
    fontStyle  FontStyle {
      size    1.5
      family  "TYPEWRITER"
      style   ""
    }
  }
}
```

Figure 4-14 shows what this file looks like.

Figure 4-14   Using a FontStyle node

Text Orientation and Placement

Three Boolean fields indicate what direction the text should be displayed in.
horizontal specifies whether the text should read horizontally or vertically;
leftToRight indicates whether the text reads left-to-right or right-to-left; and
topToBottom indicates whether the text reads top-to-bottom or bottom-to-
top. These three Boolean values, taken together, form eight possible ways to
display text, including common approaches for English (horizontal, left-to-

right, top-to-bottom) and Japanese (vertical, top-to-bottom, right-to-left—though that format may not be as common as it once was).

These field values interact with the *justify* field to determine how each line of text should be placed in relation to the specified line width (or height). *justify* takes one or two string values. The first string indicates whether the beginnings ("BEGIN"), middles ("MIDDLE"), or endings ("END") of the lines should line up with one another; the second indicates how the entire block of text should be aligned as a unit. See "FontStyle" in Chapter 11 for details. These methods taken together provide quite a bit of flexibility in choosing a format for text display.

Appearances

By now you've learned everything you need to know about creating marvelous shapes. But even if you build a perfect model of Notre Dame—or, for that matter, of an Aztec temple—it looks dull and gray until you assign colors to it.

Appearance Nodes

Just as a shape's *geometry* field contains a geometry node, which in turn contains further information about the geometry, so a shape's *appearance* field contains an Appearance node. Unlike the situation with geometry nodes, however, an Appearance node exists only as a container for other kinds of nodes that affect the shape's appearance. (This approach may seem roundabout, but it provides the very useful ability to define and reuse each part of the Appearance node as well as the Appearance node itself. Often, you define an Appearance node once in your file, give it a name, and use it in several places to give different pieces of geometry the same look.)

Each Appearance node can contain a Material node and several kinds of texturing nodes.

Materials

A Material node lets you specify what associated geometry looks like—its color, how it reflects light, and how transparent it is. You can give an object the appearance of plastic, metal, or even a reasonable approximation of stone, using just a Material node. If you want your objects to look less flat or less uniform, consider using a texturing node, described in "Textures" on page 89.

The Material node uses six fields: *diffuseColor*, *specularColor*, and *emissiveColor* (each specified as an RGB value), and *ambientIntensity*, *shininess*, and *transparency* (each specified as a single floating point value from 0 to 1, inclusive).

The *diffuseColor* field indicates more or less what you mean when you say an object "is" a certain color—it describes the color of light that reflects most from the object. The *specularColor* field gives the color of the highlights on a highly reflective object, the color of the light that reflects directly back to the eye. The *emissiveColor* field indicates that the object glows with a light of its own—though emissive objects in VRML do not cast light on other objects in the scene.

So how about finally adding some color to your heretofore gray Aztec temple? Start by making the column bases red:

Example 4-14   Using diffuse color in a Material node

```
DEF COLUMN_BASE Shape {
  appearance  Appearance {
    material  Material { diffuseColor  0.45 0.1 0.1 }
  }
  geometry  Box { size  3.75 2.5 3.75 }
}
```

Now move on to the columns themselves, which are gray-green:

```
DEF COLUMN Shape {
  appearance  Appearance {
    material  Material { diffuseColor  0.22 0.3 0.3 }
  }
  geometry  Cylinder {
    radius  1.25
    height  7.5
    top     FALSE
    bottom  FALSE
  }
}
```

Now for the roof—the top piece of the temple, the part labeled "ROOF" in the full gray temple file. Color it red like the column bases, and make it contribute some of that red color to the scene's overall ambient lighting.

Example 4-15 Ambient intensity

```
DEF ROOF Shape {
  appearance  Appearance {
    material  Material {
      ambientIntensity  0.35
      diffuseColor      0.45 0.1 0.1
    }
  }
  geometry  Box { size  37.5 1.25 20 }
}
```

Go ahead and play around with adding colors. When you're done coloring the temple, you can load the full *temple.complete* file to see the colors used in the full city model.

There's nothing shiny or transparent in the temple as it was originally modeled, but there's no reason not to use the *shiniess* and *transparency* fields as you experiment with Material nodes. They do pretty much what you would expect: make an object shinier or allow the viewer to see things through an object. Be careful with transparency; all browsers support fully transparent and fully opaque materials, but some browsers can't handle partly transparent materials.

Changing the *shininess* value works best for objects with rounded surfaces, like the columns.

Textures

If you really want your objects to look realistic, you need texture maps. A *texture map*, also called a *texture*, is a 2D image that's "mapped" onto a surface—like putting wallpaper on a wall. If the texture is exactly the same size and shape as the surface, it's obvious how it should be attached; however, textures are usually rectangular and surfaces are irregular (and often curved). A texturing node allows you to specify both the texture itself and how to map the texture onto the surface. There are three different kinds of texturing nodes: ImageTexture, which contains the URL of a *JPEG-* or *PNG*-format image in a separate file; MovieTexture, which contains the URL of an *MPEG* movie file to use as an animated texture; and PixelTexture, which lets you specify a texture as hexadecimal numbers directly in the node. For instance, the texture used on the Aztec temple is an image texture; it's specified in the *texture* field of an Appearance node, like this:

```
texture   ImageTexture {
  url   "Skull0.jpg"
  repeatS   TRUE
  repeatT   TRUE
}
```

Each shape node has a different default way of mapping textures to its surface, all described in the appropriate node descriptions in Chapter 11. Texture nodes allow you to specify whether the texture should be repeated over and over if it runs out while there's still some of the surface left to be covered, like ordinary wallpaper, or whether the texture should be stretched to fit the entire surface, like some kind of rubber wallpaper.

Unfortunately, the default mapping of textures to vertex-based geometry is not usually the best mapping to use; the Aztec temple texture, for instance, includes a full VRML description of how to apply the skull texture. For detailed information on textures, including examples of nondefault mappings, see "Advanced Textures" on page 187.

 Large, high-quality textures are slow to download across a network and can be slow to display on some systems. Keep your textures small and reuse the same texture where possible.

Prototypes

Now you've learned how to create objects using built-in VRML geometry nodes and how to modify the appearance of those objects. But using the techniques shown in this chapter so far, if you want to create several similar objects you have to create each one independently. If you want to use exactly the same object in more than one place, you can use DEF and USE, but what if you want to create several slightly varying copies of an object, each with customized parameters? The answer is *prototyping*, a method of packaging up a set of nodes (and routes between them if you wish) to provide a new custom node type.

Imagine you've defined an Aztec temple in a VRML file. Now you want to create another one, but you don't want it to be quite like the first one. Maybe you want the columns in your new temple to be a different color from the original, or to be wider. The best solution is to create a prototype of a new node type, perhaps called AztecTemple, which provides a field for each parameter you might want to vary.

Prototyping may sound like a fancy form of DEF, but they're not really the same thing. DEF simply gives a name to a particular node so that you can use that node again elsewhere. A prototype creates a new node type, not a node; if you subsequently want to create a node of that new type, you do so just as you would create a node of any standard node type. When you create an instance of the new node type, you can set values for its fields, just as you can for the standard node types.

To define a prototype, use the PROTO declaration. First give the new type a name; then list its fields and events in brackets. Finally, define the new type as a combination of previously known types. For instance, you might want to create a new node type that lets you easily create columns (colored cylinders like the ones in the Aztec temple) of any color. The first thing to do is to define a node-type name and list the fields that this new type has.

Example 4-16   Creating a prototype's interface

```
PROTO Column [
  field SFColor columnColor   .5 .5 .5
]
```

The **field** declarations (you can have as many **field** lines as you want) define the names, types, and default values for the publicly accessible fields in this new node type. In this case there's only one such field: the column's color. This field's type is specified as SFColor, which means the field can contain a single color value. The field's name is *columnColor*, and .5 .5 .5 is its default value.

Note: For information on field types and how to specify them, see Chapter 12, "Field Reference."

When you create an instance of the Column node type, you can specify a color value for the *columnColor* field or leave it at its default value, much as you can give the *radius* field a value when you create an instance of the Sphere node.

But before you can create a Column node, you have to finish defining the prototype. The rest of the prototype consists of a node or set of nodes that make up the inner workings of the new node type.

Every field (and event) that you declare in the prototype's public interface must have a corresponding field (or event) of the same type inside the prototype implementation. To set this up, list a field or event (in a node inside the prototype definition) with the word IS followed by a name given in the declaration.

Example 4-17   Prototyping a column

```
PROTO Column [
  field SFColor columnColor   .5 .5 .5
]
{
  Shape {
    appearance  Appearance {
      material  Material {
        diffuseColor  IS columnColor
      }
    }
    geometry  Cylinder { }
  }
}
```

The line that reads `diffuseColor IS columnColor` indicates that the value of the prototype's *columnColor* field is used as the value of the Material node's *diffuseColor* field—which is to say, in this case, the color of the column. Note that both *columnColor* and *diffuseColor* are SFColor fields; corresponding items in the public interface and the prototype definition must be of the same field or event type.

Once you've defined a prototype like the preceding one, you can use it just like a built-in node. For example,

```
Column { columnColor  1 0 0 }
```

gives a red column.

You've seen that certain nodes can appear only in certain places in a file. A prototyped node type acts like the first node inside the prototype definition. In this case, since the top-level node within the prototype definition is a Shape node, the Column node can appear anywhere a Shape node can in the file.

Any given prototype name can be defined only once in a given file. After you've defined a prototype, you can create as many instances of the new node type as you like, anywhere in the same file; the browser doesn't distinguish between node types defined by VRML and node types defined by prototypes. (In fact, several of the standard VRML nodes are defined as prototypes in some browsers.) You can even use DEF and USE with a prototype instance.

The prototype definition creates a sort of barrier between what's inside it and what's outside it. You don't have access to nodes inside the prototype definition from the outside. For instance, if a node is named with DEF inside the prototype, you can't USE that node name outside of the prototype. Also, if a node is named outside the prototype, you can't use it inside. The prototype acts like a black box: the public interface (the field and event declarations) provides the only contact possible between the inside and the outside.

Besides declaring fields, the public interface can declare the events that a prototype can send or receive, using **eventIn** and **eventOut** declarations. You can also specify a special kind of field called an **exposedField**, which combines an ordinary field with a pair of events, one incoming event and one outgoing event. Exposed fields are discussed in greater depth in "Events and Routes Revisited" on page 115. Note that the term "exposedField" describes a particular kind of field; the word isn't a field name, and it never occurs in a VRML file except in prototype definitions.

Fields Versus Events

The distinction between the **field** declarations and the **eventIn** and **eventOut** declarations is an important one. A field can be given an initial value when you create an instance of the node, but can't be changed subsequently. An event is, in most cases, simply a request to change the value of a field—an incoming event asks the prototyped node to change one of its own field values, while an outgoing event is a request from the prototyped node asking some other node to change one of its field values. So if you want to be able to change the color of a Column node after you've created it, you need to declare an event in the prototype interface. In this particular case, that's best done using the **exposedField** declaration.

Example 4-18   Prototyping with an exposed field

```
PROTO Column [
  exposedField SFColor columnColor   .5 .5 .5
]
{
  Shape {
    appearance  Appearance {
      material  Material {
        diffuseColor   IS columnColor
      }
    }
  }
```

```
    geometry  Cylinder { }
  }
}
```

Since *diffuseColor* is defined as an exposed field in the Material node (see "Material" in Chapter 11), it implicitly defines a *set_diffuseColor* event; in this example, an exposed field in the prototype definition (*columnColor*) corresponds to the *diffuseColor* exposed field, so there's an implicit incoming event to set the column's color called *set_columnColor*. When a Column node receives a *set_columnColor* event, the event is treated as a *set_diffuseColor* event to set the diffuse color in the internal Material node.

Note that in Example 4-17 you declared *columnColor* as a nonexposed field, while in Example 4-18 you defined it as an exposed field. The corresponding field inside the prototype definition (*diffuseColor*) is an exposed field, so *columnColor* could be declared as a field, an exposed field, an incoming event, or an outgoing event, depending on what you want to use it for. When the item inside the prototype definition is a nonexposed field, an incoming event, or an outgoing event, then the corresponding declaration must be the same. That is, you can't declare an **eventIn** in the public interface and then associate it with a nonexposed field or an **eventOut** inside the prototype definition.

EXTERNPROTO

Instead of defining your prototypes in your main scene file, you can indicate that a prototype is defined fully in an external file. You still declare the interface, but you don't give default values for fields in the external-prototype declaration. EXTERNPROTO is just a reference to a PROTO defined in another file. For instance, if the Column node prototype from the preceding code is in a file of its own called *column.wrl*, you can use it in any other file like this.

Example 4-19   External prototype syntax

```
EXTERNPROTO Column [
  exposedField SFColor columnColor
]
"column.wrl"
```

This method works a little like an Inline node. The EXTERNPROTO declaration indicates that the full prototype for the named node type is in the given URL. The file pointed to by that URL should contain nothing but the VRML header and one or more prototypes (using PROTO). If the file contains more than one prototype, the URL should indicate which one you want: `"column.wrl#DoricColumn"`, for instance, loads the prototype named DoricColumn from the file *column.wrl*.

The **field**, **exposedField**, **eventIn**, and **eventOut** declarations in the EXTERNPROTO declaration must be a subset of the corresponding declarations specified in the PROTO in the given URL. Once an EXTERNPROTO has been declared, it works just like a PROTO that's in the main file.

Chapter 5

Lighting, Sound, and Complex Shapes

Congratulations! You've built and painted an Aztec temple with your bare hands! But you're not done building your world yet. As any theater lighting designer can tell you, the most beautiful set in the world isn't much good if the audience can't see it; you need to light your temple. Furthermore, without sound it's very hard to create a convincing virtual world. And finally, as you create more advanced worlds you'll want to know how to build certain kinds of complex geometry without having to specify an indexed face set vertex by vertex.

Lights

There are three kinds of light nodes in VRML: DirectionalLight, PointLight, and SpotLight.

Lights in VRML are not like lights in the real world. Real lights are physical objects that emit light; you can see the object that emits the light as well as the light it emits, and that light reflects off of various other objects to allow you to see them. In VRML, a lighting node describes how a part of the world should be lit, but does not automatically create any geometry to represent the light source. If you want a light source in your scene to be a visible object, you need to create a piece of geometry (in the shape of a lightbulb, for instance, or of the sun) and place it in the appropriate place in the scene, which usually means at the same location as the light node. You may also want to assign an *emissiveColor* to the geometry (as part of the associated Appearance node) in order to make it look like the object is glowing;

otherwise there's no indication that the object is associated with the light source.

You can turn this lack of geometry to your advantage. You may sometimes want to place a light close to an object without a lighting fixture getting in the way of users looking at the object. This sort of setup is ideal for situations in which making the world look nice is more important than a strict adherence to real-world physics. Theater lighting designers would be overjoyed to be able to light a set without the audience seeing the light fixtures.

Another difference between VRML lights, as currently implemented, and lights in the real world is that objects in VRML don't cast shadows. This fact is due to the way current VRML browsers (and the renderers they're based on) handle lighting; they don't attempt to simulate photons rushing around and bouncing off of things, but instead apply a *lighting equation* to each piece of geometry drawn, in order to shade surfaces realistically. The lighting equation combines the colors of the object in question (as indicated in the shape's Appearance node) with the colors of light available (as indicated by light nodes). This computation ignores the effects of opaque objects between the light and the geometry being lit.

It's possible to simulate shadows under some circumstances. You have to figure out what shape each shadow would be, and place flat dark semitransparent polygons where the shadow should be. This approach makes it difficult to simulate moving shadows; it's probably best not to bother creating explicit shadows, except possibly for objects that can't be moved and lights that can't be moved. You can create shading effects using per-vertex coloring (see "Colors" in Chapter 8).

Scope of Lights

A VRML lighting node lights only certain objects. Each PointLight and SpotLight node has a *radius* field that indicates how far the node's light can spread; any object outside that radius is not lit by the node, no matter how bright the light may be.

DirectionalLight nodes have a different kind of scope. A directional light affects only sibling objects, objects that are children of the light's parent grouping node. It doesn't affect anything outside of the parent grouping node. You can use this fact to ensure the right scope for a directional light—to keep ceiling lights that are inside a room, for instance, from lighting up anything outside the room. However, the results of this scoping are not always intuitive; a directional light won't affect objects if they're not under the same grouping node as the light, even if the objects are right next to other objects that are lit. If you find that your scene doesn't seem to be lit properly—if objects seem to be lit that shouldn't be, or seem not to be lit when they should be—check to make sure that your directional lights are in the right grouping nodes.

Common Attributes of Lights

There are four fields that all three light nodes contain: *on*, *color*, *intensity*, and *ambientIntensity*.

The *on* field indicates whether the light is currently turned on or not. When a light is off, it doesn't contribute to the light in the scene at all. At first glance, you might wonder why you would want a light in your world if it's turned off; the answer is that you can change the value of this field (and thereby turn a light on or off) by sending an event to the light node with the appropriate value (TRUE or FALSE). For information on how to send events, see "Events and Routes Revisited" in Chapter 6.

If you use an object with an *emissiveColor* to represent the light source in your scene, be sure to modify the *emissiveColor* (by sending it an event) every time you turn the light node on or off. Otherwise, the light bulb geometry continues to glow even after the light source has been turned off.

The *color* field indicates the color of the light. The light's color interacts with the various colors specified in an object's Material node to determine the color(s) of the object's surface.

intensity is a floating point value indicating how bright the light is, from 0 (emits no light at all) to 1 (maximum brightness).

The *ambientIntensity* field affects the ambient (indirect) lighting for lit objects. Its use is somewhat complex; at first you may wish to leave it at its default value of 0. Ambient light in VRML simulates light that doesn't go directly from a light source to an object, including light that's been scattered or reflected before it reaches an object. As such, ambient light does originally come from the light sources in the scene; although it may appear to be sourceless, it's not really.

If a light is on, its contribution to the scene's overall ambient lighting is computed (for each of red, green, and blue values) by multiplying the light's intensity by its *ambientIntensity*, and multiplying the result by the light's value for that color component. For instance, this light node:

```
PointLight {
  on                  TRUE
  intensity           .75  # three-quarters maximum brightness
  ambientIntensity    .5
  color               1 0 0  # red
}
```

contributes $.75 \times .5 \times 1 = .375$ to the red portion of the ambient lighting for the scene. All of the ambient light values for all of the lights in the scene are added up and applied to objects within the lights' scopes. Note that this means that changing the light's intensity also changes its contribution to the scene's ambient lighting.

 Note that some browsers (and their underlying rendering systems) may consider ambient lighting to be an attribute of the scene rather than of individual lights; such browsers are likely to set up ambient lighting when the scene is loaded and not subsequently change it. Thus, if you change your ambient lighting after the scene is loaded (by routing events to the lights), you risk some users not being able to see the changes.

Attenuation

In the real world, light *attenuates*: it gets fainter (loses intensity) the farther you are from the light source. Specifically, the intensity of light at a given point is proportional to the inverse of the square of the distance from the light source. VRML can simulate attenuation for lights that have a location (the PointLight and SpotLight nodes), using the *attenuation* field. That field specifies three coefficients to be used by the browser in calculating an attenuation factor; the browser multiplies the attenuation factor by the light's *intensity* value to determine intensity at a given distance. The default is no attenuation. Not all browsers can handle full lighting attenuation; if you use attenuation in your scene, some users may not experience it.

Since directional lights don't have a specific location, it's impossible to calculate the distance from the light source, so you can't use attenuation for such lights.

DirectionalLight Nodes

A directional light is a light considered to be far away, or "at infinity," and that therefore illuminates a scene with parallel rays, all from one direction. In a DirectionalLight node, in addition to the standard *on*, *intensity*, *ambientIntensity*, and *color* values, you specify the direction the light moves toward (as a vector from the origin that parallels the light rays) in the node's *direction* field.

Directional lights don't take as much processing power as other kinds of lights. You can use them to get reasonably good general lighting for a scene with very little impact on performance.

PointLight Nodes

A point light is located at a specific point in space and illuminates in all directions, like a light bulb. Besides the four common lighting fields, a PointLight node contains fields to specify the light's *location*, its *radius* of effect (beyond which nothing is lit by it), and its *attenuation*.

Point lights are reasonably fast, but some systems can't handle more than a couple of them in a world at once. Every time you add a light to your world, try navigating through the world to make sure performance hasn't dropped too much.

SpotLight Nodes

A spotlight is located at a specific point in space and illuminates in a cone pointed in a specified direction. The intensity of the illumination drops off exponentially toward the edges of the cone. The rate of drop-off and the angle of the cone are controlled by the *dropOffRate* and *cutOffAngle* fields. Note that SpotLight nodes are often slow to render.

Spotlights are slow and take a lot of processing power. It's probably best to use them as little as you can. Be sure to test for performance every time you add one to your world.

Sound

In addition to placing lights, you can place sounds in a scene—anything from audio loops of ambient background noise (such as crickets or rain), to sound effects (bumping into things, explosions), to music, to speech. There are two sound-related nodes: the Sound node, which specifies the spatial parameters of a sound—such as its location and how far away it can be heard—and the AudioClip node, which provides information about a specific sound file to be played. (The MovieTexture node, described in Chapter 8, can also be used as a sound source.) An AudioClip node may occur only in the *source* field of a Sound node.

A Sound node is located at the specific place in the scene indicated by its *location* field (in local coordinates, of course). At and near that location, the sound can be heard at maximum volume, which is to say at its recorded volume scaled by the value of the *intensity* field. The *intensity* field's value can range from 0 to 1, with 1 indicating the full volume of the sound as given in the sound file, and 0 indicating total silence. An *intensity* of greater than 1 amplifies the sound but is likely to distort it; if you need the sound to be louder than the original recording, re-record it at a higher volume rather than increasing *intensity* over 1.

The region in which the sound can be heard is defined by two ellipsoids, each of which has *location* as a focus. (In most cases, one of these ellipsoids is completely contained within the other.) The inner ellipsoid defines the region in which the sound is played at the given *intensity* value; moving around within that region produces no change in the sound's volume. In the region between the inner and outer ellipsoids, the sound's volume fades as a function of distance from the inner ellipsoid's surface, into near-inaudibility just inside the edge of the outer ellipsoid. A user outside the outer ellipsoid can't hear the sound at all.

Each ellipsoid is defined by the distances from the *location* focus to the ends of the ellipsoid along its major axis. The major axis is parallel to the vector given in the *direction* field, as shown in Figure 5-1.

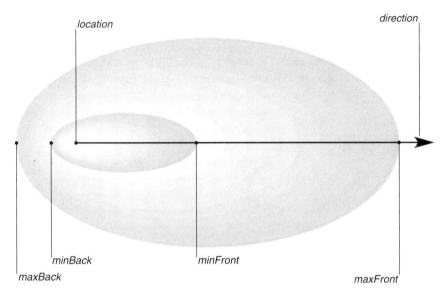

Figure 5-1   A Sound node and where it can be heard

The major axis of the inner ellipsoid is defined by the *minFront* and *minBack* fields: *minFront* indicates the distance from *location* of the forward end of the ellipsoid (the end toward the direction that the *direction* vector points), and *minBack* indicates the distance of the other end (in the direction opposite that of the *direction* vector). Similarly, the major axis of the outer ellipsoid is defined by *maxFront* and *maxBack*.

If *maxFront* is less than *minFront* or *maxBack* is less than *minBack*, the sound can be heard at the given intensity out to the edge of the inner ellipsoid in the appropriate direction, and can't be heard at all beyond that edge.

> If you want an omnidirectional sound (where the audible region is a sphere instead of an ellipsoid), just set *minFront* equal to *minBack* and *maxFront* equal to *maxBack*. In that case, *direction* is ignored. Omnidirectional sounds are likely to result in improved sound performance, at the cost of a measure of realism.

Note that these ellipsoids do not provide a precisely accurate physical model of how sound propagates in the real world, any more than the VRML lighting model accurately simulates real-world lighting. However, both the sound model and the lighting model are accurate enough to be useful, and simple enough to be computed quickly for use in a real-time environment. You can create realistic sound attenuation by setting *maxFront* equal to ten times *minFront* and *maxBack* equal to ten times *minBack*; if the outer ellipsoid is more than ten times as long as the inner one, attenuation is slower than in the real world, while if it's less than ten times as long, attenuation is faster.

If your sound ellipsoids are long and thin, the inner and outer ellipsoid surfaces can be very close to each other in places. Users traveling between the ellipsoids anywhere other than the front or back of the ellipsoids may experience abrupt increases or decreases in volume, because the full attenuation (from zero to full volume) occurs over a brief distance. If you want to avoid this phenomenon, use ellipsoids that are closer to being spherical.

You can include multiple sounds in your scene, but be aware that some browsers may be able to play only a limited number of sounds simultaneously. If there are more sounds to be played than can be played at once, browsers use a priority scheme to determine which ones to use. The prioritization method is somewhat complex, but the most important part is that sounds with a high *priority* field value are more likely to be played, given limited resources, than low-priority sounds. The *priority* value defaults to 0; if you have a sound that you want to guarantee is played even if there are other sounds playing, you can set its priority higher. Leave *priority* at 0 for continuous background sounds, such as crickets; set it to 1 for nonlooping event sounds, such as a doorbell. There may be occasions when you need to give a sound a fractional priority, but in most cases 0 or 1 should suffice.

Humans can usually tell what direction a sound is coming from; a sound coming from the left side, for instance, sounds louder in the left ear than in the right. By default, sounds in VRML are spatially localized, so that they sound like they're coming from a particular direction. A monaural sound with its *spatialize* field left at the default value of TRUE is added into the stereo mix based on the angle from the user's location and orientation to the sound's location. To produce ambient sounds—sounds which don't seem to come from any particular direction—set *spatialize* to FALSE.

AudioClip

The Sound node provides a location in your world and information on where a sound can be heard; you can think of it as a speaker attached to a stereo system. The AudioClip node, in that analogy, is a tape deck or a CD changer—it specifies which sound is to be played and how to play it.

The usual specification method is to use the *url* field to give a URL from which to read the sound to be played. You can list multiple URLs in that field, as with all fields that contain URLs; the list should be in order of preference. You can thus provide an audio file in several different formats; each browser then downloads and plays the highest-preference file that's in a format that it understands. Besides the URL of the sound file, you can also provide a string in the *description* field, a text description of the sound to be displayed in addition to or instead of playing the sound itself.

You can provide sound files in almost any format, but browsers are required only to support WAVE files in uncompressed PCM format; if you want all users to be able to hear your sound files, make sure that at least one of the URLs you list is for a WAVE file. Most browsers support MIDI type 1 format as well.

Along with the sound, you can specify information about when the sound should start playing, its duration, and whether it loops. If you set the value of *loop* to TRUE (the default is FALSE), the sound is repeated indefinitely. *startTime* contains a time in SFTime field format (see "SFTime and MFTime" in Chapter 12 for details) indicating when the sound should start; you should almost always set this field interactively rather than giving it a value in the file. (For information on changing a field's value by sending it an event, see Chapter 6, "Animation and User Interaction.") You can set *stopTime* to the current time (again by routing events to it) to stop a sound.

The final field you can set in an AudioClip node is *pitch*, which allows you to control the pitch, or frequency, of a sound. A *pitch* of 1.0, the default, means that the sound should be played at its recorded pitch; 2.0 means all frequencies in the sound file are doubled, which corresponds to playing the sound twice as fast and an octave higher.

AudioClip nodes generate outgoing events called *duration_changed* and *isActive*, to let other interested nodes know the total duration (before any changes of pitch) of the current sound, and whether the sound is playing at the current moment, respectively. For instance, if the sound has finished playing (and *loop* is FALSE), or hasn't started yet, or has been stopped by setting *stopTime*, then the *isActive* outgoing event is set to FALSE.

Example 5-1 illustrates a Sound node that might be used in the Aztec city to play the sound of the ceremonial drumming going on in the Great Temple. Note that for demonstration purposes, the *startTime* and *stopTime* fields are set so that the drums start playing as soon as you load this scene; normally, you would leave those fields at their default values and set them interactively using events.

Example 5-1   Using a Sound node and an AudioClip node

```
#VRML V2.0 utf8
Sound {
  source  AudioClip {
    description   "temple drums"
    url           "drums.wav"
    loop          TRUE
    startTime     1
    stopTime      0
  }
  minFront   10
  maxFront   100
  minBack     0.4
  maxBack     4
}
```

In this example, the drums can be heard faintly up to a hundred meters away from the front but can't be heard from behind unless the user is fairly close. These specifications simulate the fact that the drummers are inside a mostly enclosed room with an open front; if the drummers were out in the open, it would make more sense to set *minBack* equal to *minFront* and *maxBack* equal to *maxFront* to make the drums equally audible in all directions.

 If a sound is completely inside a rectangular walled-off space, you can ensure its inaudibility outside that space by using a ProximitySensor to activate the sound. See Chapter 6 for details of ProximitySensor use.

Complex Shapes

A couple of shape nodes are more complex than the ones you've seen so far, and require more explanation. The ElevationGrid node makes it easy to model terrain in a compact form. The Extrusion node allows you to create compact representations of various complex shapes such as extrusions and surfaces of revolution.

Terrain Modeling with the ElevationGrid Node

If you want to represent terrain features—from mountains to tiny irregularities in the ground surface—the ElevationGrid node is your best choice. This node provides a compact way to represent ground that varies in height over an area.

The node specifies a rectangular grid and the height of the ground at each intersection in that grid. The *xDimension* and *zDimension* fields specify the number of grid points in the x and z directions, respectively, defining a grid of *zDimension* by *xDimension* lines in the *xz* plane.

Note: Many people are used to modeling terrain in the *xy* plane, with height values in z. In VRML, however, the *xz* plane is considered to be horizontal, and vertical distances are measured along the y axis. The horizontal grid of the ElevationGrid node therefore lies in the *xz* plane, with height values in y, so that you won't have to rotate the terrain to make it horizontal. If you're used to grids with rows that parallel the x axis and columns that parallel the y axis, be careful to remember that the columns of an elevation grid in VRML are parallel to the z axis.

Figure 5-2 shows a diagram of a sample ElevationGrid node; of course when a real elevation grid is displayed by a browser, the grid lines and numbers aren't shown.

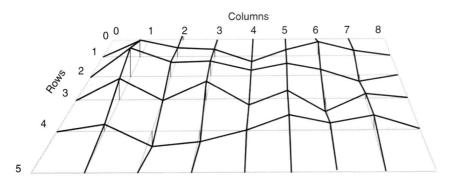

Figure 5-2   Diagram of an elevation grid

In this figure, there are six rows in the *z* direction (numbered 0 through 5), so *zDimension* is 6. Similarly, *xDimension* is 9, because there are nine columns (numbered 0 through 8) in the *x* direction.

The *height* field is a list of height values, one for each vertex in order. The vertices of row 0 are listed first, followed by the vertices in row 1, then row 2, and so on up through the last row. For the elevation grid shown in Figure 5-2, for instance, the heights at grid points in the first row are given by the first nine values in the *height* field; the next nine values give heights in the second row (row 1), and so on.

The *xSpacing* and *zSpacing* fields allow you to scale the entire grid to whatever size you want in each horizontal direction. The *xSpacing* value listed in that field gives the distance in the *x* direction between adjacent columns, and the *zSpacing* value gives the distance in the *z* direction between adjacent rows.

If the diagram were translated into an ElevationGrid node, the node would look something like this:

```
ElevationGrid {
   xDimension   9
   zDimension   6
   xSpacing     2.1
   zSpacing     2
   height [ 0, 0,    0.2, 0,    0,    0,    0,    0,    0, # row 0
            0, 0.8,  0.4, 0.2, -0.2, 0.2,  0.4,  0.2, 0, # row 1
            0, 1,    0.6, 0.4,  0.2, 0.4,  0.2, -0.2, 0, # row 2
            0, 0.8,  0,   0.4, -0.2, 0.2, -0.4,  0.1, 0, # row 3
            0, 0.2, -0.4, -0.2, 0,   0.4,  0.2,  0.4, 0, # row 4
            0, 0,    0,   0,    0,    0,    0,    0,   0 # row 5
          ]
}
```

The fields uniquely determine a set of vertices to use for the terrain. It's then the browser's job to create the terrain surface to display by interpolating surfaces between the given vertices. Since the quadrilaterals of the terrain surface are unlikely to be planar, each one is broken up by the browser into a pair of triangles. Note that different browsers may perform this triangulation differently, resulting in slightly different terrain displays from browser to browser.

Extrusions

There's one further type of geometry node besides those discussed so far: the Extrusion node.

An Extrusion node is something like a more general version of a cylinder. It consists of a 2D polygon, defined in the *crossSection* field, which sweeps out a path through space (as indicated by the *spine* field and modified by the other fields) to define a surface in three dimensions.

The *crossSection* and *spine* paths are both *piecewise linear*; that is, they're composed of straight line segments. You specify each of them as a series of vertices to be connected in order. To produce a cylinder or other shape with a curved cross-section using an Extrusion node, you have to specify many points spaced close together to approximate a curve.

Figure 5-3 illustrates a simple example of an Extrusion node: a 2D path, defined by the *crossSection* field, extruded through space along a short linear *spine*. A *spine* path may, of course, consist of more than one linear segment.

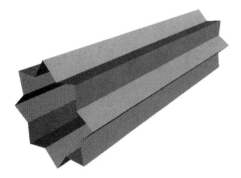

Figure 5-3   An extruded star

Here's the VRML file that describes the object:

Example 5-2   Using an Extrusion node

```
#VRML V2.0 utf8

Shape {
  appearance  Appearance { material  Material { } }
  geometry  Extrusion {
    crossSection [
       1   0,   .67  -.27,    .71  -.71,   .27   -.67,
       0  -1,  -.27  -.67,   -.71  -.71,  -.67   -.27,
      -1   0,  -.67   .27,   -.71   .71,  -.27    .67,
       0   1,   .27   .67,    .71   .71,   .67    .27,  1 0
    ]
    spine      [ 0 0 0, 0 0 -6 ]
    beginCap   FALSE
    endCap     FALSE
    solid      FALSE
  }
}
```

The browser follows these steps to form an extruded surface:

1. Start with a 2D cross-section in the *xz* plane, usually with vertices given in counterclockwise order when looking down at the *xz* plane.

2. Scale the cross-section by the first amount given in the *scale* field. Rotate it so that it'll be oriented correctly when it's moved to the start of the spine. Then translate it by the 3D vector given as the first vertex of the spine path. This translation has the effect of placing the cross-section at the beginning of the spine, with the first vertex of the spine corresponding to the origin in the cross-section's coordinate space. In

Figure 5-4 and Figure 5-5, the spine path for an extruded snake is shown in solid black for reference; the spine isn't actually displayed when you view an Extrusion node.

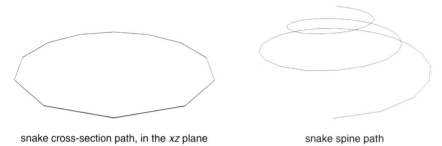

snake cross-section path, in the *xz* plane   snake spine path

Figure 5-4   Cross-section and spine

Figure 5-5   Cross-section moved to start of spine

3.   Place another copy of the cross-section at the next vertex of the spine. For the *n*th joint, this procedure involves scaling the cross-section by the *n*th value in the *scale* field, rotating the result through space to the proper angle to form a joint, then translating it by the *n*th vector in the spine path. Finally, the resulting cross-section is twisted counterclockwise about its local origin (that is, about the current spine vertex, in the plane of the cross-section) by the *n*th value in the *orientation* field.

4. Connect the cross-section at one joint to that at the next joint with a surface. The result is shown in Figure 5-6.

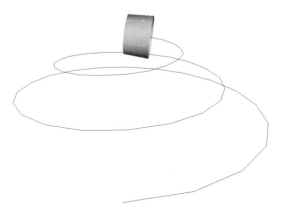

Figure 5-6   Placing a cross-section at the second joint

5. Repeat steps 3 and 4 until you reach the end of the spine path.

Besides the extruded surface, an Extrusion can have a cap at either end. If *beginCap* is TRUE, a cap is placed across the end of the Extrusion corresponding to the first vertex in *spine*; if *endCap* is TRUE, a cap is placed across the other end. The caps are generated by filling in the shape formed by *crossSection*; if *crossSection* isn't a closed path (that is, if the first and last points listed aren't the same), the cap is generated as if the first point in *crossSection* were added to the end (that is, it connects the final point to the initial point).

You can use Extrusion nodes to create many different sorts of shapes. A nonclosed *crossSection* with caps, for instance, could describe a cylinder sliced lengthwise, like a Quonset hut. A spine that approximates a helix could provide a basis for a 3D DNA model. And by coiling the spine and varying the scale factor, you can produce a snake like the snake statue in the Aztec temple, as shown in Figure 5-7.

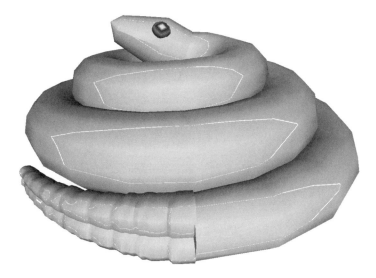

Figure 5-7   An extruded snake

The head of the snake is an indexed face set; the body is an extrusion; and the tail is another extrusion using a differently shaped cross-section.

What's Next?

Now you understand the basics of modeling a static scene. VRML allows you to go one step further and bring your scene to life, using the animation techniques discussed in Chapter 6. If you want to construct a simple static scene and publish it, just to try out all you've learned so far, you can skip ahead at this point to Chapter 9 to learn how to publish a VRML file on the World Wide Web. But static scenes usually aren't very interesting; to get the full potential out of your scenes, be sure to come back to read Chapters 6 and 7 to learn about animation and Chapter 8 to learn about advanced use of colors and textures.

Animation and User Interaction

Until now, most of what you've learned to create has been static: 3D worlds that users can travel through but that don't include life or motion. This chapter shows you how to make your worlds richer and more convincing by animating objects and detecting and responding to user activity.

Interaction with a world can range from something as straightforward as a user running into a wall (which might result in a muffled "thud" sound effect), to letting the user click objects to invoke some sort of behavior (turning on a light to see the wall, opening a door to get through the wall), to encounters with complex animated creatures (whatever lives on the other side of the wall).

Events and Routes Revisited

The basis for animation is the ability to change the world over time—which, in VRML, amounts to changing the values of a given object's fields. (Note that these changes take place only in a browser's internal representation of the world, not in the VRML file itself.) The way to change a field in VRML is to send an event, by way of a route, to that field. The browser handles all the actual event generation and routing, but in your VRML file you have to describe what events the browser should generate and where the browser should route them. In "Interacting with the Scene" on page 54, you learned about the basics of events and routes. This section goes into a little more detail about them.

Events that each node can send or receive are listed in the node descriptions in Chapter 11, "Node Reference." Recall from the description in Chapter 3 that incoming events are labeled **eventIn**, and outgoing events are labeled **eventOut**.

The node descriptions often include fields labeled "exposed field." This term is a convenient shorthand to describe a field for which there are two implicitly defined associated events: a *set_* incoming event that lets you set the field's value and a *_changed* outgoing event that sends out the new value when the field's value changes. For instance, the *translation* field of the Transform node is an exposed field, so the events *set_translation* and *translation_changed* are implicitly defined; if you want to change the value of the *translation* field, you set up a route to *set_translation*, and if you want another node to be notified whenever the value of *translation* changes, you set up a route from *translation_changed*.

For simplicity and ease of typing, the *set_* and *_changed* parts of the event names for exposed fields can be left out; if you route to or from the name of an exposed field, the browser understands to use the appropriate *set_* or *_changed* event name. For instance, if XFORM1 and XFORM2 are Transform nodes, each of the following ROUTE statements sets the *translation* field of XFORM2 equal to the *translation* field of XFORM1 whenever the latter changes:

```
ROUTE XFORM1.translation_changed TO XFORM2.set_translation

ROUTE XFORM1.translation TO XFORM2.set_translation

ROUTE XFORM1.translation_changed TO XFORM2.translation

ROUTE XFORM1.translation TO XFORM2.translation
```

This chapter uses this last form of the statement, for simplicity.

Note: This syntax works only with exposed fields. Some event names that aren't associated with exposed fields use *set_* or *_changed* names; for such events, you can't leave off the *set_* or *_changed*. When in doubt, use the full event name.

If a field isn't exposed, it has no implicit associated events and you can't route to or from it. Unless an unexposed field has an explicit *set_* or *_changed* event associated with it, the value given in the file for that field can't be changed.

When you route one event to another event, they don't have to have the same name, but you do have to make sure the types of the events match. Events use the same set of types as fields. For example, you can route any outgoing Boolean event (type SFBool) to any incoming event of the same type, but not to an incoming multiple-integer event (type MFInt32). A *set_* or *_changed* event is the same type as the exposed field it's associated with.

Note: You can't route a single-valued event to a multi-valued event, or vice versa, even if the types of the individual values match; for instance, you can't route an SFColor event to an MFColor event.

To indicate which node to route an event to, you have to use the node's name as defined with DEF. Of course this means you're routing to all places the node is used with USE as well, since it's the same node in all of those places. Be aware that you can't route an event to just one of the places that a node occurs; if you want to route to just one instance, use a prototype instead of DEF and USE.

It's perfectly legal to send events to a node that's not currently displayed, such as a child of an LOD or of a Switch. There's no easy way, however, to send events to a node from another file that's been brought in with an Inline node.

Besides the implicit *set_* and *_changed* events, several kinds of nodes define events explicitly (as indicated by **eventIn** or **eventOut** in the node description). These events have types as indicated in the node description. For example, one such node is the TouchSensor node, which produces a Boolean event named *isActive*; when the user clicks some geometry associated with the sensor, the browser generates an *isActive* event with the value TRUE. It generates another *isActive* event with the value FALSE when the mouse button is released. (That's all you need to know about sensors for now; they're explained in detail in later sections of this chapter.) Here's an example of how to use routes and events to turn on a light while the user holds the mouse button down over a light switch (represented as an inlined object here for simplicity):

```
Group {
  children  [
    DEF LIGHT_CONTROL TouchSensor { }
    Inline {
      url  [ "lightswitch.wrl" ] # click this to light the light
    }
  ]
}
DEF LIGHT PointLight {
  location  -6 4 2
  on         FALSE
}
Inline { url  [ "table.wrl" ] } # objects to be lit
ROUTE LIGHT_CONTROL.isActive TO LIGHT.on
```

Now whenever the user presses the mouse button while pointing to the light switch, the touch sensor named LIGHT_CONTROL generates a Boolean *isActive* event with value TRUE. The ROUTE statement sends the value of that event to the node named LIGHT, calling it a *set_on* event (*on* for short). The PointLight node receives the *set_on* event with value TRUE, and sets its exposed *on* field (also of type SFBool) to that value, turning on the light. The PointLight node then generates an *on_changed* event, but as there's no ROUTE set up to send that event elsewhere, the event is ignored by the browser.

When the user releases the mouse button, LIGHT_CONTROL generates an *isActive* event with value FALSE; the ROUTE sends that event to LIGHT as a *set_on* event. LIGHT sets its *on* field to FALSE, turning off the light.

A realistic light switch is more complex than this; this example is merely intended to show how routes work. If you want a light switch in your world, you probably want to have the light turn on after the user clicks and releases, instead of only having it on while the mouse button is held down. You can also keep track of whether the light is on or off, animate the switch when it's activated, and include geometry for a light bulb that starts to glow when the light turns on.

A ROUTE statement creates a message path across the scene structure; routes are not themselves part of the scene hierarchy, even though they are part of the VRML file. In fact, the only requirement for the placement of a ROUTE statement is that both the source node and the destination node must be defined earlier in the file than the statement defining a route between them. Usually, it's best to place all routes together near the end of the file, in functional groups with comments to explain what they're doing.

The Animation Event Path

Animation in VRML consists of sending events through a series of steps, though most kinds of animation can skip one or more of the steps. Figure 6-1 provides a diagram of the flow of events from each step to the next.

Figure 6-1   Flow of events through the animation event path

Here's an explanation of the steps:

1. Trigger. Something generates an event to set the animation in motion. Usually, a Trigger is a sensor that sends an event when a user performs a particular action.

2. Logic. This step is usually unnecessary for simple animations; it involves doing some processing on the event sent by the Trigger before starting the Timer. To start the Logic stage, the browser passes the event sent by the Trigger to a Script node—a node that contains a program or *script*—and calls the appropriate routine inside that node's script. The script processes the event and (usually) sends out a time event to start the Timer. Script nodes are described in Chapter 7.

3. Timer. The browser forwards the outgoing time events from the Logic or Trigger stages to the *startTime* of a TimeSensor node. The time sensor then generates time events, either for a specified duration or else continuously until it's explicitly stopped. The Timer, Engine, and Target stages occur repeatedly as long as the animation runs.

4. Engine. The browser sends the time sensor's outgoing events to a node or set of nodes that determine the exact parameters of the animation at the given moment and generate more events accordingly. An Engine most often consists of an *interpolator* node, but can instead or additionally include a Script node to do anything from simple datatype conversion to complex processing. Interpolators are more efficient than scripts, but not as general.

5. Target. The browser sends the Engine's output to a relevant node in the scene hierarchy, whose field values change accordingly. In its most common form, this step involves changing the fields of a Transform node to translate or rotate that node's children.

Scripts are described in detail in Chapter 7; you don't need them to do basic animation. This section describes most of the above stages, starting with the simplest possible "animations" (involving only a Trigger and a Target) and increasing in complexity to use all the stages except Logic.

Triggers and Targets

The simplest time-based user interactions require only two of the five animation stages: Trigger and Target, as diagrammed in Figure 6-2.

Figure 6-2   Simplified animation event path

The Trigger is almost always a sensor node. The various kinds of sensors provide a means of generating events. Sensors can detect a user's proximity to a given location or region, detect various kinds of clicks and drags from a mouse or other input device, and indicate the passage of time. Another way of looking at sensors is that they detect changes—changes in user position, changes in time, changes in user input, and so on.

When a sensor is triggered—whether by a user's action or by time passing—it generates an event, which can then be redirected into another node's incoming event by using routes. If you route the event into a standard node, the event changes a field value. If you route it into a Script node or a complex prototyped node, you can perform all sorts of processing on the data before passing it on to its final destination.

Pointing-Device Sensors

A class of sensors called pointing-device sensors generate events based on user input from a pointing device (such as a mouse, joystick, or trackball). There are a variety of such sensors, to detect pointing-device clicks and drags of various sorts; they allow users to manipulate objects within your world.

A pointing-device sensor occurs in a VRML file as a child of a grouping node. The sensor detects user interaction with any geometry that's also a child of the same grouping node. Note that a sensor by itself has no geometry or other visible manifestation; if you don't explicitly include some geometry as a sibling of your pointing-device sensor, the user can't click anything and the sensor is useless. Note too that though the geometry corresponding to the sensor must be a sibling of the sensor, the objects controlled by the sensor can be anywhere in the file. For instance, if you want a light switch to control a distant light, you include the light switch's geometry as a sibling of the touch sensor, but the light itself (and the light bulb geometry) may be somewhere else in the file entirely.

Pointing-device sensors may have slightly different semantics depending on whether the user's input device gives 2D input (such as a mouse or trackball) or 3D input; the descriptions of these sensors in this book assume 2D input devices.

The simplest pointing-device sensor is the TouchSensor node, which detects a click from the pointing-device button. Whenever the user points to an object that's a sibling of a touch sensor, the sensor generates certain events:

- Every time the user moves the pointing device to point to part of the sensor's sibling geometry, the sensor generates an *isOver* event with value TRUE. Every time the user moves the pointing device off the geometry, the sensor generates an *isOver* FALSE event.

- When the user presses the pointing-device button while pointing to the geometry, the sensor issues an *isActive* TRUE event. When the user releases the button (regardless of what the pointing device is now pointing to), the sensor issues an *isActive* FALSE event.

- Whenever the user moves the pointing device while pressing the button, the sensor generates further events to indicate the point on the surface of the geometry that the device is pointing to, the normal at that point, and the corresponding coordinates in the geometry's texture map (if any). When the user releases the button, the most recent value for each of these events gives information about where the button release took place. For instance, the most recent value of the sensor's *hitPoint_changed* event after an *isActive* FALSE event indicates the location on the geometry's surface where the button release occurred.

- If the user presses the button while pointing to the geometry and releases it while still (or again) pointing to the geometry, the sensor generates a *touchTime* event with a value equal to the time of the button release.

Most of those events aren't much use without a script to handle them. The last event listed above, however, *touchTime*, can be used without a script. It's often the most useful of the above events, because it's generated only when a sequence of actions occurs, a sequence that corresponds to the most common interface for clicking things: the user presses and releases the mouse button, and if the press and release were over the same user-interface item, the item is activated. You can route the *touchTime* time values directly to inputs of other nodes to make things happen as soon as the button is released.

For example, here's one way to implement a doorbell.

Example 6-1   Using a TouchSensor node

```
Group {
  children  [
    DEF PUSH TouchSensor { }
    Inline { url  [ "doorbell.geom.wrl" ] } # doorbell geometry
  ]
}
Sound {
  source  DEF BUZZ AudioClip { url  [ "doorbell.wav" ] }
  maxFront  50
  minFront  5
}
ROUTE PUSH.touchTime TO BUZZ.startTime
```

This example is one of the simplest "animations" possible: a Trigger (the TouchSensor and its associated geometry) sends a time event (type SFTime), which is routed to the corresponding incoming event of a Target (the audio clip). When the user clicks the doorbell geometry, a buzzer sound plays. Because of the semantics of *touchTime*, this doorbell doesn't work like some real-world doorbells; it buzzes only after the user lets go of the button. More realistic behavior requires more routes.

Figure 6-3 shows a diagram of the event and its route in this example. Wiring diagrams like this one show nodes as large boxes, outgoing events as smaller boxes projecting from the right sides of the nodes, incoming events on the left sides of nodes, and routes as arrows between events.

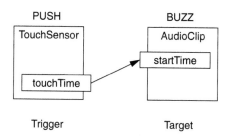

PUSH   BUZZ

Trigger   Target

Figure 6-3 Doorbell wiring diagram

An almost identical setup provides a sound effect when the user runs into a wall; that effect would be achieved by putting the wall geometry inside a Collision node, and routing the outgoing *collideTime* event to the *startTime* of an audio clip.

Note: Collision detection is on by default in VRML worlds. In other words, if you don't include a Collision node in your world, users can't go through solid objects. If you want to allow users to travel through solid objects, use a Collision node to turn off collision detection. If you don't want collisions with solid objects to trigger animations, the only reason to use a Collision node is to improve rendering speed; for more information on that use, see "Turn Off Collision Detection and Use Collision Proxies" on page 252.

The above example uses only the *touchTime* event from the touch sensor. The more sophisticated information that touch sensors provide—such as *isActive* and *hitTexCoord_changed* events—can be used (for instance) to create 3D image maps corresponding to HTML image maps, allowing users to click different parts of an object to achieve different results. This sort of information could even be used, with drag sensors, to allow users to create and modify VRML objects within your world.

Drag Sensors

There are several other pointing-device sensors besides the touch sensor. The others are all *drag sensors*: they generate events when a user moves a pointing device while holding down the device's button. Each of the drag sensors maps the input from the pointing device onto a 3D surface. Such interpretation of the input is necessary because dragging across a 2D display results in motion data in only two dimensions, and you usually want to interpret such motion as if it were motion in three dimensions. For instance, if your world includes a globe of the Earth in a standard globe stand, users are likely to click the globe and drag in an attempt to spin it. Don't interpret that 2D dragging as 2D motion; interpret it as a rotation around the globe's axis, as if the user were dragging around the circumference of an imaginary cylinder (not an imaginary sphere, because a globe on a stand is constrained to rotate around only one axis, like a cylinder). The CylinderSensor node interprets dragging motion as rotation around the sensor's local y axis; this sensor is what you'd use to let users spin that globe.

Note that drag sensors do not constrain where the pointing device may go; the user can drag anywhere on the display. Drag sensors simply interpret that dragging as motion of a particular kind (and therefore may ignore certain components of the drag direction).

The most common drag sensor is the PlaneSensor. It interprets dragging motions as translations in the local xy plane. If you ignore one of those axes, a plane sensor becomes a linear sensor, interpreting dragging as a translation along a single axis.

In the Aztec city, users can examine a rack of skulls left by the ancient Aztecs, as shown in Figure 6-4.

Figure 6-4   The skull rack

A user can click one of those skulls and drag it along the bar it's attached to. To indicate that the skull can be manipulated, it should highlight as the user moves a pointing device across it, but highlighting requires a Script node—see "Locate-Highlighting: A Glowing Skull" in Chapter 7. Ignoring the highlighting for now, here's how to make the skull slide.

First, you need the sensor and the geometry to be dragged. This simplified version of the skull rack leaves out the rack itself and all the other skulls.

Example 6-2 Using a PlaneSensor node

```
#VRML V2.0 utf8
Group {
  children  [
    DEF SKULL_DRAG PlaneSensor {
      minPosition   0 0
      maxPosition   5 0
    }
    DEF SKULL Transform {
      translation  0 0 0
      children  [
        Inline { url  [ "skull.wrl" ] }  # skull geometry
      ]
    }
  ]
}
```

Note that in the plane sensor shown, the y components of *minPosition* and *maxPosition* are equal; that tells the sensor to ignore all motion in the y direction. The slider's motion in the x direction is constrained (or *clamped*) to be between 0 and 5 in the local coordinate system; that is, the user can drag the skull only up to five units to the right.

When the user drags the skull, the plane sensor emits a *translation_changed* event (a 3D vector, type SFVec3f, showing the distance to translate along each axis) that provides a clamped translation in the x direction only. This event can be routed to the translation of the geometry itself:

ROUTE SKULL_DRAG.translation_changed TO SKULL.translation

You can't abbreviate *translation_changed* as *translation* here; remember that you can only abbreviate *set_* and *_changed* event names if they're associated with an exposed field of the same name. In this case, there's no "translation" field in a plane sensor, so you must give the full event name. There is an exposed *translation* field in a transform, so you can abbreviate the implicit *set_translation* incoming event in SKULL as simply *translation*.

Figure 6-5 shows a diagram of the event and route for this example.

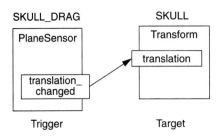

Figure 6-5   Skull-dragging wiring diagram

Most of the time, if the user drags some geometry, lets go of it, and then drags it again, you want the new drag to pick up where the old drag left off—that is, if the user drags and lets go, clicking to drag again shouldn't reset the geometry to its initial position. All drag sensors contain an *autoOffset* field which indicates whether or not a new drag should pick up where the last one left off. If *autoOffset* is TRUE (as it is by default), then when the user stops dragging, the new position (or orientation) of the object is stored in the drag sensor's *offset* field; the *offset* field is then added to the initial position (or orientation) of the object when the next drag begins. Since *autoOffset* is TRUE by default, you only need to set it explicitly (to FALSE) if you want your object to jump back to its initial position or orientation when the user lets go and starts to drag a second time.

Note: Place drag sensors carefully in your scene hierarchy; in particular, be sure not to put a drag sensor inside the transform whose values are affected by that sensor. The sensor interprets dragging in terms of its local coordinate system; if that coordinate system is changing as the user drags, the interface can become unusable.

In the sliding-skull example no script is necessary, but for more complicated uses of drag sensors, scripts are required. For instance, if you want to allow a user to move an object around in 3D space, you have to build your own "space sensor" out of plane sensors and scripts. One way to do this is to place six plane sensors as the sides of a box and track motion in all three dimensions; it's up to you how to interpret the resulting translations to make the dragging "feel" right to the user.

Timers

The next simplest stage of an animation is the Timer stage. Figure 6-6 illustrates the event path so far.

Figure 6-6   Animation event path with Timer stage

The Timer stage consists of a TimeSensor node. A time sensor does nothing until a given *startTime*, when it starts generating events. The *startTime* field is almost always initialized by an event when the user starts the animation; there's no point in putting an explicit *startTime* in your file, since *startTime* is an absolute time and you have no way of knowing what time a user is going to start an animation. The default value for *startTime* is 0; the time sensor doesn't generate events until after *startTime* is set to a new time. The time sensor generates the *time* and *fraction_changed* events.

The *time* events are floating point values indicating the current time at the moment the event is generated; thus, the first *time* event has a value equal to or slightly greater than *startTime*. There's no guarantee of how often *time* events are issued by the browser, but most browsers issue such events as often as possible, usually about once per frame. Note that this means there's no guarantee an event will be issued exactly at *startTime*; you shouldn't rely on a time sensor to give precisely accurate times.

The *fraction_changed* events are floating point values ranging between 0 and 1, used to control animation that goes from a beginning to an end, or that repeats cyclically. These events are independent of *time* events; they don't measure seconds. Instead, they indicate the fraction of a cycle that has elapsed since the current cycle started. The duration of a cycle (in seconds) is given by the *cycleInterval* field. Thus, if *cycleInterval* is 3, *fraction* events increase steadily from 0 to 1 over the course of three seconds.

If the time sensor's *loop* field is set to FALSE (the default), the time sensor stops running at the end of one cycle; when *loop* is TRUE, the time sensor keeps running until the current time reaches *stopTime*, or runs forever if *stopTime* is less than *startTime*.

> It's usually not a good idea to let animations run forever; they take a lot of processing power.

If *loop* is TRUE, the *fraction_changed* values increase from 0 to 1 during the first cycle; in all subsequent cycles the values start at a little more than 0 and increase up to 1. That is, the value at the end of each cycle is 1, not 0.

Most of the time, you use *fraction_changed* as input to an Engine. For some particularly simple cases, though, you can route *fraction_changed* directly to a Target that has a floating point (SFFloat) incoming event or exposed field. For instance, the brightness of a point light source is defined mostly by the PointLight node's *intensity* field, which is a floating point (SFFloat) exposed field that takes values between 0 and 1, just like the values that the *fraction_changed* event can have. If you want a light to get gradually brighter rather than turning on all at once, you can use a time sensor to adjust the intensity.

This is a good opportunity to introduce a new sensor, the ProximitySensor, which generates events whenever the user enters or leaves a defined box-shaped region. It also generates events whenever the user moves within that volume.

 Sizes for box shapes can be difficult to estimate. The box-shaped region of sensitivity for a proximity sensor often turns out to be smaller than you think it ought to be for a given *size* value. If your proximity sensor doesn't seem to be working, try expanding its *size* field, or placing a Box node of the same size at the same location to get a better idea of the exact region covered.

If you want a light to come on gradually whenever the user enters a room, you might use an arrangement like the one illustrated in Figure 6-7.

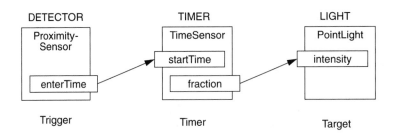

Figure 6-7   Dimmer-switch wiring diagram

Here's a simple example of a set of VRML nodes to implement this auto-lighting system. For best effect, turn off your browser's headlight before viewing this file.

Example 6-3   Using a ProximitySensor node

```
#VRML V2.0 utf8
Viewpoint { position  0 0 15 }
DEF DETECTOR ProximitySensor { size  25 25 25 }
DEF TIMER TimeSensor { cycleInterval  2 }
DEF LIGHT PointLight {
  intensity  0
  location   3 3 3
}
Inline { url  [ "chacmool.wrl" ] }  # objects to be lit
ROUTE DETECTOR.enterTime TO TIMER.startTime
ROUTE TIMER.fraction_changed TO LIGHT.intensity
```

Whenever the user enters a twenty-five-meter cube centered around the origin, the time of entry is sent to the time sensor to start it running. The time sensor generates *fraction_changed* events for one full cycle (two seconds, as indicated by the *cycleInterval* field) and then stops (because its *loop* field, which tells it whether to repeat, is set to FALSE by default).

When the animation finishes, at the end of the two seconds, the light is at full intensity. But note that if the user leaves the region and re-enters it, the timer starts over again generating *fraction_changed* events, starting with an event with value 0. This means that when the user re-enters the region, the light suddenly goes out and then gradually comes back on again. To make this light action look good, the light should turn off as the user leaves the region. To implement that, though, you need an Engine, because there's no way to get a time sensor to run backwards.

Under most circumstances, you don't want an animation to start over again if a user triggers it while it's already running. A time sensor ignores all events that attempt to set its *startTime* while it's running. If you want re-triggering to interrupt the animation and start it over, you need to set *stopTime* to stop the time sensor, then set *startTime* again; this procedure probably requires a script in the Logic stage of your animation. See "Logic" in Chapter 7.

Engines

Most of the time, animations require changing values that are neither single floating point values nor time values. Thus, you usually need to transform the output of a time sensor into a change in some other type of value. That's what the Engine stage of the animation is for, as shown in Figure 6-8.

Figure 6-8   Four stages of the animation event path

Complex engines usually require the use of scripts, but you can create many interesting animations using just an *interpolator* for the Engine stage.

The most common way to create animation is to use *keyframes*: specific key moments in the animation sequence. You define these keyframes and decide what happens at each one; then you allow the browser (with the help of the Engine stage) to generate the necessary frames to get from each keyframe to the next. Interpolator nodes take a set of key values (one value for each keyframe) and create a sequence of values in between the key values, linearly interpolating between each key value and the next.

For instance, in an animation of a fish swimming in a tank, you might define a keyframe at time 0 (with value equal to the fish's initial position), another at time 4 (the fish reaching the far end of the tank), another at time 6 (the fish turned around and ready to come back), and a fourth at time 10 (the fish reaching the first end of the tank again). You could then use interpolator nodes to generate intermediate positions along the way. You might even use two interpolators for this task: one to generate position values, the other to rotate the fish when it reaches the far end of the tank.

You often may want to do nonlinear interpolation, based on complex curves—for instance, it's usually best to start motion slowly, accelerate into it, and then end slowly, rather than maintaining a constant speed throughout with an abrupt start and stop. There are two ways you can do nonlinear interpolation in VRML:

- Use a script instead of an interpolator, to generate values based on a particular function instead of by keyframes.

- Use an interpolator, but provide many keyframe values close together to simulate a curve by connecting several short straight lines. For instance, you could make each keyframe the same amount of time after the previous one, but move only half as far in the first and last keyframes as in the middle ones.

There are a variety of interpolators, one for each kind of value that animators are most likely to want interpolated. There's an interpolator for color values, another for positions, one for orientations, and so on. Each works pretty much the same way: you give it a set of key values and send it an event indicating what fraction of the animation has completed, and it sends out an event giving an interpolated value.

For example, at the Great Temple in the Aztec city, there are braziers containing hot coals. When a user clicks a brazier, the fire begins to burn and to shoot sparks up into the sky; after it's burned for a little while, it stops, ready to be started again by another click. Each "frame" of that animation is generated with the help of an interpolator. Figure 6-9 shows a still image from the animation.

Figure 6-9   Fire in the brazier

The flames and sparks are animated using several sets of interpolators. Here's a simplified version of the animation, in which clicking sends a single pair of sparks into the sky. The animation is started by a touch sensor attached to the brazier and coals geometry.

Example 6-4   Using an interpolator

```
#VRML V2.0 utf8

Group {
  children   [
    DEF SPARK_TOUCH TouchSensor { }
    Inline { url   [ "brazier.wrl" ] }
    Transform {
      translation  0 1.5 0
      children   [
        Inline { url   "coals.wrl" }
      ]
    }
  ]
}
DEF SPARK Transform {
  children   [
    Shape {
      appearance  Appearance {
        material  Material { diffuseColor  1 1 0 }
      }
      geometry  PointSet {
        coord  Coordinate {
          point  [ 0    1.3  .5,
                   0    1.41 .5,
                   0.01 1.41 .5 ]
        }
      }
    }
  ]
}
```

The sparks are modeled as three yellow points in a point set, two of which are extremely close together (presenting the illusion of a single brighter spark).

There are still three pieces missing: a time sensor to run the animation, an interpolator to act as the engine, and routes connecting all of the pieces. Figure 6-10 shows the flow of events in this animation.

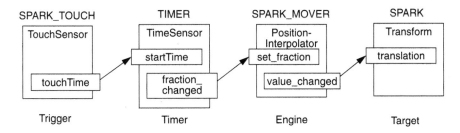

Figure 6-10   Fire-lighting wiring diagram

When activated by the touch sensor, the time sensor feeds time events through an interpolator:

```
DEF TIMER TimeSensor { cycleInterval  1.5 }
DEF SPARK_MOVER PositionInterpolator {
  key        [ 0, 1 ]
  keyValue   [ 0 0 0, 0.8 5 0 ]
}
```

The position interpolator sends out events of type SFVec3f, each signifying (in this case) a translation value. These values are forwarded to the *translation* field of the SPARK transform, setting the new location for the sparks at each frame.

Finally, a set of routes connects everything:

```
ROUTE SPARK_TOUCH.touchTime TO TIMER.startTime
ROUTE TIMER.fraction_changed TO SPARK_MOVER.set_fraction
ROUTE SPARK_MOVER.value_changed TO SPARK.translation
```

There are millions of other uses for sensors and interpolators. In the brazier in the Tenochtitlán world, for instance, interpolators create a flickering effect by changing a flame-shaped polygon: an OrientationInterpolator rotates the polygon, a ColorInterpolator shifts its color through various shades of yellow, orange, and red, and two ScalarInterpolator nodes change the flame's size and transparency. Another example: you can morph objects with a CoordinateInterpolator by animating the coordinates in a Coordinate node inside an indexed face set. (Note that when animating a Coordinate node you have to give values for all of the vertices for each keyframe, even if a given vertex doesn't move throughout the animation; there's no way to animate only some of the vertices of a vertex-based geometry node using interpolators.)

Check your key values carefully when using an orientation interpolator. Each key value must be a rotation of less than π radians (180 degrees) from the previous key value, or the rotation may go in the wrong direction.

There's no standard interpolator that sends out integer or Boolean values, but it's easy to write a script to do handle either of those situations. For an example of an integer interpolator, see "Switching among Choices: The Eagle Has Landed" in Chapter 7.

Advanced Engines

The Engine stage of an animation can be much more complex than just a single interpolator. For instance, you can run multiple interpolators off of the *fraction_changed* events from a single time sensor; you can even have multiple time sensors running at once, each operating a separate interpolator. In most cases it's probably not a good idea to have more than one interpolator affecting the same field of a given Target at the same time, but it is useful to have multiple interpolators running at once—to affect different Targets or different fields of the same Target. If you wanted to create a car model, for instance, you could run the wheel rotations from orientation interpolators and the car's forward motion from a position interpolator.

If you want to do animation that can't be handled by linear interpolation, you have to use a script in the Engine stage. If you don't feel that you're up to learning to program, however, never fear: there are a variety of prepackaged scripts to do simple but common tasks that interpolators can't handle. For information on scripts in general, see Chapter 7, "Scripting"; if you don't want to write your own scripts, start with "Scripting and Animation" on page 141.

Animation Hints

A course in traditional animation techniques is far beyond the scope of this book; if you're going to do a lot of animation, you may want to learn more about animation in general by reading a book such as *The Art of 3-D Computer Animation and Imaging* by Isaac Victor Kerlow (see "About This Book").

However, here are a few simple tips that can make your animations more realistic:

- Accelerate and decelerate over the course of the animation; don't maintain a constant speed. Usually the best approach is to ease into an animation with a slow start, pick up speed in the middle, and ease out with a slow finish.

- A slow ease-in and ease-out makes objects appear heavy; quicker ease-in and ease-out give the impression of less weight.

- By judicious choice of key values in an interpolator, you can simulate effects such as gravity. This requires pre-calculating the position of a falling object over time—the first frame moves only a little, the next moves a greater distance, and so on until the object reaches terminal velocity or hits the ground. It's easier to use a script for this sort of interpolation-by-formula, but a script slows down the browser more than an interpolator.

- If you want an object to appear to be a character, give it a personality. Make it move in particular ways. Also, decide what part of it corresponds to the human head or face; people can identify more easily with something that has a head.

- Use sounds in your animation. Even simple sound effects can greatly improve the illusion of reality. (But be judicious in your choice of sounds, since playing sounds may slow down a browser.)

- Try to synchronize the sound with the animation. This can be difficult, but try anyway. For instance, if you wait until a door has finished closing to set off a *click* or *slam* sound effect signaling the close, it'll be too late: the sound won't start until after the door is already closed, when really it should start just before the door finishes closing (as the door enters the doorframe and the latch begins to move). Use a script to set up the audio clip just before you start the animation; set the start time of the audio clip to a time that occurs shortly before the animation ends. For instance, if the door takes three seconds to close, as you're starting the animation you can set the start time for the audio clip to (say) 2.9 seconds from now. The more advance notice you give the browser, the more likely it can start the sound at the desired time.

- Squish and otherwise deform animated objects by scaling or by transforming their vertices. This effect can be useful in giving the impression of acceleration, creating the illusion of bumping into or bouncing off of surfaces, and generally giving animated objects more character.

- Exaggerate motion and make your animation pause to create anticipation for an important motion or sequence.

- Living creatures never sit entirely still; constant subtle motion is better than no motion.

- Note, though, that animation uses up precious processing time; if there's too much else going on, it may be best to sacrifice a degree of realism in order to keep your world usable. Use animation sparingly, and only where it really adds to the world.

- On a related note, if your world is too complex, a browser may drop frames. If you animate a short sharp motion that goes from point A to point B and then back to point A in a brief time, and frames get dropped during that time, the motion may not appear to the user at all. The only things you can do about this situation are to optimize your worlds (see Chapter 10, "Improving Performance") and to be aware that frames may get lost at times. There's no way in VRML to make an animation last a certain number of displayed frames rather than a certain length of time.

Chapter 7

Scripting

The Script node provides a way for you to include more complex forms of interaction. A Script node can be used for a variety of tasks but is most likely to fill one of five roles:

- acting as the Engine stage to control an animation (often with one or more interpolators)

- processing input to act as the Logic stage in an animation

- interacting with the browser in certain ways (such as binding the browser to a Viewpoint node to animate the viewer along a path)

- manipulating the scene hierarchy (adding or removing a grouping node's child nodes, for instance)

- communicating with a server or another VRML world across a network

Like other nodes, a Script receives incoming events and generates outgoing events; unlike other nodes, a Script can perform some processing before producing those outgoing events. The part of the node that does that processing is called a "script" (or sometimes a "program") and can be written in any programming language a browser supports. A browser can't execute a script in a language it doesn't support.

At the time of this writing, browsers aren't required to support any particular scripting language; some browsers support one language, some support another, so if you write scripts in just one language you can't be certain that your world works with all browsers. For maximum portability across browsers, use a commonly supported scripting language, or provide multiple versions of your scripts in different languages. The languages most likely to be supported are JavaScript and Java™.

This chapter uses JavaScript for all examples. If a browser doesn't support JavaScript, it can't execute the example scripts in this chapter. If the browser you use doesn't support JavaScript, try the Java versions of the scripts, given in Appendix B.

Note: JavaScript is a scripting language, developed by Netscape Communications, that uses a somewhat Java-like syntax. Despite some similarities, however, Java and JavaScript are two different languages. JavaScript is easier to use, especially for small tasks; Java is more powerful and more general.

If you're unfamiliar with programming, you should probably read a good introduction-to-programming book before reading the rest of this chapter. If you're familiar with programming (especially in C or C++) but unfamiliar with JavaScript, you can probably understand the examples in this chapter easily, but you may want to learn more about JavaScript before trying to write your own scripts.

Script Node Syntax

The most important built-in field in a Script node is the *url* field, which contains either the script itself or a URL where the script can be found. Two other Script fields, *directOutput* and *mustEvaluate*, help the browser improve performance.

In addition to the built-in fields of a Script node, you can define as many other fields, incoming events, and outgoing events as you wish, in the same format you would use to define a prototype. You can't define an exposed field in a Script; an exposed field is simply shorthand for a field plus an associated *set_* incoming event and *_changed* outgoing event, so if you want the same effect in your Script, you have to explicitly list the field, the *set_* event, and the *_changed* event, and then handle those events in your script just as you would any other events.

Exposed fields aren't allowed because of the implementation difficulties that arise when the fields of a Script node get changed by an event from another node while the script is running.

How Scripts Handle Events

A Script node receives incoming events and passes the event values to the script specified in the *url* field. The script can then set the values of the Script node's outgoing events.

Every time a Script node receives a set of incoming events, the browser delivers them to the node's script. Through various methods (depending on the language used for the script), each event is handled in turn. The usual approach to handling an incoming event, and the one used in JavaScript, is to define a function in the script for each incoming event listed in the Script node; when an incoming event arrives, the browser calls the function with the same name. (In some languages you may be allowed to override this general event-handling approach, but usually there's no need to do so, and it's not possible in JavaScript.) The function receives as its parameters the event's value and a time stamp indicating (usually) when the event was sent; the time stamp is usually irrelevant for simple tasks, and in JavaScript you can ignore that parameter if you wish. The examples in this chapter ignore time stamps.

For each field and outgoing event defined in the Script node, the browser creates a global variable with the same name and type, to be used in the script. To set the value of an outgoing event, just assign the desired value to a variable with the same name as the outgoing event. In JavaScript you don't have to declare variables, and type conversion is automatic so you don't even have to indicate the type of the variable.

For example, if your Script node contains an incoming event called *touchTime* and an outgoing event called *startTime*, your script might contain a function that looks something like this:

```
function touchTime (timeValue) {
  startTime = timeValue + 5;
}
```

The function has the same name as the incoming event, so whenever a *touchTime* event arrives, the browser calls that function and passes it the value of the incoming event as its *timeValue* parameter. (You can name a function parameter anything you want, as long as it's not the name of an event or a field.) The function adds five seconds to *timeValue* and sends the new value out as the value of the *startTime* outgoing event. A Script node containing this function could be used to start an animation five seconds after the user clicks something.

Note: The easiest mistake to make in writing a script is to confuse the function name (that is, the incoming event name) with the name you give the function's parameter (that is, the incoming event value). If your script doesn't seem to be working, examine your functions and make sure that you aren't trying to use the function name as a variable. In the function in the example, be sure to use `timeValue + 5` instead of `touchTime + 5` inside the function.

You can't send more than one value for a given outgoing event during a single execution of the script; in JavaScript, and probably in most other languages, the most recent value assigned when the script finishes executing is the value that's sent. You can think of scripts as saving up outgoing events until they finish executing, then sending all the events at once. If no value was assigned to a variable for an outgoing event, no corresponding event is sent. Note that only variables with the same names as events cause events to be sent; you can create and use as many other variables as you want in the script, with other names, but no events are sent out for those.

Sometimes you may want variables to keep their values from one script invocation to the next. To retain variable values, store the values in fields of the Script node. For more information on how to store values in fields and why you might want to, see "Retaining State: Putting Out Fires" on page 150.

Special Functions

In addition to the individual event-handling functions, you can define functions with certain special names which the browser automatically calls under particular circumstances.

If you define a function called **initialize**(), the browser calls that function as soon as the containing Script node is loaded, and before any events are processed. The function takes no parameters. You can use it to set up geometry or do anything else that needs to be done before the script starts receiving events.

If you define a function with the special name **eventsProcessed**(), the browser automatically calls it after one or more incoming events have finished being processed. The **eventsProcessed**() function performs any post-processing that might be necessary. For instance, the incoming-event functions can collect data in global variables, leaving **eventsProcessed**() to process all the data at once. Since you can't tell how many or which incoming events have been processed at the time **eventsProcessed()** is called, you should only use this in scripts that don't rely on events being received in any particular order.

The **shutdown()** function you define, if any, is called when the Script node is deleted or when the world containing the Script node is unloaded.

Field Types in JavaScript

JavaScript treats data types as largely interchangeable; you can assign a number to a variable, and later assign a string to the same variable. Most VRML field types are represented in JavaScript as objects, a data type which contains a set of other data types. For almost all VRML purposes, however, it's convenient to think of each VRML field type as having a corresponding data type in the script (which is the way strongly typed languages are likely to handle VRML field types). For instance, you can think of JavaScript in a VRML browser as providing an SFFloat data type that corresponds to the SFFloat field type in VRML.

Single-valued (SF) fields that contain more than one number (such as SFColor fields) are represented in scripts as arrays. Multiple-valued (MF) fields are also represented as arrays. To assign the color red (the RGB value 1 0 0) to an outgoing event of type SFColor, for instance, you might use these JavaScript statements:

```
color[0] = 1;
color[1] = 0;
color[2] = 0;
```

Be sure to assign values to all the elements of a variable. If, for instance, you don't assign a value to *color[2]* in this example, the browser is unlikely to correctly guess the amount of blue you intended.

If you want to assign a value to the green element (subscript 1, since red is subscript 0) of the fifth color (subscript 4) in an MFColor field, you can do it like this:

```
colors[4][1] = .5;
```

Scripting and Animation

This section describes several ways you might use a Script node either in the Engine stage or the Logic stage of animation. Other uses of scripts—such as moving a user's viewer through the world—are covered in "Advanced Scripting" on page 153.

A script can be used as an Engine any time you want more complex behavior than linear interpolation. Interpolators don't do anything a prototyped script couldn't do; the only reason interpolators are built into VRML is that they're likely to be faster when implemented directly in the browser than when implemented as scripts. If you want to do nonlinear interpolation, and tightly spaced keyframes with linear interpolation between them isn't good enough for your purposes, you can easily write a script that takes an incoming-event *set_fraction* value, interpolates among a set of key values, and sends out a *value_changed* event to be passed on to the Target. In fact, one of the examples in this section provides a simple prototyped "switch interpolator" that acts just like a scalar interpolator but sends out integer values, for use with a Switch node, instead of floating point values.

In Chapter 4, you saw how to create a new node type, using the PROTO command to package existing nodes for re-use. Prototypes can also be used to package frequently used script nodes, or to bundle scripts with sensors, interpolators, routes, and geometry. Standard prototypes exist for certain kinds of behavior that are used over and over again. Such prototyped scripts that do a simple task and can be plugged in anywhere are called *fittings* or *utilities*.

Locate-Highlighting: A Glowing Skull

Here's an example of how you might use a Script to improve user interaction.

When a user moves the cursor across a piece of geometry that's linked to an Anchor node, some browsers highlight the geometry automatically. However, browsers don't highlight other geometry, such as that connected to a pointing-device sensor. If you want to highlight such geometry when the user points to it—which is usually a good idea—you have to do it yourself. This section shows how to build a simple highlighter fitting.

Note: You might think that attaching an empty Anchor node to geometry would achieve automatic locate-highlighting, but not all browsers highlight anchored geometry. For maximum cross-browser generality, use the method described here to highlight geometry.

Example 6-2 demonstrated a plane sensor that allowed the user to drag a skull back and forth. Recall that the skull gave no indication, when the user moved the cursor across it, that it could be moved. With a script, you can create a simple "animation" to highlight the geometry. Note that highlighting usually means simply replacing colors with brighter colors. Highlighting a complex delicately colored object might require more work, and if you want to highlight an object that uses a three- or four-component texture (see Chapter 8), you need to replace the texture with another, brighter, one. But such details aren't covered here; the following example assumes the skull has only one color and no texture.

First, set up a Group that contains a touch sensor, a plane sensor, and a transform containing the skull shape. Recall that the plane sensor shouldn't be inside the transform affected by it.

Example 7-1   Locate-highlighting with a Script node

```
Group {
  children [
    DEF SKULL_TOUCH TouchSensor { },
    DEF SKULL_DRAG PlaneSensor {
      minPosition 0 0
      maxPosition 5 0
    },
    DEF SKULL Transform {
      translation  0 0   0
      scale        1 0.8 0.8
      children  [
        Shape {
          appearance Appearance {
            material DEF SKULL_COLOR Material {
              diffuseColor .5 .5 .5
            }
          }
          geometry IndexedFaceSet {
            .
            # skull geometry goes here
            .
          }
        }
      ]
    }
  ]
}
```

Note: You can't use an Inline to bring in the skull geometry, because you have to be able to change the *diffuseColor* field to do highlighting, and you can't change anything inside an Inline. A more elegant approach than putting the skull geometry in the file is to create a prototype of a skull Shape node (including a color and an incoming event to change the color), and then create an instance of that prototype with the desired color. However, the prototyped-geometry approach partly obscures details that are relevant for this example.

Here's a prototyped Script that does simple highlighting:

```
PROTO Highlighter [
  eventIn SFBool isActive
  eventOut SFColor color
  field SFColor activeColor     .8 .8 .8
  field SFColor inactiveColor   .5 .5 .5
]
{
  Script {
    eventIn SFBool isActive IS isActive
    eventOut SFColor color IS color
    field SFColor activeColor   IS activeColor
    field SFColor inactiveColor   IS inactiveColor
    url [
      "javascript:
        function isActive(eventValue) {
          if (eventValue == true)
            color = activeColor;
          else
            color = inactiveColor;
        }",
      "HighlightOnTrue.class"
    ]
  }
}
```

The special URL protocol "javascript:" indicates that the rest of the string is to be interpreted as JavaScript source code. Other languages may define other analogous special protocols.

The *url* field of the Script in this example contains two items: the JavaScript version of the script, and the URL for the Java version of the script (the source code for which is given in Appendix B, "Java Notes and Examples"). If you list multiple scripts in the *url* field, the browser executes the first script that's written in a language it understands. Providing both JavaScript and Java versions of a script increases the likelihood that browsers can execute the script. In this example, if the browser can interpret JavaScript it uses the first script; if it doesn't understand JavaScript but can execute Java, it loads the Java program in the file *HighlightOnTrue.class*.

To use this prototype, include it in your file (either directly, as above, or from an external file using EXTERNPROTO), then instantiate it:

```
DEF SKULL_LIGHTER Highlighter { }
```

The reason to make it a prototype is to allow you to reuse it in other contexts. In particular, if you want to do locate-highlighting for another object that's a different color, you can create a new Highlighter node and give different values for the *activeColor* and *inactiveColor* fields.

To round out the highlighting example, of course, you need to add the routes to connect all the pieces together:

```
ROUTE SKULL_DRAG.translation_changed TO SKULL.set_translation
ROUTE SKULL_TOUCH.isOver TO SKULL_LIGHTER.isActive
ROUTE SKULL_LIGHTER.color TO SKULL_COLOR.diffuseColor
```

Figure 7-1 shows a wiring diagram for highlighting, leaving out the plane sensor wiring previously shown in Figure 6-5. Note that unlike the earlier animation examples, this example contains no Engine stage; there's no continuing animation to be kept running, just a discrete state change from one color to another. Such state changes are more in the realm of the Logic stage, which interprets or modifies data from the Trigger before passing it on to later stages.

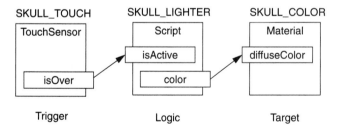

Figure 7-1   Locate-highlighting wiring diagram

Switching among Choices: The Eagle Has Landed

The Aztec story of the founding of Tenochtitlán involved an eagle landing on a cactus; the guided tour of the VRML model of Tenochtitlán includes a re-enactment of that event. It was created using a technique called *flipbook animation*, involving a time sensor, a script, and a set of texture maps. It also provides an example of a prototyped interpolator fitting, a node that interpolates among integers.

Flipbook animation consists of displaying a series of texture maps on the same piece of geometry—much like projecting a series of frames of a movie onto a screen. The textures can contain transparent pixels so that the surface doesn't appear to be a polygon. This technique is clearly a form of 2D animation, not animation of 3D geometry, but it can look fairly convincing without being as slow as detailed 3D animation. A similar effect can be achieved using a MovieTexture node (see "Advanced Textures" in Chapter 8), but most movie formats don't support transparency, so the shape of the underlying polygon in that case is obvious.

For this example, first create a series of texture maps that can be used as frames in the animation and save them as images in separate files. One such texture is shown in Figure 7-2.

Figure 7-2   A frame of eagle animation

The textures can be listed in the VRML file as part of a Switch node under a grouping node, along with a touch sensor to trigger the animation. In this example, the textures are applied to flat rectangles in external (inlined) files, to reduce the example's length.

Example 7-2   Animating the choices under a Switch node

```
#VRML V2.0 utf8
Group {
  children  [
    DEF EAGLE_TOUCH TouchSensor { },
    DEF EAGLES Switch {
      whichChoice  0
```

```
        choice   [
          Inline { url   "texture1.wrl" },   # 1st texture,
                                             #   on a flat rectangle
          Inline { url   "texture2.wrl" },   # 2nd texture,
                                             #   on same rectangle
          Inline { url   "texture3.wrl" },
          Inline { url   "texture4.wrl" },
          Inline { url   "texture5.wrl" }
        ]
      }
    ]
}
```

Once the textures are ready, add a time sensor.

```
DEF EAGLE_TIMER TimeSensor { cycleInterval 1 }
```

Now add the script, a prototyped interpolator that sends out integer values
for use in switching among choices in a Switch node.

```
PROTO SwitchInterpolator [
  eventIn SFFloat set_fraction
  eventOut SFInt32 value_changed
  field MFFloat key        [ ]
  field MFFloat keyValue   [ ]
]
{
  DEF INTERP ScalarInterpolator {
    set_fraction IS set_fraction
    key IS key
    keyValue IS keyValue
  }
  DEF INTEGERIZE Script {
    eventIn SFFloat scalarValue
    eventOut SFInt32 value_changed IS value_changed
    url [
      "javascript:
        function scalarValue(scalar) {
          value_changed = Math.floor(scalar);
        }",
      "Float2Int.class"
    ]
  }
  ROUTE INTERP.value_changed TO INTEGERIZE.scalarValue
}
```

There are several ways an integer-value interpolator can be set up,
depending on when you want the outgoing values to change from one

integer to the next. In this version of the interpolator, the scalar interpolator inside the prototype generates a floating point value and the script truncates it (using Javascript's **Math.floor()** function) to produce an integer. You might prefer to round to the nearest integer instead, which requires changing the script slightly. A more complete implementation might do the actual interpolation in a script rather than relying on an interpolator. But this version will do for the purposes of this example.

To use the interpolator, of course, you have to instantiate it:

```
DEF EAGLE_ANIMATOR SwitchInterpolator {
  key         [ 0, 1 ]
  keyValue    [ 0, 4 ]
}
```

When the user arrives at the spring and clicks the cactus, the touch sensor generates a time event that's routed to the time sensor's *startTime*. The animation works just like the animation you've seen previously, except that the Engine includes a Script instead of only an interpolator.

These routes complete the animation:

```
ROUTE EAGLE_TOUCH.touchTime TO EAGLE_TIMER.startTime
ROUTE EAGLE_TIMER.fraction_changed TO
EAGLE_ANIMATOR.set_fraction
ROUTE EAGLE_ANIMATOR.value_changed TO EAGLES.whichChoice
```

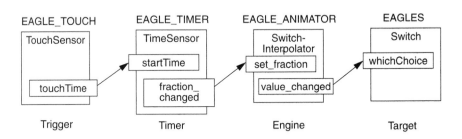

Figure 7-3   Eagle animation wiring diagram

You can use a similar approach to make geometry appear when the user moves to a certain area and disappear as the user moves out of that region: hook up a proximity sensor's *isActive* outgoing event to a script that translates FALSE to 0 and TRUE to 1, then send the result of that script to the *whichChoice* field of a Switch node. An LOD node could be used to achieve this effect, but that's not really what LODs are designed for. Using them that way may result in unfortunate behavior on some browsers that substitute lower levels of detail for higher ones when frame rate starts to fall.

> If you want one child of a Switch node to display nothing, use `Shape { }` for that child—an empty Shape node, containing no geometry. You can't specify NULL as a child of a Switch node. Another way to display nothing with a Switch node is to set *whichChoice* to –1.

Other Fittings

There are many other uses for simple fittings. You can fairly easily build, for instance,

- an Inverter node that takes a Boolean incoming event and inverts its value, sending out TRUE if the incoming event is FALSE and vice versa

- an Accumulator or Averager node that takes several incoming events and averages their values or combines them in another way to produce an outgoing value

- any of various oscillators, which can be used in the Engine phase to produce more complex periodic interpolations (or more specific interpolations in which you specify only one or two parameters):

    - various waveforms (such as sine, cosine, square wave, or triangular wave)

    - shuttles, which generate a series of translations away from and back to the initial location

    - pendulums, which generate a series of rotations away from and back to the initial orientation

In general it's a good idea to create a general-purpose prototype rather than a special-purpose script that you can use only once. The general prototype usually doesn't take much longer to write, and you and others can use it again and again. Of course, in some circumstances it may be more efficient and easier to write a specific script to solve a specific problem.

Logic

The one remaining stage of the animation event path that hasn't been discussed in detail is the Logic stage. This section describes how to process information given by a Trigger before passing it on to a Timer or Target.

Retaining State: Putting Out Fires

In "Engines" on page 130, you saw how to make sparks fly from a brazier. That animation ran once through and then stopped; it would be better to let users click the brazier once to start a fire, and click again to put the fire out. But without some logic to keep track of the current state of the fire (lit or unlit), there's no way for the animation to know whether to start the fire or stop it when the user clicks.

Here are the geometry, time sensor, and interpolator for the sparks again; only this time the time sensor has *loop* set to TRUE, so when you click, sparks rise out of the brazier repeatedly. Also, the spark geometry is contained within a Switch node, so that when the user clicks to put the fire out, the spark won't be left hovering in mid-air.

Example 7-3   Keeping track of state with a script

```
Group {
  children [
    DEF SPARK_TOUCH TouchSensor { },
    Inline { url  [ "brazier.wrl" ] },
    Transform {
      translation  0 1.5 0
      children [
        Inline { url  "coals.wrl" }
      ]
    }
  ]
}
DEF TIMER TimeSensor {
  cycleInterval  1.5
  loop    TRUE
}
DEF SPARK_MOVER PositionInterpolator {
  key        [ 0, 1 ]
  keyValue  [ 0 0 0,  0.8 5 0 ]
}
DEF SWITCHER Switch {
  whichChoice  0
  choice  [
```

```
  Shape { },
  DEF SPARK Transform {
    children   [
      Shape {
        appearance  Appearance {
          material  Material { diffuseColor  1 1 0 }
        }
        geometry  PointSet {
          coord  Coordinate {
            point  [ 0    1.3  .5,
                     0    1.41 .5,
                     0.01 1.41 .5 ]
          }
        }
      }
    ]
  }
  ]
}
```

Here's a script that keeps track of whether the fire is currently lit or unlit and starts or stops the animation as appropriate. This script also switches to a different child of the Switch node when starting or stopping the animation, to make the sparks visible or invisible.

```
DEF SPARK_TOGGLE Script {
  eventIn SFTime touchTime
  eventOut SFTime startTime
  eventOut SFTime stopTime
  eventOut SFInt32 whichChoice
  field SFBool isAnimating  FALSE
  url  [
    "javascript:
      function touchTime(time) {
        if (!isAnimating) {
          isAnimating = true;
          startTime = time;
          whichChoice = 1;
        }
        else {
          isAnimating = false;
          stopTime = time;
          whichChoice = 0;
        }
      }",
    "AnimationToggle.class"
  ]
```

}

This script contains a field, *isAnimating*, which keeps track of information about the current state of the animation. Maintaining state is necessary for any animation that has two or more separate states that you want to treat differently—such as a door that can swing open or closed. An animated door might involve four distinct states with different click responses in each state: an open state (clicking starts the closing animation), a closing state (door is animating from open to closed; clicking is ignored), a closed state (clicking starts the opening animation), and an opening state (door is animating from closed to open; clicking is ignored).

In the case of the spark animation, there are only two states: animating and not animating. Clicking during animation stops the sparks; clicking while not animating starts the sparks.

When the user clicks the brazier the first time, the script determines that *isAnimating* is FALSE (the default value given in the VRML file), sets *isAnimating* to TRUE, reveals the spark geometry by setting *whichChoice*, and starts the animation by sending out a *startTime* event. When the user clicks the brazier again, the script determines that *isAnimating* is TRUE, sets it to FALSE, hides the spark geometry by setting *whichChoice*, and sends out a *stopTime* event to turn off the time sensor and the interpolator.

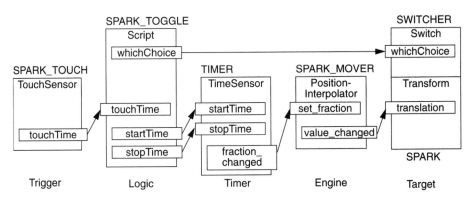

Figure 7-4   Fire-lighting wiring diagram

Here are the routes described by the diagram:

```
ROUTE SPARK_TOUCH.touchTime TO SPARK_TOGGLE.touchTime
ROUTE SPARK_TOGGLE.startTime TO TIMER.startTime
ROUTE SPARK_TOGGLE.stopTime TO TIMER.stopTime
```

```
ROUTE SPARK_TOGGLE.whichChoice TO SWITCHER.whichChoice
ROUTE TIMER.fraction_changed TO SPARK_MOVER.set_fraction
ROUTE SPARK_MOVER.value_changed TO SPARK.translation
```

Other uses for a Logic-stage script include:

- delayed-activation Timer stage (the script adds to the incoming time value before sending it out again)

- combining information from multiple triggers before starting an animation (only start if the user presses two buttons in sequence, or if a precondition has already been satisfied)

- clickable texture maps (deciding what to do based on the *hitPoint_changed* or *hitTexCoord_changed* events from a touch sensor)

- any other case in which you want to process data before starting an animation

Computed Animation

Scripts can perform most of the computations that a full-fledged computer program can. You can therefore use them for very sophisticated control of animated creatures or characters.

For instance, you could use a script to compute an irregular path for a self-propelling creature to follow through a world. Proximity sensors and collision detection apply only to users; no objects or creatures in your world have any way of directly detecting the location of a wall, and nothing prevents an animated character from walking right through the walls. You might therefore want to program animated creatures with some "knowledge" of where the walls and other solid objects in the world are, or design the motion algorithm to stay away from certain areas (to avoid walking across ponds, for example).

Once you've gone that far, you could proceed to design sophisticated *heuristics* for character actions—changing facial expressions, say, or making an animated dog wag its tail when a user approaches. You're limited only by the processing speed of scripts; advanced artificial intelligence algorithms might be too much for a browser to handle while it's trying to keep up a minimum frame rate.

Advanced Scripting

Animation control and processing are probably the most common uses for scripts, but you can use them for many other things that have nothing to do with animation.

The Browser Script Interface (Browser API)

Besides interacting with the containing Script node, scripts can also interact with the user's browser by using the browser *API* calls, a set of function calls that provide an interface to the browser. The Browser API is also known as the browser script interface.

Some of these functions allow a script to determine information about the current state of the user's browser, including the name and version number of the browser (**getName()** and **getVersion()**), the current speed at which the user's viewer is traveling (**getCurrentSpeed()**), and the current frame rate at which the browser is displaying the world (**getCurrentFrameRate()**). You can also find out the URL of the currently loaded world by using **getWorldURL()**. Note that the name and version number have no defined format; each browser is free to return whatever data the browser writers deemed appropriate. Speed and frame rate are returned as floating point numbers; the other information is returned in the form of string values. For details of parameters and return values, see "Script" in Chapter 11.

Scene Hierarchy Manipulation

Scripts allow you to modify other nodes, and even to modify the structure of the scene hierarchy.

Direct (Routeless) Node Access

Fields and events in a Script node can be of any VRML field type, including SFNode or MFNode. When a Script node contains an SFNode or MFNode field, the script in a Script node can get direct access to events in another node, without having to establish a route.

You can provide a previously named node as the value of an SFNode or MFNode field in the Script node. For instance:

```
DEF MY_NODE Transform { }
Script {
```

```
directOutput  TRUE
field SFNode transformNode  USE MY_NODE
eventIn SFVec3f set_position
url
  "javascript:
  function set_position(value) {
    transformNode.set_translation = value;
  }"
}
```

In this example, the value of the Script node's *transformNode* field is the Transform named MY_NODE. The *directOutput* field is set to TRUE, indicating that the script can both send events to and receive events from MY_NODE by referring to the desired event as *transformNode.eventName*. If *directOutput* were FALSE (the default), the script could only receive events from MY_NODE.

> When *directOutput* is left at FALSE, the browser can perform certain optimizations to improve performance. If you don't need to send events to another node directly, leave *directOutput* set to FALSE. You can still send events to other nodes using outgoing events from the Script node and ROUTE statements.

You can read the value of an outgoing event from a node that the script has direct access to using the same syntax. In the given example, `transformNode.translation_changed` would return the most recent value sent out on the *translation_changed* outgoing event from MY_NODE. If no such event has yet been sent, the value returned is the *initial value* for the event type, as described in Chapter 12, "Field Reference."

Instead of putting an SFNode field in a Script node, you can use an SFNode incoming event in that Script node. Then, using an established route, you can send nodes from one script to another. You can even route MFNode values to the *children* exposed field of a Transform node (and corresponding fields of other grouping nodes) to replace the grouping node's entire set of children.

You can add or remove individual child nodes in some grouping nodes if you prefer, instead of changing the entire set of children at once: send an outgoing MFNode event to the *addChildren* or *removeChildren* incoming events of the grouping node. Not all grouping nodes allow those events, however; if you want to change the children of an Inline, LOD, or Switch node you need to replace all the children at once by routing to *set_url*, *set_level*, or *set_choice*, respectively.

Modifying the Scene Hierarchy Using the Browser API

There are browser API functions that allow a script to modify the current world in a variety of ways.

The **loadURL**() function loads the file specified by the URL you pass it. That URL doesn't have to point to a VRML file; you can use **loadURL**() to open an HTML file or any other file that has a URL. Loading a new URL doesn't necessarily mean replacing the current VRML world with the given URL, because you can also specify parameters (similar to the *parameter* field of an Anchor node) that tell the browser to do something else with the new URL. For instance, you can specify a different frame as a parameter; the browser then loads the new URL and places it in the specified frame. If you don't specify parameters, the loaded URL replaces the current world. You can provide multiple alternate URLs as arguments, just as you can provide multiple URLs for any VRML field that contains URL values. You can build your own variations on the Anchor node by using this function in conjunction with a sensor and the **setDescription**() function, which sets a description string much like the one in the Anchor node.

The **replaceWorld**() function replaces the current world with a new world consisting of a set of nodes passed to the function. In this case the argument you pass to the function is an MFNode value, not a URL. When you call **replaceWorld**(), the function doesn't normally return from the function call, because the world that's making the call has been replaced.

Sometimes you may want to create new nodes and add them to the current world, rather than loading in an entire new world. Such additions can be useful in creating new portions of the world based on user actions, for instance. You can do this with the **createVrmlFromString**() and **createVrmlFromURL**() functions. The former takes a string consisting of text in the VRML file format, and parses it to turn it into a node; for instance, after this line executes:

```
newNode = createVrmlFromString("Box{ }");
```

then the variable *newNode* contains a default-valued Box node. That variable's value can then be passed to some other node using an outgoing event, or can be further manipulated within the script.

The **createVrmlFromURL**() function is more complex: you pass it the URL of the VRML file you want to incorporate into your world, and a node that the script has access to, and a string containing the name of an incoming event of type MFNode in that passed node. The browser fetches the VRML file specified by the URL and passes its contents, as a set of nodes, to the specified MFNode event in the specified node. For instance, you can use this function to set a grouping node's children to the contents of a particular file.

There may be situations in which you can't fully determine what routes you need to establish between nodes at the time of creating a world. For such occasions, the browser API provides the **addRoute()** and **deleteRoute()** functions. You specify the names of the nodes and events to route to and from.

For more information on Browser API functions, see "Script" in Chapter 11.

Binding the Browser to a Node

Background, NavigationInfo, Fog, and Viewpoint are special node types known as *bindable* types. Only a single node of each bindable type can be active at a given time. You can send an event to a particular bindable node to *bind*, or activate, that node, thereby deactivating whatever node of that type was previously bound (if any). When you no longer want a bound node to be active, you can send another event to unbind it. You can, for instance, bind a new Background node to change the world's current background; when you want to switch back to the previous Background node, you unbind the current one.

For each of the bindable node types, the browser maintains a *stack* of nodes. All four stacks work approximately the same way.

Background Binding

When the browser initially reads in the VRML file, it binds the first Background node it finds. It pushes that node onto the top of the Background stack, and the node issues an *isBound* outgoing event with value TRUE. (A bindable node sends out an *isBound* event whenever it becomes bound or unbound.) The browser doesn't automatically bind any Background nodes other than the first one; thus, the background displayed when the user first arrives in the world is the first background listed in the file.

When a particular Background node that isn't already at the top of the stack receives a *set_bind* event with value TRUE, the browser places that node on top of the Background stack and makes it the current Background node. The previously displayed background is replaced with the one described in the newly bound node. The Background node previously at the top of the stack (now in the second position on the stack) sends an *isBound* event with value FALSE; the new current Background node sends an *isBound* event with value TRUE.

Note: If the newly bound node was already somewhere on the Background stack, it's moved from wherever it was in the stack to the top; a bindable-node stack never contains more than one copy of any given bindable node. If the newly bound node was already at the top of the Background stack, the *set_bind* TRUE event has no effect.

When a Background node anywhere in the stack receives a *set_bind* event with value FALSE, it's removed from the stack, whether or not it's at the top of the stack. If it was at the top of the stack, the node sends out an *isBound* event with value FALSE, and the new top of the stack (formerly the second item on the stack) becomes bound and sends out an *isBound* TRUE event. If a node not at the top of the stack is removed from the stack, the current node at the top of the stack doesn't change and no *isBound* events are sent.

If there's only one node on the stack and it receives a *set_bind* FALSE event, it unbinds (sending an *isBound* FALSE event). The browser then behaves as if there's a default-valued Background node still on the stack.

If a node not in the stack receives a *set_bind* event with value FALSE, it ignores the event and doesn't send an *isBound* event.

Once a Background node is bound, you can change its fields using the ordinary events-and-routes method. If you want to use only one background in your world, you never have to explicitly bind or unbind a Background node; the first Background node in the file is automatically bound.

NavigationInfo Binding

The NavigationInfo stack works exactly like the Background stack. When you change the fields of the current NavigationInfo node, however, it usually affects the way the browser behaves rather than changing the display as such. If you want to change only a single parameter of a NavigationInfo node, such as the type of viewer to be used, you can send an event to the current NavigationInfo node giving the new value of the field to be changed. If you want to be able to switch easily between two different viewers with different characteristics, though, you can set up the viewing parameters in two separate NavigationInfo nodes and bind or unbind the second one as appropriate. For instance, if part of your world involves walking around in a small area and another part involves flying across a great distance, you can use one NavigationInfo with "WALK" for *type*, 1.0 for *speed*, and 100 for *visibilityLimit*, and another NavigationInfo node with `"FLY"` for *type*, 10.0 for *speed*, and 0 (meaning infinite) for *visibilityLimit*. Whenever the user initiates the flying mechanism, you bind the flying NavigationInfo node; when the user switches back to walking, you unbind the flying node.

Fog Binding

The Fog node allows you to reduce visibility to simulate the effects of fog, smoke, clouds, or other obscuring atmospheric phenomena. When a Fog node is bound, the further away an object is the less visible it is.

You can specify the *color* of the fog to produce various effects (such as smog or smoke). Beyond the distance specified in the Fog node's *visibilityRange* field, fog obscures everything (which is to say, everything is the color given in *color*).

> The Fog node can't create swirling eddies of mist; it's implemented by simply blending the given color with everything the browser draws.

You can also specify, in the *fogType* field, how rapidly the thickness of the fog increases with distance; `"LINEAR"` allows gradual fades over distance, while `"EXPONENTIAL"` decreases visibility more rapidly as distance increases.

> Using fog can improve rendering performance, because no geometry further away than *visibilityRange* gets rendered at all.

The Fog binding stack works similarly to the other binding stacks. To bind a Fog node, send it a *set_bind* event with value TRUE; to unbind it, send it a FALSE value on *set_bind*.

Since the background given in a Background node is conceptually infinitely far away, fog ought to completely obscure any background. Fog, however, doesn't have any effect on Background nodes; the background shows through everywhere it would be visible if there were no fog. Therefore, whenever you bind a Fog node in a place where the background is visible, you should also bind a Background node with a background the same color as the fog. The background still shows through, but it looks just like the fog. Remember to unbind the Background node when you unbind the fog. Of course, if your background is the same color as the fog in the first place, you don't have to change it.

Viewpoint Binding

Viewpoint binding works much like binding other nodes but provides an additional feature: you can animate the position and orientation of a bound viewpoint in order to move the viewer around in the world. A bound viewpoint behaves like a transform that contains the viewer as a child; when you change the viewpoint's position or orientation, the user's view changes accordingly. If the bound viewpoint is a descendant of a transform, any change made to the transform also affects the viewer.

Viewpoints generate an outgoing event that the other bindable nodes don't. Whenever a viewpoint is bound, it sends out the current time as *bindTime*; that time can be used to start a viewpoint animation.

If the user enters a vehicle or conveyance—a train, for instance, or an elevator, or a moving sidewalk—you can bind the viewer to a viewpoint and then animate that viewpoint, causing the viewer to move as well. Guided tours, like the one you've seen of Tenochtitlán, can be implemented using viewpoint binding. Some browsers may provide an interface to automatically animate users from one viewpoint to another without using a script, but not all browsers support such functionality. Even browsers that do support automatic animating between viewpoints are likely to provide straightforward linear interpolation between where the user is standing and the next stop on the guided tour; such a path might not be what you want, and may even take the user through solid objects. (Collision detection is usually turned off during such animation.) So it's a good idea to set up your own guided tours.

First, set up signposts. Each should indicate in some way that clicking it carries the user to the next stop on the tour. Signposts can look like old-fashioned wooden pointing road-signs, high-tech holographic displays, or anything else—such as the pointing hands used in the Tenochtitlán world. Decide where all the stops on the tour are, and place a signpost at each stop. Reuse whatever geometry you can; if all the signposts are identical, use DEF and USE to display them, or create a Signpost prototype. Include a Viewpoint node, under its own Transform, close to each signpost. (The Viewpoint node itself is invisible; the location you give for it should be where you want the user to end up when animating from the previous tour stop to the current one.) The value of each viewpoint's *description* field should be a descriptive string rather than (for instance) the number of the stop, for two reasons: first, because some browsers list all named viewpoints in a form the user can see; and second, because if you number the stops it's harder to add and remove stops later without renumbering all the rest of them.

Each signpost needs an associated touch sensor to start the animation. Here's a prototype for a tour stop, combining a signpost, a touch sensor, a viewpoint, and a proximity sensor to detect where the viewer is when the user clicks the signpost.

Example 7-4   *Animating a viewpoint*

```
PROTO TourStop [
  field SFString description  "Tour Stop"
  field SFVec3f signLocation  0 0 0
  field SFVec3f viewpointLocation  0 0 0
  field SFRotation viewpointOrientation  0 1 0  0
  eventIn SFBool set_bind
  eventOut SFTime touchTime
  eventOut SFVec3f position_changed
  eventOut SFRotation orientation_changed
  eventOut SFBool isInRange
]
{
  Transform {
    translation  IS signLocation
    children  [
      TouchSensor { touchTime  IS touchTime }
      Signpost { } # assuming this has been PROTOd elsewhere
    ]
  }
  ProximitySensor {
    size  50 50 50                    # picked randomly
    position_changed IS position_changed
    orientation_changed IS orientation_changed
    isActive IS isInRange
    center IS signLocation
  }
  Viewpoint {
    description IS description
    set_bind IS set_bind
    position IS viewpointLocation
    orientation IS viewpointOrientation
    jump FALSE
  }
}
```

This prototype is set up to animate the fields of the viewpoint itself. If you want, you can instead animate the fields of a transform that contains the viewpoint; that approach allows you to change the direction the browser treats as "up" (for simulating gravity, for instance). A transform can change the up vector but a viewpoint can't. In general, though, it's simpler to animate the fields of the viewpoint than to animate the fields of the transform.

Viewpoint animation changes the position and orientation of the viewer, but the user can still navigate using the browser's GUI controls. Any motion the user initiates during the viewpoint animation is cumulative with the animation. Viewpoint-animating scripts should always be written to handle user input during animation. You can take any of several approaches:

- Turn off the user interface entirely during animation by setting the current NavigationInfo node's *type* field to "NONE". This approach gives you complete control over the user's movements, but can be disorienting if the user has been using a GUI to navigate. It can also cause discontinuities in the animation when the GUI is removed and when it's redrawn at the end of the animation.

- Place a proximity sensor around the viewpoint; if the user moves a certain distance from the viewpoint during animation, unbind the viewpoint. For instance, on a moving sidewalk without rails, the user can step off at any point and stop the animation.

- Place invisible walls (with collision detection turned on) around the user for the duration of the animation.

- Place visible barriers (with collision detection turned on) around the user for the duration of the animation. Such barriers might include the walls of an elevator or bus (allowing the user a certain amount of freedom of movement within the confines of the conveyance), the guide rail of a moving sidewalk, or the seat belt in a roller coaster car. Visible walls are better than invisible walls, but walls of any kind may be inappropriate for nonvehicular guided tours like the one in the Tenochtitlán world.

For simplicity, this example assumes that the distance between stops on the tour is short enough that you don't need to worry about the user navigating too far off the path during animation.

The next step is to set up a script to control animation from one tour stop to the next, as shown in the following prototype. A pair of functions, **set_position()** and **set_orientation()**, track the user's position and orientation, storing them in fields of the script. Another function, **set_inRange()**, keeps track of whether the user is inside the proximity sensor's range; if the user is far away from the signpost, clicking the signpost shouldn't activate the tour. The **touchTime()** function executes when the user clicks the signpost: if the user is close enough to the signpost, the function sets up the viewpoint and interpolators, binds the viewpoint, and starts the animation. When the viewpoint has been moved to the next stop on the tour—usually the same position and orientation as the viewpoint of the next tour stop—the animation ends, signaling yet another function, **set_animating**(), to unbind the viewpoint.

Here are the functions, combined into a prototype:

```
PROTO TourAnimator [
  eventIn SFVec3f set_position
  eventIn SFRotation set_orientation
  eventIn SFTime touchTime
  eventIn SFBool set_inRange
  eventIn SFBool set_animating
  field SFNode orientInterp OrientationInterpolator { }
  field SFNode posInterp PositionInterpolator { }
  eventOut SFBool isBound
  eventOut SFTime startTime
  eventOut SFVec3f position_changed
  eventOut SFRotation orientation_changed
]
{
  Script {
    eventIn SFVec3f set_position IS set_position
    field SFVec3f position  0 0 0
    eventIn SFRotation set_orientation IS set_orientation
    field SFRotation orientation  0 0 1  0
    eventIn SFTime touchTime IS touchTime
    field SFBool inRange   FALSE
    eventIn SFBool set_inRange IS set_inRange
    field SFNode orientInterp  IS orientInterp
    field SFNode posInterp  IS posInterp
    eventIn SFBool set_animating IS set_animating
    eventOut SFBool isBound IS isBound
    eventOut SFTime startTime IS startTime
    eventOut SFVec3f position_changed IS position_changed
    eventOut SFRotation orientation_changed IS
            orientation_changed
    directOutput   TRUE
    url [
      "javascript:
        function set_position (newPos) {
          position = newPos;
        }
        function set_orientation (newOri) {
          orientation = newOri;
```

```
        }
        function touchTime (timeVal) {
          if (inRange == true)
          {
            position_changed = position;
            orientation_changed = orientation;
            isBound = true;
            posInterp.keyValue[0] = position;
            orientInterp.keyValue[0] = orientation;
            startTime = timeVal;
          }
        }
        function set_inRange (isClose) {
          inRange = isClose;
        }
        function set_animating (isAnimating) {
          if (isAnimating == false)        # animation has finished
            isBound = false;
        }",
      "HandleTour.class"
    ]
  }
}
```

Most of the functions here are straightforward. The only complex one is
touchTime(). It first checks that the user is close enough to the signpost to
start the animation (as detected by the proximity sensor and set by the
set_inRange() function); if so, the function stores the user's current
position and orientation (as detected by the proximity sensor and tracked
by **set_position()** and **set_orientation()**) in both the viewpoint and the
interpolators. It then binds the viewpoint and starts the animation.

A more detailed description of the intended scenario may help in
understanding how the interpolators are set up. Consider a user standing at
point A, as shown in Figure 7-5. Nearby, at point B, stands a signpost. Near
the signpost is viewpoint C. The viewpoint and signpost are part of a
TourStop node. Far off, probably not visible from here, is the next stop on
the guided tour: another TourStop node, containing viewpoint D.

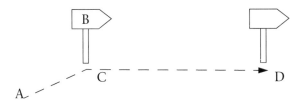

Figure 7-5   Setting up a viewpoint animation

Viewpoint C is the starting point for this segment of the guided tour, but the user has navigated through the scene to this point without using the tour animation, and therefore isn't precisely at C. The interpolators for the tour were designed to carry users from C to D, but for them to work properly, the user has to start at C. If the user clicks signpost B while standing at point A, you have to move the viewer to C before you can start the animated tour.

Thus the need for placing the viewer's position and orientation in the interpolators. If you didn't care about getting the user to C smoothly, you could start the interpolators at C and set the viewpoint's *jump* field to TRUE. As soon as the animation began the user would teleport from A to C.

Discontinuous jumping around in a guided tour can be disorienting, though. So instead, the script finds out the user's current location (point A) from the proximity sensor, and inserts that location as the first value in the position interpolator; the interpolator already has point C as its second value. Thus, starting the animation animates from point A to point C, arriving at C by the second keyframe of the animation, then from point C to point D. All this is complicated further by animating orientation as well as translation, which requires another event and interpolator doing analogous work.

Also, as soon as you bind the viewpoint, the viewer becomes a conceptual child of the viewpoint. As long as the viewpoint is bound, the viewer remains the same distance from the viewpoint as it was at bind time. If you leave the viewpoint in its original position (point C in the previous diagram), bind it, and then move it to A to begin the animation, when you move it the viewer moves the same distance. Thus, before you bind the viewpoint you must set its position to that of the viewer, so that when the animation begins the viewpoint and viewer are in the same place.

The wiring diagram for this animation, shown in Figure 7-6, is more complex than any you've seen before. To slightly improve its readability, the pieces of the TourStop node (the touch sensor, the proximity sensor, the viewpoint, and the viewpoint's transform) have been shown as separate nodes.

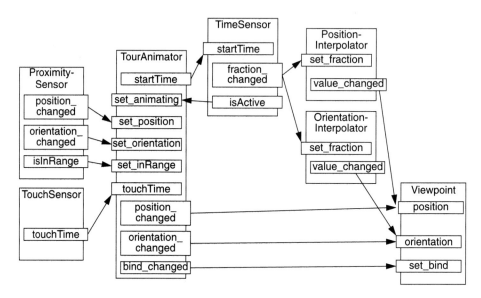

Figure 7-6   Wiring diagram for viewpoint animation

Now that everything's prototyped, instantiate it and put it all together:

```
DEF STOP1 TourStop {
  description "West Gate"
  viewpointLocation 10 3 12    # location of viewpoint 1
  viewpointOrientation 0 1 0   1.57
  signLocation 11 4 11         # location of signpost 1
}
DEF STOP2 TourStop {
  description "Top of Wall"
  viewpointLocation 50 5 82    # location of viewpoint 2
  viewpointOrientation 0 1 0   3.14
  signLocation 50.5 5 81.5     # location of signpost 2
}
DEF TIMER TimeSensor { cycleInterval 10 }
DEF TRANSLATOR1 PositionInterpolator {
  key   [ 0, .1, 1 ]
  keyValue [ 0 0 0, 10 3 12, 50 5 82 ]
}
```

```
DEF ROTATOR1 OrientationInterpolator {
   key [ 0, .1, 1 ]
   keyValue [ 0 1 0 0, 0 1 0 1.57, 0 1 0 3.14 ]
}
DEF SCRIPT TourAnimator {
   orientInterp USE ROTATOR1
   posInterp USE TRANSLATOR1
}
```

Note that both interpolators start out with a dummy value at time 0. That value is replaced (by the **touchTime()** function in the script) with the viewer's current location at the time of clicking the signpost. The first tenth of the animation (from 0 to .1 in *fraction_changed* values) is spent animating from that location to the real starting point of the animation. The rest of the animation goes from the specified starting point (the first viewpoint given) to the specified ending point (the next viewpoint on the tour). This example moves the user in a straight line from the first tour stop to the second; you could make the path more interesting than that by creating a more complex pair of interpolators.

Finally, you need routes to hook it all together:

```
ROUTE STOP1.position_changed TO SCRIPT.set_position
ROUTE STOP1.orientation_changed TO SCRIPT.set_orientation
ROUTE STOP1.touchTime TO SCRIPT.touchTime
ROUTE STOP1.isInRange TO SCRIPT.set_inRange
ROUTE SCRIPT.position_changed TO STOP1.viewpointLocation
ROUTE SCRIPT.orientation_changed TO STOP1.viewpointOrientation
ROUTE SCRIPT.isBound TO STOP1.set_bind
ROUTE SCRIPT.startTime TO TIMER.startTime
ROUTE TIMER.fraction_changed TO TRANSLATOR1.set_fraction
ROUTE TIMER.fraction_changed TO ROTATOR1.set_fraction
ROUTE TIMER.isActive TO SCRIPT.set_animating
ROUTE TRANSLATOR1.value_changed TO STOP1.viewpointLocation
ROUTE ROTATOR1.value_changed TO STOP1.viewpointOrientation
```

As with most animation, the motion complexity is handled by the interpolators. This time, the trick is to define a useful and smooth path from one tour stop to the next, preferably a path that doesn't pass through solid objects.

You have to define new interpolators for each pair of consecutive tour stops, and set up new routes, but using the prototyped nodes should make viewpoint animation relatively painless.

Viewpoint binding is a powerful feature. With it, you can simulate any kind of vehicle—users can "travel" from one virtual place to another by way of virtual buses, boats, airplanes, trains, or even smaller user-controlled vehicles such as cars or bicycles. All you need to do is bind a viewpoint to the user's viewer as the user enters the vehicle, then animate the vehicle's transform (including its child Viewpoint node) to propel the user along with the vehicle.

It's similarly easy to simulate other kinds of closed conveyances—elevators, monorails, overhead trams, and roller coasters all operate on the same principle in VRML. As suggested earlier, collision detection prevents users from stepping out of these virtual devices while in motion.

You can move users around with open-air conveyances too—from airport-style slidewalks to merry-go-rounds (in which the user moves up and down as well as around and around). If you do, though, be careful to decide ahead of time what happens if the user navigates away from the moving objects, and make sure your script handles that situation.

 Many users find navigating freely through 3D spaces to be difficult. Providing a method for getting around in your world using animated viewpoints can make your world easier to use and more fun.

Network Access

The VRML API doesn't define any special networking capabilities. Scripts are expected to use the networking functions provided by the scripting language to connect to and communicate with a remote location. There are a variety of reasons you might want to connect to a program on a remote site, rather than simply downloading a file from a given URL. For instance, you might want to process data about the user's actions using a CGI script in order to decide what other world to link to, or you might want to provide a centralized server for a multiuser VRML world.

Note: JavaScript has no networking capabilities, and is therefore inappropriate as a scripting language for applications that require networking. Work is underway on an "External API" to allow programs outside of a VRML file to communicate with a script in any language inside the file, but at the time of this writing, this API is not fully defined.

Multiuser Worlds

VRML 2.0 doesn't provide explicit support for multiple users interacting in a single world; handling multiuser environments is scheduled to be part of the VRML 3.0 specification. In the meantime, you can set up your own multiuser world if you're willing to do some fairly extensive programming. A full description of implementing a multiuser world is beyond the scope of this book, but this section provides an outline of what's necessary.

Providing access to multiple users at once means that all users' browsers must be kept informed about the current state of the world, and some effort must be made to keep that state consistent. For instance, if two users both attempt to pick up a particular object at the same time, some mechanism must arbitrate and decide which of them (if either) ends up with the object. The most likely model for implementing such a system is a client-server setup, in which each user's browser communicates with a central server program connected to the Web; it's then the server's job to keep all users informed of the current state of the world.

If multiple users are connected at once, providing geometry to represent each user (probably bound somehow to each user's viewer location) is probably a good idea. Such geometry is commonly called an *avatar* (a term borrowed from Hinduism). Several complex issues must be resolved by any implementation of avatars, such as whether the user or the world gets to choose the user's avatar within a given world.

Thus, each avatar's location and geometry is part of the state-of-the-world that the server must keep track of. The idea is that each user's browser connects to the server and sends it information about intended changes to the world to the server, and the server sends that information back out to all other browsers connected to the world. Each browser then makes changes to the local copy of the world (as described in "Scene Hierarchy Manipulation" on page 154) to reflect changes sent by the server.

Many more issues are involved in building a multiuser world. Before embarking on building your own, you may wish to see what others have done. Plates 34 and 35 illustrate several implementations of multiuser worlds.

Chapter 8

Using Colors, Normals, and Textures

In Chapter 4, "Building Objects," you learned how to use the Material and ImageTexture nodes to change an object's appearance. This chapter shows additional ways to color an object—for example, how to use a variety of colors on one shape, and how to combine textures with colors for a rich effect. It also discusses the different ways you can specify normals to affect whether a surface looks faceted or smooth.

Colors

The Material node allows you to specify overall material characteristics of a piece of geometry—shininess, transparency, color. In many cases, you can achieve the desired effect by using a Material node to describe the overall appearance of a given shape. For certain types of geometry, though, you have the option of specifying different colors for different parts of the geometry. Nodes that allow you to specify a variety of colors for pieces of the same shape are the IndexedFaceSet, IndexedLineSet, PointSet, and ElevationGrid nodes. The following sections describe how to use the color fields within these geometry nodes to achieve a variety of effects.

Specifying Colors Per Face

This discussion focuses on using the color fields of the IndexedFaceSet node. Once you understand how that node's *color, colorIndex,* and *colorPerVertex* fields work, you'll be able to use these fields in other geometry nodes as well.

The *colorPerVertex* field in the IndexedFaceSet node lets you specify whether to apply colors to each face of the object or to each vertex of the object. The colors themselves are specified in the *color* field.

The simplest case is to apply a different color to each face of an object, as shown in Figure 8-1 and Plate 9. To apply colors per face, specify FALSE in the *colorPerVertex* field and specify red/green/blue values for the colors in the *color* field. The following example creates a pyramid with red, green, blue, and yellow sides and a cyan base. The five colors are applied to the faces in order—that is, the first face gets the first color, the second face gets the second color, and so on. When you use this technique, be sure to specify a color for each face.

Example 8-1   Specifying colors per face

```
#VRML V2.0 utf8

Transform {
  children   [
    Shape {
      geometry  IndexedFaceSet {
        coord  Coordinate {
          point  [
            -5 -5 0,
             5 -5 0,
             5  5 0,
            -5  5 0,
             0  0 5
          ]
        }
        coordIndex  [
          0, 1, 4, -1,      # face 0: side
          1, 2, 4, -1,      # face 1: side
          2, 3, 4, -1,      # face 2: side
          3, 0, 4, -1,      # face 3: side
          3, 2, 1,  0, -1   # face 4: base
        ]
```

```
        color   Color {
          color   [
            1 0 0,      # red
            0 1 0,      # green
            0 0 1,      # blue
            1 1 0,      # yellow
            0 1 1       # cyan
          ]
        }
        colorPerVertex   FALSE
      }
    }
  ]
}
```

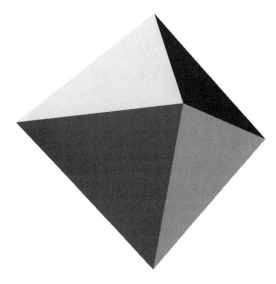

Figure 8-1   Specifying colors per face

If your object has many faces that reuse a small number of colors, it may be more efficient to specify colors by index rather than simply using them in the order they're listed in the *color* field. Each color has an implicit *index* associated with it, starting with 0. In the previous example, red is color 0, green is color 1, blue is color 2, and so on. To create a pyramid with cyan and blue sides and a red bottom, you add the *colorIndex* field and specify the color indices for each face of the polygon, as shown in Example 8-2 (Figure 8-2).

Example 8-2   Specifying indexed colors per face

```
#VRML V2.0 utf8

Transform {
  children  [
    Shape {
      geometry  IndexedFaceSet {
        coord  Coordinate {
          point  [
            -5 -5 0,
             5 -5 0,
             5  5 0,
            -5  5 0,
             0  0 5
          ]
        }
        coordIndex  [
          0, 1, 4, -1,      # face 0: side
          1, 2, 4, -1,      # face 1: side
          2, 3, 4, -1,      # face 2: side
          3, 0, 4, -1,      # face 3: side
          3, 2, 1,  0, -1   # face 4: base
        ]
        color  Color {
          color  [
            1 0 0,    # color 0
            0 0 1,    # color 1
            1 1 0,    # color 2
          ]
        }
        colorIndex  [
          2,    # applied to face 0
          1,    # applied to face 1
          2,    # applied to face 2
          1,    # applied to face 3
          0     # applied to face 4
        ]
        colorPerVertex  FALSE
      }
    }
  ]
}
```

Figure 8-2   Specifying indexed colors per face

Note: When you are using indexed colors, you do not need to have the same number of colors and faces. The polygon in Example 8-2 has five faces, but only three colors (red, blue, and cyan) are used. You must, however, specify a color index for each face.

Specifying Colors Per Vertex

Specifying colors per vertex is another way to achieve sophisticated effects economically (see Plate 10). When you specify colors for vertices, the browser interpolates the colors between the vertices and across the faces of the polygon to achieve smooth gradations of color across each polygon. This type of shading is also referred to as *Gouraud shading*.

To apply colors per vertex, specify TRUE in the *colorPerVertex* field and list the red/green/blue color values in the *color* field. (If you do not specify any colors, the *colorPerVertex* field is ignored.) Then, use the *colorIndex* field as in the previous example to pull values out of the color list and apply them to the vertices. In the following example, vertex 0 has color 3, vertex 1 has color 4, vertex 2 has color 0, and so on. Be sure that the end-of-face markers (–1) in the *colorIndex* list match up exactly with the end-of-face markers in the *coordIndex* field.

The following example shows applying colors per vertex. The resulting object is shown in Figure 8-3.

Example 8-3   Specifying colors per vertex

```
#VRML V2.0 utf8

Transform {
  children  [
    Shape {
      appearance  Appearance { material  Material { } }
      geometry  IndexedFaceSet {
        coord  Coordinate {
          point  [
            -5 -5 0,
             5 -5 0,
             5  5 0,
            -5  5 0,
             0  0 5
          ]
        }
        coordIndex  [
          0, 1, 4, -1,     # face 0: side
          1, 2, 4, -1,     # face 1: side
          2, 3, 4, -1,     # face 2: side
          3, 0, 4, -1,     # face 3: side
          3, 2, 1,  0, -1 # face 4: base
        ]
        color  Color {
          color  [
            1 0 0,    # color 0
            0 1 0,    # color 1
            0 0 1,    # color 2
            1 1 0,    # color 3
            0 1 1     # color 4

          ]
        }
        colorIndex  [
          3, 4, 1, -1,
          4, 0, 1, -1,
          0, 2, 1, -1,
          2, 3, 1, -1,
          2, 0, 4,  3, -1
        ]
        colorPerVertex  TRUE
      }
    }
  ]
}
```

Figure 8-3   Specifying colors per vertex

Since the default is TRUE for *colorPerVertex*, you can omit this field entirely if you want to specify colors per vertex.

A shortcut is to use the *coordIndex* field to pull values out of both the coordinate list *and* the color list. If you specify TRUE for *colorPerVertex* and do not fill in the *colorIndex* field, the browser automatically uses the *coordIndex* field to index into both coordinates and colors. In the following example, the *colorIndex* field is omitted, since it's identical to the *coordIndex* field.

Example 8-4   Specifying indexed colors per vertex

```
#VRML V2.0 utf8

Transform {
  children  [
    Shape {
      appearance  Appearance { material  Material { } }
      geometry  IndexedFaceSet {
        coord  Coordinate {
          point  [
            -5 -5 0,
             5 -5 0,
             5  5 0,
```

```
              -5   5 0,
               0   0 5
          ]
      }
      coordIndex  [
        0, 1, 4, -1,      # face 0: side
        1, 2, 4, -1,      # face 1: side
        2, 3, 4, -1,      # face 2: side
        3, 0, 4, -1,      # face 3: side
        3, 2, 1,  0, -1 # face 4: base
      ]
      color  Color {
        color  [
          1 0 0,     # color 0
          0 1 0,     # color 1
          0 0 1,     # color 2
          1 1 0,     # color 3
          0 1 1      # color 4
        ]
      }
      colorPerVertex   TRUE
    }
  }
 ]
}
```

In the previous example, vertex 0 gets color 0, vertex 1 gets color 1, and so on. This technique works well when each vertex has a unique color.

Whenever you use indexed colors, be sure that you have a color corresponding to each index. For example, if you use indices 0 through 7 in your *colorIndex* or *coordIndex* field, you need at least eight colors in the *color* field.

If you don't specify a material for an object, lighting calculations are not performed. In some cases, this technique may speed up performance since complex lighting effects can be "built in" to the vertex colors of an object. The scene shown in Plate 19 uses radiosity techniques, which precompute the colors that would simulate the lighting in a scene. Once the shading has been computed, colors are explicitly assigned to the objects' vertices, and lighting can be turned off.

Lines and Points

The IndexedLineSet node has *color*, *colorIndex*, and *colorPerVertex* fields that are analogous to the fields in the IndexedFaceSet node. If *colorPerVertex* is TRUE (the default), colors are applied to each vertex of the line set using either the *colorIndex* field or the *coordIndex* field (if there is no *colorIndex* field). If *colorPerVertex* is FALSE, one color is used for each polyline in the line set.

The PointSet node has only a *color* field, which, if used, must contain a color for each point, in order.

Normals

A *normal vector* ("normal," for short) is a vector perpendicular to a surface. A vector is a directional line formed by the given point and the origin (0 0 0). The length of a normal vector is 1.

Normals are used in determining how a surface reflects light. Figure 8-4 shows the same object, with normals specified for each face (top) as well as normals specified for each vertex (bottom). When you specify normals per face, you generally see a sharp crease between adjoining faces because the colors of the adjacent faces are so different. When you specify normals per vertex, the renderer computes a different normal for each point on the surface to create a smooth variation between the normals at the vertices. This interpolation causes the shading to appear smooth. Specifying normals per vertex allows you to achieve curved effects without using lots of tiny polygons (which are expensive in terms of performance).

The IndexedFaceSet node has *normal*, *normalIndex*, and *normalPerVertex* fields. The ElevationGrid node has *normal* and *normalPerVertex* fields.

Using Default Normals

If you don't specify any normals for a shape, the browser generates the normals automatically. If the geometry node has a *creaseAngle* field, the browser looks at the value of this field to decide whether the "seams" between faces should be faceted or smooth. The IndexedFaceSet, ElevationGrid, and Extrusion nodes all have *creaseAngle* fields.

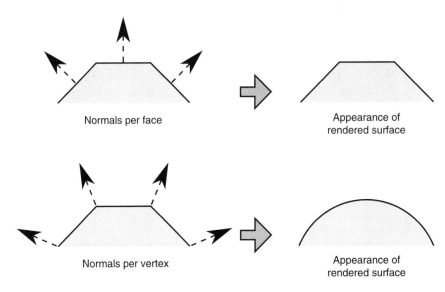

Normals per face

Appearance of
rendered surface

Normals per vertex

Appearance of
rendered surface

Figure 8-4   Specifying normals

The *crease angle* is a tolerance angle (in radians) that is compared to the normals for two adjacent faces of a shape. If the angle between two normals is less than or equal to the specified value for *creaseAngle*, the edge between the two adjacent polygonal faces is smooth shaded. (The faces will share the same normal.) If the angle between two normals is greater than the specified value for *creaseAngle*, the edge is faceted, and a separate normal is calculated for each face. For example, if *creaseAngle* equals .8 radians (approximately 45 degrees), any two faces whose normals form an angle less than or equal to .8 radians are smooth-shaded, as shown in Figure 8-5. If two normals form an angle greater than .8 radians, they appear faceted.

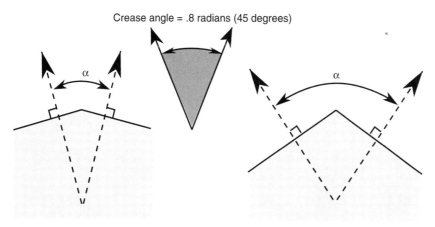

Crease angle = .8 radians (45 degrees)

α < 45 degrees : edges appear smooth   α > 45 degrees : edges appear faceted

Figure 8-5   Crease angle

A high crease angle can reduce the number of polygons necessary to create a smooth look, but note that if you look at an angle edge-on, you can often see it clearly even if it's smooth-shaded from the front. (For instance, a smooth-shaded, low-resolution sphere often has clearly defined edges around the rim of the circle.) In the Tenochtitlán scene, there are *creaseAngle* values specified in several places: the top of the Temple of Quetzalcoatl, for instance, looks smoother than it really is, because there's a crease angle specified to smooth out the facets.

Figure 8-6 shows the Temple of Quetzalcoatl using a crease angle of .401 radians. Figure 8-7 shows the same object with the default crease angle of 0 radians, which always produces faceted edges.

Plate 7 shows the use of the default crease angle. Plate 8 shows use of a crease angle of 2 radians, which produces smooth-shaded curves on the same model.

Figure 8-6   Smoothly shaded edges (crease angle = .401)

Figure 8-7   Faceted edges (crease angle = 0)

Specifying Normals Per Face

To achieve special effects, such as combinations of smooth-shaded and faceted faces on the same shape, you can explicitly specify your own normals. As with colors, you can specify normals for each face or normals for each vertex of a polygon. Both the IndexedFaceSet and ElevationGrid nodes have a *normal* field that contains the normal vectors, and a *normalPerVertex* field that specifies whether the normals are per vertex (TRUE) or per face (FALSE).

Here is an example of applying normals per face. In this example, normals are applied to the faces of the polygon, in the order the normals are listed.

Example 8-5   Specifying normals per face

```
#VRML V2.0 utf8

Group {
  children  [
    Shape {
      appearance  Appearance { material  Material { } }
      geometry  IndexedFaceSet {
        coord  Coordinate {
          point  [
            0 0 0, 1 0 .5, 2 0 .5, 3 0 0,
            0 1 0, 1 1 .5, 2 1 .5, 3 1 0
          ]
        }
        coordIndex  [
          0, 1, 5, 4, -1, # face 0
          1, 2, 6, 5, -1, # face 1
          2, 3, 7, 6, -1  # face 2
        ]
        normalPerVertex  FALSE
        normal  Normal {
          vector  [
            -0.45 0 0.89,      # normal 0, for face 0
             0    0 1,         # normal 1, for face 1
             0.45 0 0.89       # normal 2, for face 2
          ]
        }
      }
    }
  ]
}
```

Figure 8-8 shows the indexed face set generated by this file.

Figure 8-8   Specifying normals per face

If you have a large number of faces that share the same normal, you will probably want to use indexed normals per face, filling in the *normalIndex* field of the IndexedFaceSet node. This field is analogous to the *colorIndex* field. The following section shows use of the *normalIndex* field with vertex normals.

Specifying Normals Per Vertex

Normals per vertex are useful if you want to produce the effect of a curved surface without using large numbers of polygons. If different vertices share the same normal, or if a vertex is shared by different polygons and has a different normal for each polygon, you'll probably want to use indexed normals.

As with the colors, if you specify vertex normals and leave the *normalIndex* field blank, the *coordIndex* field is used to choose normals from the *normal* field.

The following example shows applying normals per vertex, without normal indexing. Since there are eight vertices in the polygon, there are eight normals in the normals list. The *coordIndex* field is used to select normals from the *normal* field.

Example 8-6   Specifying normals per vertex

```
#VRML V2.0 utf8

Group {
  children  [
    Shape {
      appearance  Appearance { material  Material { } }
      geometry  IndexedFaceSet {
        coord  Coordinate {
          point  [
            0 0 0, 1 0 .5, 2 0 .5, 3 0 0,
            0 1 0, 1 1 .5, 2 1 .5, 3 1 0
          ]
        }
        coordIndex  [
          0, 1, 5, 4, -1,
          1, 2, 6, 5, -1,
          2, 3, 7, 6, -1
        ]
        normalPerVertex  TRUE
        normal  Normal {
          vector  [
            -.45 0 .89,
            -.23 0 .97,
             .23 0 .97,
             .45 0 .89,
            -.45 0 .89,
            -.23 0 .97,
             .23 0 .97,
             .45 0 .89,
          ]
        }
      }
    }
  ]
}
```

Figure 8-9 shows the indexed face set generated by this file.

Figure 8-9   Specifying vertex normals

Example 8-7 shows specifying indexed vertex normals. The polygon, shown in Figure 8-10, has three faces. The edge between the first and second faces is faceted. The edge between the second and third faces is smooth-shaded.

Example 8-7   Specifying indexed vertex normals

```
#VRML V2.0 utf8

Group {
  children  [
    Shape {
      appearance  Appearance { material  Material { } }
      geometry  IndexedFaceSet {
        coord  Coordinate {
          point  [
            0 0 0, 1 0 .5, 2 0 .5, 3 0 0,
            0 1 0, 1 1 .5, 2 1 .5, 3 1 0
          ]
        }
        coordIndex  [
          0, 1, 5, 4, -1,
          1, 2, 6, 5, -1,
          2, 3, 7, 6, -1
        ]
        normalPerVertex  TRUE
        normal  Normal {
          vector  [
            -0.45 0 0.89,
             0     0 1,
             0.23 0 0.97,
```

```
              0.45 0 0.89
         ]
    }
    normalIndex  [
      0, 0, 0, 0, -1, # this face is faceted
      1, 2, 2, 1, -1, # these next two faces are smooth
      2, 3, 3, 2, -1  # because they share some normals
    ]
  }
 }
]
}
```

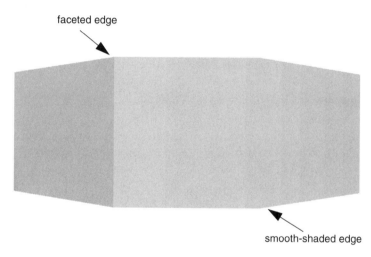

faceted edge

smooth-shaded edge

Figure 8-10   Specifying indexed vertex normals

Advanced Textures

Chapter 4 describes how to apply textures to shapes using default texture mapping. For boxes, cones, spheres, cylinders, and extrusions, default texture mapping is the only technique available to you. For indexed face sets and elevation grids, though, you can specify exactly how to apply a given texture to the shape. You can also transform the texture—for example, stretching, shrinking, rotating, or offsetting it—before you apply it to any shape.

Different systems use different algorithms for displaying textures. Some of the texture examples in this chapter may look different on your system.

Textures, like materials, are specified in the Appearance node, which occurs only within the *appearance* field of a Shape node. Here is the basic syntax for the Appearance node:

```
Appearance {
  material          # contains a Material node
  texture           # contains a texturing node
  textureTransform  # contains a TextureTransform node
}
```

The texture can be specified using an ImageTexture, MovieTexture, or PixelTexture node.

Materials and textures can sometimes be used together, and you will often reuse materials and textures on different objects. Be sure to name materials, textures, and Appearance nodes with DEF and reuse them with USE to shorten the file and reduce transmission time.

What Is a Texture Map?

A texture is specified as a two-dimensional image that extends from 0 to 1 in the horizontal (s) and vertical (t) directions. This two-dimensional image is referred to as a *texture map*. In fields that require texture coordinates, the horizontal coordinate, s, is specified first, followed by the vertical t coordinate. As shown in Figure 8-11, the lower-left corner of the texture map is (0, 0), and the upper-right corner is (1, 1).

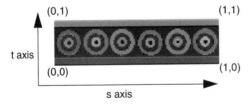

Figure 8-11   Texture map

The ImageTexture node defines a texture map. It also contains fields that allow you to repeat the texture horizontally (*repeatS*) or vertically (*repeatT*) if the texture needs to be expanded to fill the shape (see the section "Using Explicit Texture Mapping" on page 197 for more information on repeating a texture). The texture file itself can be in JPEG or PNG image file format. In addition, some browsers support the GIF format. Only the PNG format supports one-component textures.

The texture file containing the image data is specified in the *url* field of the ImageTexture node. The *url* field contains one or more URLs for the texture maps, in decreasing order of preference.

An alternative to using the ImageTexture node is the PixelTexture node. This node defines a 2D image-based texture map in its *image* field. In a PixelTexture node, the texture is defined as a field in the node itself, not as an external file to be brought in (see the section "How to Specify a Pixel Texture" on page 204 for more information on how to specify a texture in a PixelTexture node). In most cases, you'll simply use the ImageTexture node to specify the texture.

Movie Textures

The MovieTexture node defines an animated movie texture map. It has *repeatS* and *repeatT* fields, as well as other fields for specifying the speed at which to play the movie, the start and stop times, and whether to replay the movie when it ends. If you want both the video and the audio for the movie, name the MovieTexture node with DEF and then USE the same node as an AudioClip node (see Chapter 5, "Lighting, Sound, and Complex Shapes," for more information on the AudioClip node). The MovieTexture node supports MPEG1-Systems format (audio and video are interleaved into a single stream) as well as MPEG1-Video format (video-only in a single stream).

Components of a Texture

Textures can have from one to four components:

- *One-component texture:* contains intensity values, which are used to modulate the object's color
- *Two-component texture:* contains intensity values plus transparency values (intensity map plus transparency)
- *Three-component texture:* contains three colors (full red, green, blue color)
- *Four-component texture:* contains three colors plus transparency values

JPEG textures are always three-component textures. PNG textures can have from one to four components, and PNG is the only format that supports one-component textures. GIF textures can have either three or four components.

For an interesting effect requiring minimal performance overhead, try applying a one-component texture to an object with colors per vertex. This combination achieves a more interesting effect than that of a simple repeated RGB texture. In the Aztec city, the sacrificial knife at the top of the Great Temple combines color per vertex on the knife with a one-component texture (Figure 8-12).

Example 8-8   Combining color per vertex with a one-component texture

```
Group {
  children DEF Knife Transform {
    children Shape {
      appearance Appearance {
        material Material {
          ambientIntensity .20
          diffuseColor     .81 .81 .81
        }
        texture ImageTexture {
          url "textures/sac.knife.jpg"
          repeatS FALSE
          repeatT FALSE
        }
        textureTransform TextureTransform {
        }
      }
      geometry IndexedFaceSet {
        coord Coordinate {
          point [ .37 -.1 .17,
          ...
          ]
        }
        color Color {
          color [ .55  0     .04,   # red
                  1    1     1,     # white
                  .21  .33   .23    # green
          ]
        }
        coordIndex   [ 5, 4, 6, 7, -1, 4, 5, 3, 1, -1,
          ...
        ]
        colorIndex   [ 2, 2, 2, 2, -1, 2, 2, 2, 2, -1,
          ...
        ]
```

```
      normal  Normal {
        vector [ .87 -.42 .25,
          . . .
        ]
      }
      texCoord TextureCoordinate {
        point [ .57 .13,
          . . .
        ]
      }
      normalIndex [ 9, 8, 9, 10, -1, 5, 7, 6, 4, -1,
        . . .
      ]
      texCoordIndex [ 5, 4, 6, 7, -1, 4, 5, 3, 1, -1,
        . . .
      ]
      creaseAngle .52
      }
    }
    scale .25 .25 .25
  }
}
```

Figure 8-12   Sacrificial knife illustrating color per vertex with a one-component
                texture

Plate 11 illustrates the use of vertex colors with a one-component texture.

Three-component textures are used to stamp a color image, such as a brick wall, wood grain, or a painting, onto an object. Two- and four-component textures are analogous to one- and three- component textures, with transparency values added. When a pixel is transparent, you can see through it to the objects behind it. Four-component textures are useful for creating objects such as the leaves on a tree. The texture contains the pixels for the leaves, leaving transparent spaces between them where the objects behind the tree can show through. If you create a Billboard node that is always facing the viewer, you can use a two-dimensional tree texture to simulate a full model of a three-dimensional tree (see Chapter 10, "Improving Performance," for more information on the Billboard node).

 For simple, one-color objects, specify only a Material. For simple texture-mapped objects, specify a Material and an ImageTexture (or PixelTexture). For optimized objects where lighting is built in to the texture map, specify only an ImageTexture (or PixelTexture) and no Material.

Combining Textures, Colors, and Materials

The appearance of a piece of geometry when it is finally displayed on the screen is a result of the textures, colors, and materials specified for that geometry. Browsers are expected to follow certain general guidelines, depending on what combination of textures, colors, and materials you supply. As a general rule, textures have priority over vertex and face colors. Vertex and face colors, in turn, have priority over the diffuse material color. The following paragraphs describe in more detail how textures, colors, and materials interrelate.

No Textures

If you don't specify any textures, colors specified in the Color node replace the *diffuseColor* values in the Material node.

No Materials

If you don't specify a material, no lighting calculations are performed. Face and vertex colors are used to color the objects.

If you don't specify any colors, materials, or textures, the result is a black, unlit object.

Note: Lines and points are not texture mapped or affected by light sources.

Three- and Four-Component Textures

If you specify a three- or four-component texture, the red/green/blue values replace both face and vertex colors for that object (if they are specified) as well as the *diffuseColor* values of the Material node. Remember, though, that if you want lighting calculations to be performed, you need to include a Material node for the object. The texture is used instead of the diffuse color, and the *ambientIntensity*, *specularColor*, *emissiveColor*, and *shininess* fields from the Material node are used in the lighting calculations. The transparency values in the texture replace the Material node's *transparency* values.

If you specify a three- or four-component texture and no material for an object, lighting calculations are not performed, and the texture colors are used as is.

It's not a waste of time to specify a diffuse color and a texture, because the diffuse color can be used while the texture is being loaded. The diffuse color can also be used in the lower-resolution children of an LOD node as a substitute for the more complex texture. In this case, try to match the diffuse color closely with the texture's coloring.

One- and Two-Component Textures

A one- or two-component texture does not contain color values. It contains intensity values that are used to modulate the color values, which are specified elsewhere. If you specify vertex or face colors in a geometry node, those color values are multiplied by the intensity values specified in the one-component texture. If you do not specify vertex or face colors, the values in the diffuse color field of the Material node are multiplied by the intensity values of the texture.

If you do not specify any colors, the values in the texture are used to modify the default diffuse color (.8 .8 .8), which produces a gray-scale effect.

To create the effect of shadows on a surface without the cost of expensive lighting calculations, combine a one-component texture with a Material node. This technique is also a useful way to simulate spotlights.

Specifying Texture Coordinates

Default texture mapping may be adequate for your needs. The best recommendation is to try using the default mapping first. If you're not satisfied, you can add a TextureCoordinate node to explicitly map texture coordinates (*s*, *t* pairs) to the vertices of the object (*x*, *y*, *z* coordinate values).

Using Default Texture Mapping

For example, try mapping a texture onto a piece of the Aztec temple. You can get the texture from

```
http://vrml.sgi.com/handbook/examples/textures/GoggleEyes.jpg
```

or substitute one of your own.

Example 8-9   Using default texture mapping

```
#VRML V2.0 utf8

Shape {
  appearance  Appearance {
    material  Material {
      ambientIntensity  .5
      diffuseColor   .70 .70 .70  # texture replaces this field
      emissiveColor  .13 .13 .13
    }
    texture  ImageTexture {
      url  "textures/GoggleEyes.jpg"
    }
  }
  geometry  IndexedFaceSet{
    coord  Coordinate {
      point  [
         17.5 11.25  -1.25,
         17.5 15      -1.25,
        -17.5 15      -1.25,
        -17.5 11.25  -1.25,
         17.5 15     -18.75,
         17.5 11.25 -18.75,
        -17.5 11.25 -18.75,
        -17.5 15     -18.75
      ]
    }
```

```
coordIndex  [
    0, 1, 2, 3, -1,
    4, 1, 0, 5, -1,
    6, 7, 4, 5, -1,
    2, 7, 6, 3, -1,
    4, 7, 2, 1
  ]
 }
}
```

The textured object is shown in Figure 8-13.

Figure 8-13   Using default texture coordinates

If you don't specify texture coordinates, the browser generates them for you using the following technique. First, it computes the *bounding box* of the object. A bounding box is the smallest rectangular shape that encloses an object, as shown in Figure 8-14. It is aligned with the object's coordinate system.

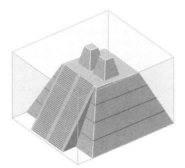

Figure 8-14   Bounding box for an object

Then, it uses the longest edge of the box as the horizontal (s) axis of the texture. It uses the next longest edge as the vertical (t) axis of the texture. The value of the s coordinate ranges from 0.0 to 1.0, from one end of the bounding box to the other. The value of t ranges from 0 to n, where n equals the ratio of the second longest side of the bounding box to the longest side. The effect is that the texture is applied to the longest side of the box once and not distorted for the other dimension (it may need to be clipped or repeated in that direction to preserve the scale).

Note that the two largest faces of the bounding box show a rectangular region of the texture (one of them is a mirror image of the other), and the other faces of the bounding box are striped with the pixels at the edges of the largest faces, as shown in Figure 8-15.

Finally, the bounding box texture is projected onto the shape. At this point, some parts of the texture may remain unused if the shape doesn't fill up the entire bounding box.

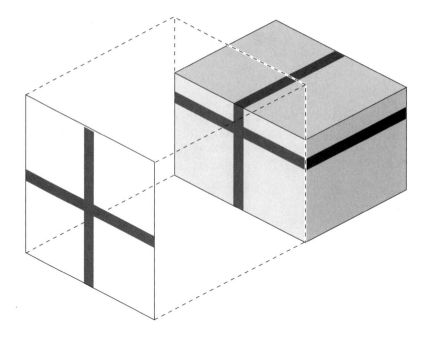

Figure 8-15   A texture and its default projection onto a shape (with bounding box)

Note: For shapes such as box, cone, cylinder, and sphere, the default texture is applied differently. Each shape has its own texturing algorithm, described in Chapter 11, "Node Reference."

Using Explicit Texture Mapping

The default texture mapping shown in Figure 8-13 is probably not exactly what you wanted in this case. You may want the texture to be applied to each face of the object, and you don't want the banded distortions that appear on some of the faces. To improve the results, you can add a TextureCoordinate node to the middle layer of the roof in the *temple.wrl* file to indicate which points within the texture should be mapped to each vertex of the shape. The TextureCoordinate specifies *s,t* points in the texture map that should be "attached" to each vertex of an IndexedFaceSet or ElevationGrid node. (Think of a very flexible rectangle of wallpaper that you want to tack onto the different vertices of the face set.)

This example uses the texture coordinates in order, so it must list exactly as many texture coordinates as there are vertices in the shape (in this case, there are eight). For purposes of illustration, this example adds a top to the sides of the face set and applies a texture to it as well. Contrast this effect, shown in Figure 8-16, with the default texture mapping shown in Figure 8-13.

Example 8-10   Specifying texture coordinates

```
#VRML V2.0 utf8

Transform {
  children  [
    Shape {
      appearance  Appearance {
        material  Material {
          ambientIntensity  .5
          diffuseColor   .70 .70 .70  # texture replaces this
                                      # field
          emissiveColor  .13 .13 .13
        }
        texture  ImageTexture {
          url  "textures/GoggleEyes.jpg"
        }
      }
      geometry  IndexedFaceSet{
        coord  Coordinate {
          point  [
             17.5 11.25  -1.25,    #0
             17.5 15      -1.25,    #1
            -17.5 15      -1.25,    #2
            -17.5 11.25  -1.25,    #3
             17.5 15      -18.75,   #4
```

```
        17.5 11.25 -18.75,     #5
       -17.5 11.25 -18.75,     #6
       -17.5 15    -18.75 ]    #7
        }
    coordIndex  [
       0,  1,  2,  3,  -1,
       4,  1,  0,  5,  -1,
       6,  7,  4,  5,  -1,
       2,  7,  6,  3,  -1,
     ]
    texCoord  TextureCoordinate {
      point  [ 1 0, 1 1, 0 1, 0 0, 0 1, 0 0, 1 0, 1 1 ]
    }
   }
 },
 Shape {
   appearance  Appearance {
     texture  ImageTexture {
       url  "textures/GoggleEyes.jpg"
     }
   }
   geometry  IndexedFaceSet{
     coord  Coordinate {
       point  [
         17.5 15   -1.25,   #0
         17.5 15  -18.75,   #1
        -17.5 15  -18.75,   #2
        -17.5 15   -1.25,   #3
       ]
     }
     coordIndex  [
       0,  1,  2,  3,  -1
     ]
     texCoord  TextureCoordinate {
       point  [ 1 0, 1 1, 0 1, 0 0 ]
     }
    }
   }
  ]
}
```

Although this example uses the corners of the texture as the texture
coordinates, you can also specify texture coordinates from any other place
in the texture map. Also note that you can reuse the same texture
coordinates for different vertices in the shape.

Figure 8-16   Specifying texture coordinates explicitly

As with colors and normals, the IndexedFaceSet also has a field for specifying indexed texture coordinates (*texCoordIndex*). This field indexes into the texture coordinates in exactly the same way that the *colorIndex* field indexes into the color values.

Note: Generating texture coordinates is not easy. You will probably need an authoring tool to facilitate this task.

Transforming a Texture

The TextureTransform node allows you to translate, rotate, and scale the texture coordinates before they are applied to a shape. The syntax for this node is

```
TextureTransform {
   translation   0 0
   rotation      0
   scale         1 1
   center        0 0
}
```

Note that the *translation, scale,* and *center* fields are all specified as *s,t* pairs, since they refer to a 2D texture. The *center* field specifies the center for the rotation and scale texture transformations. The default is (0 0), the lower-left corner of the texture. The rotation field specifies a rotation in radians about the center, in a counterclockwise direction. Note that transformations specified in a TextureTransform node also affect any texture coordinates you specify.

The *scale* field specifies how to scale the texture on the object. In Figure 8-17, the TextureTransform nodes specify a texture scale of (2 2). This means that the texture coordinates (0 0) to (1 1) are multiplied by 2, which results in coordinates from (0 0) to (2 2). The texture is thus repeated twice in *s* and *t*.

Example 8-11   Scaling a texture

```
Transform {
  children  [
    Shape {
      appearance  Appearance {
        material  Material {
          ambientIntensity  .5
          diffuseColor    .70 .70 .70
          emissiveColor   .13 .13 .13
        }
        texture  ImageTexture {
          url  "textures/GoggleEyes.jpg"
        }
        textureTransform  TextureTransform {
          scale  2 2
        }
      }
      geometry  IndexedFaceSet{
        coord  Coordinate {
          point  [
            17.5 11.25  -1.25,      #0
            17.5 15     -1.25,      #1
           -17.5 15     -1.25,      #2
           -17.5 11.25  -1.25,      #3
            17.5 15    -18.75,      #4
            17.5 11.25 -18.75,      #5
           -17.5 11.25 -18.75,      #6
           -17.5 15    -18.75 ]     #7
          }
        coordIndex  [
          0, 1, 2, 3, -1,
          4, 1, 0, 5, -1,
          6, 7, 4, 5, -1,
          2, 7, 6, 3, -1,
        ]
        texCoord  TextureCoordinate {
          point  [ 1 0, 1 1, 0 1, 0 0, 0 1, 0 0, 1 0, 1 1 ]
        }
      }
    },
```

```
Shape {
  appearance  Appearance {
    texture  ImageTexture {
      url  "textures/GoggleEyes.jpg"
    }
    textureTransform  TextureTransform{
      scale  2 2
    }
  }
  geometry  IndexedFaceSet{
    coord  Coordinate {
      point  [
        17.5 15  -1.25,   #0
        17.5 15 -18.75,   #1
       -17.5 15 -18.75,   #2
       -17.5 15  -1.25,   #3
      ]
    }
    coordIndex  [
      0, 1, 2, 3, -1
    ]
    texCoord  TextureCoordinate {
      point  [ 1 0, 1 1, 0 1, 0 0 ]
    }
  }
}
]
}
```

Figure 8-17   Scaling a texture

Since the *translation*, *rotation*, and *scale* fields of the
TextureTransform node are exposed fields, you can animate
them with an interpolator to simulate waterfalls, smoke, or
moving clouds.

Repeating or Clamping a Texture

The ImageTexture node has two fields that allow you to specify how the texture wraps onto an object. If the *repeatS* field is TRUE, the texture map is repeated in the *s* direction, if necessary to fill the object. If *repeatT* is TRUE, the texture map is also repeated in the *t* direction, if necessary to fill the object. (You'll need to scale the texture down to see this effect.)

If either field is FALSE, the texture is *clamped* in that direction—that is, the last row of pixels is repeated to cover the rest of the face.

 To avoid smearing the last row of pixels across the rest of the polygon, use a border of white pixels, or a colored border that matches the color of the polygon. Another alternative is to use a row of transparent pixels so that the underlying polygon color shows through.

In the following example, the texture on the sides of the box is repeated in the *s* direction and clamped in the *t* direction. On the top of the box, it is clamped in the *s* direction and repeated in the *t* direction. The results are shown in Figure 8-18.

Example 8-12   Repeating and clamping textures

```
#VRML V2.0 utf8

Transform {
  children  [
    Shape {
      appearance  Appearance {
        material  Material {
          ambientIntensity  .5
          diffuseColor    .70 .70 .70
          emissiveColor   .13 .13 .13
        }
        texture  ImageTexture {
          url  "textures/GoggleEyes.jpg"
          repeatS   TRUE
          repeatT   FALSE
        }
        textureTransform  TextureTransform {
          scale  2 2
        }
      }
```

```
geometry  IndexedFaceSet{
  coord  Coordinate {
    point  [
       17.5 11.25  -1.25,     #0
       17.5 15     -1.25,     #1
      -17.5 15     -1.25,     #2
      -17.5 11.25  -1.25,     #3
       17.5 15    -18.75,     #4
       17.5 11.25 -18.75,     #5
      -17.5 11.25 -18.75,     #6
      -17.5 15    -18.75 ]    #7
    }
  coordIndex  [
    0, 1, 2, 3, -1,
    4, 1, 0, 5, -1,
    6, 7, 4, 5, -1,
    2, 7, 6, 3, -1,
  ]
  texCoord  TextureCoordinate {
    point  [ 1 0, 1 1, 0 1, 0 0, 0 1, 0 0, 1 0, 1 1 ]
  }
  }
},
Shape {
  appearance  Appearance {
    texture  ImageTexture {
      url  "textures/GoggleEyes.jpg"
      repeatS  FALSE
      repeatT  TRUE
    }
    textureTransform  TextureTransform{
      scale  2 2
    }
  }
  geometry  IndexedFaceSet{
    coord  Coordinate {
      point  [
         17.5 15  -1.25,  #0
         17.5 15 -18.75,  #1
        -17.5 15 -18.75,  #2
        -17.5 15  -1.25,  #3
      ]
    }
    coordIndex  [
      0, 1, 2, 3, -1
    ]
```

```
        texCoord  TextureCoordinate {
          point   [ 1 0, 1 1, 0 1, 0 0 ]
        }
      }
    }
  ]
}
```

Figure 8-18   Repeating and clamping textures

How to Specify a Pixel Texture

On rare occasions, you may want to specify the texture data in the *image* field of the PixelTexture node. An important use of the PixelTexture node is to allow Script nodes to generate textures programmatically. The Script node sends the texture as an event to the *image* field of the PixelTexture node. Casual readers can skip this section, which describes exactly how to specify the inline data.

The *image* field contains an uncompressed color or intensity-mapped image (see SFImage in Chapter 12, "Field Reference").

The first three values in this field are the width of the texture (in pixels), the height of the texture, and the number of components (1, 2, 3, or 4). Values are separated by white space.

Next, list the values for each pixel in the image, starting with the lower-left pixel of the image and moving from left to right, bottom to top. The last pixel specified is the upper-right pixel of the image. Values can be either hexadecimal values from 0x00 to 0xFFFFFFFF or integer values from 0 to $2^{32}-1$.

A one-component image has one-byte hexadecimal values or decimal values representing the intensity of the image. For example, 0xFF (or 255) is full intensity, and 0x00 (or 0) is no intensity.

A two-component image lists the intensity value first, followed by the transparency value. A value of 0xFF is completely transparent. A value of 0x00 is completely opaque—that is, no transparency.

A three-component image lists the red, green, and blue components for each pixel (for example, 0xFF0000 is full red, no green, no blue). Four-component textures list the transparency value after the RGB value (for example, 0x0000FF80 is semi-transparent blue).

The following example shows a very simple three-component pixel texture composed of four pixels (red, black, blue, green). Figure 8-19 shows the resulting object.

Example 8-13   Specifying a pixel texture

```
#VRML V2.0 utf8

Shape {
  appearance Appearance {
    texture PixelTexture {
      image  2 2 3 0xFF0000 0x000000 0x0000FF 0x00FF00
    }
  }
  geometry Sphere { }
}
```

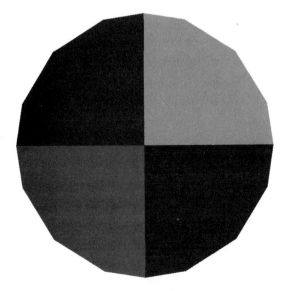

Figure 8-19   Specifying a pixel texture

Backgrounds with Textures

Texture images can also be used in the Background node, which allows you to specify an environment texture, or *panorama*, showing distant scenery that does not translate or scale with respect to the viewer. In the Aztec scene, this distant panorama contains the mountains that are always visible in the distance. The trees of a forest or a set of tall skyscrapers are other items commonly found in a panorama.

Creating the Panorama Scene

Conceptually, the panorama is a sphere with an infinite radius. This sphere is mapped onto the six planes that form a cube enclosing the scene, as diagrammed in Figure 8-20. The viewer is always at the exact center of this cube. Although viewers can never get any closer to this background, they can examine all sides of the panorama. For example, when users look up, they see the *topUrl* (+y) image of the texture cube. Figure 8-21 shows a flattened version of the six planes of the texture cube. In the Background node, these planes are labeled *rightUrl*, *leftUrl*, *topUrl*, *bottomUrl*, *frontUrl*, and *backUrl*.

If you render a series of images with a 90-degree field of view and a 1/1 aspect ratio (ratio of width to height), you can use those images to create the six image textures for the panorama. If you use photographs, you'll probably need an image-processing tool to "stitch" the photos together at the seams of the cube. Or you can create the panorama using techniques such as off-screen rendering, ray tracing, or ray casting, to map the spherical sample onto the six faces of the cube.

Figure 8-20   Projecting a spherical image onto the sides of a cube

Here is a sample Background node with three-component textures specified for each of the six panorama fields.

Example 8-14   Specifying a background panorama

```
Background {
  # Scenery specification
  leftUrl     "mountainsNegX.png"    # mtns West
  rightUrl    "mountainsPosX.png"    # mtns East
  topUrl      "mountainsPosY.png"    # sky Up
  bottomUrl   "mountainsNegY.png"    # ground Down
  backUrl     "mountainsPosZ.png"    # mtns North
  frontUrl    "mountainsNegZ.png"    # mtns South
}
```

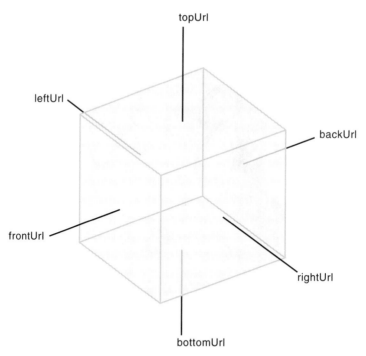

Figure 8-21   Six texture-mapped images form the panorama cube

Adding Ground and Sky Colors

The Background node also allows you to specify a set of smoothly graded colors for both the ground and sky in your scene. Conceptually, the sky forms a sphere (with an infinite radius) around your scene. This sphere has horizontal gradations of color, as specified in the *skyColor* field of the Background node. Similarly, the ground forms a semi-spherical "bowl" under your scene, with an infinite radius but drawn as though inside the sky sphere. The bowl has horizontal gradations of the colors specified in the *groundColor* fields. (Usually, most of this bowl is hidden under your scene.) The subtle gradations of color add a sense of perspective to your scene but are easy for you to specify. Typically, the horizon is at 1.57 radians (about 90 degrees), but you are free to specify other values.

The following paragraphs describe exactly how to specify ground and sky colors and ranges.

Specifying Ground Colors

You can specify any number of ground colors in the *groundColor* field. The following example specifies three colors, ranging from dark green to light green.

Example 8-15 Specifying ground colors

```
Background {
  groundColor [
    0 .6  0, # A: dark green
    0 .8  0, # B: medium green
    0  1  0  # C: light green
  ]
  groundAngle [1.05, 1.57] # MFFloat
}
```

The first color begins at the "South Pole," or the base of the bowl that forms the ground colors. Measurements for cutoff angles of the colors you specify are made relative to this direction, as shown in Figure 8-22.

In the previous example, *groundAngle* values are 1.05 radians (about 60 degrees) and 1.57 radians (about 90 degrees). These values indicate that the area between 0 and 1.05 radians (60 degrees) gradually ranges from dark green to medium green. The area between 1.05 radians (60 degrees) and 1.57 radians (90 degrees) ranges from medium green to light green.

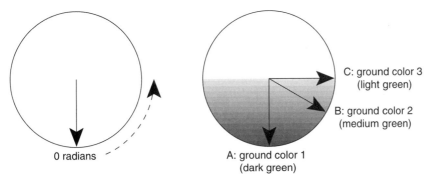

Figure 8-22   Cutoff angles for ground colors

Specifying Sky Colors

Specifying sky colors is analogous to specifying ground colors, except that the *skyAngle* values are specified relative to the "North Pole," with 0 radians directly overhead, as shown in Figure 8-23. The color value at the last sky angle specified is repeated from that angle to the "South Pole," or until it meets the ground color. (Interpolation from one color to the next stops at the last sky angle specified, and the last sky color is clamped to its value to fill the remaining space.)

Example 8-16   Specifying sky colors

```
Background {
  skyColor   [
     0   0 .2,   # D: dark blue
    .1 .1 .8,   # E: medium blue
    .2 .2  1    # F: light blue
  ]
  skyAngle  [1.05, 1.57]  # MFFloat
}
```

Here, the sky colors range from dark blue to medium blue to light blue at the horizon.

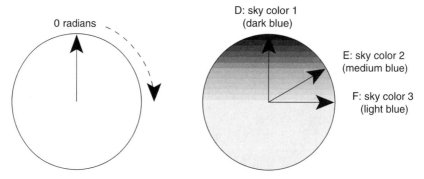

Figure 8-23   Cutoff angles for sky colors

Combining a Panorama with Ground and Sky Color

You can specify ground and sky colors as well as a panorama if your panorama has a transparency component, which will allow the ground and sky colors to show through at certain points. (If the panorama does not have a transparency component, you won't be able to see the ground and sky colors at all.) When the scene is rendered, the panorama is inserted between the viewer and the ground/sky backdrop.

Example 8-17   Specifying ground and sky colors and a background panorama

```
Background {
  # Ground specification
  groundColor [
    0 .6  0,
    0 .8  0,
    0  1  0  # MFColor
  ]
  groundAngle [1.05, 1.57] #MFFloat

  # Sky specification
  skyColor [
    0   0 .2,
    .1 .1 .8,
    .2 .2  1  # MFColor
  ]
  skyAngle [1.05, 1.57] #MFFloat

  # Scenery specification
  rightUrl   "forestPosX.png"
  leftUrl    "forestNegX.png"
  topUrl     "forestPosY.png"
  bottomUrl  "forestNegY.png"
  frontUrl   "forestPosZ.png"
  backUrl    "forestNegZ.png"
}
```

Chapter 9

Publishing Your Work

To publish your VRML files on the Web, you need access to a *server*, a computer connected to the Internet and dedicated to providing data over the Web. This chapter provides information on the basics of setting up a server and refers you to additional resources for the details of server setup, administration, and maintenance. When you publish your work, you'll need to organize and name your files according to certain conventions, copy your files to the proper location on the server, and announce your new URL and content to the world.

The first section in this chapter, "Setting Up a Server," discusses some of the issues involved in setting up your own Web server. Setting up a server is not for the faint of heart or for computer novices. If you aren't familiar with system administration, consider having your Internet service provider (ISP) handle this task. If you don't need to set up your own server, skip directly to the second main section, "Organizing and Publishing Your Files." The third section, "Using the Common Gateway Interface (CGI)," describes how to use CGI scripts to process user input and create VRML worlds based on that input.

Setting Up a Server

Setting up a server for VRML documents is the same as setting up a server for HTML documents, and many good descriptions of this task have been written. *HTML for Fun and Profit* by Mary E. Morris (Englewood Cliffs, NJ: Sunsoft Press, 1995) describes setting up *httpd*, a Web server written for UNIX® platforms, as well as setting up a Windows NT™ server.

Versions of *httpd* are available from both CERN and NCSA. Both servers are freeware, and you can obtain them from the Web at the following locations:

```
http://info.cern.ch/hypertext/WWW/Daemon/Status.html
```

```
http://hoohoo.ncsa.uiuc.edu/docs/Overview.html
```

Other servers are available from commercial sources, such as Netscape Communications. For a detailed list of available servers, check the following location:

```
http://www.webcompare.com
```

Security Issues

If you decide to maintain your own server, you'll need to learn about network security issues and set up the appropriate safeguards. If your server is connected only to other computers within your company, security is probably not a concern, since the computers already have access to one another. But if you want external sources to have access to your server, you'll need to connect to the Internet, which will then allow anyone to connect to the computers within your company. Since serious security breaches could result, you'll probably want to set up a *firewall*, which allows external sources to access the server but denies them access to all other internal computers.

Firewalls are systems that control the flow of traffic between the Internet and internal networks and systems. A firewall can consist of a router, a computer system, or a combination of the two. There is much debate on which approach to use, but it's generally agreed that a combination of both mechanisms is best.

A firewall uses a router to screen the connection between your internal network and the Internet. A table specifies which packets should be passed on to the other side of the router and which should be thrown away. This approach is convenient because it's an extension to what the router already does: routing IP packets from one side to the other. Most of the large router manufacturers, such as Cisco and Bay Networks, offer packet filtering on their routers.

Another approach to creating a firewall is to use a separate computer, called a *proxy server*, to route the packets between the internal network and the outside world. All browsers point to the proxy, and the proxy passes on requests for the browsers. There is no direct connection between the two networks. The *httpd* server provided by CERN can run as a proxy server. The

Gauntlet™ Internet Firewall, from Trusted Information Systems, is a commercially available firewall product.

For more information on security issues and building a firewall, see William R. Cheswick and Steven M. Bellovin, *Firewalls and Internet Security: Repelling the Wily Hacker* (ISBN 0-201-63357-4). Also, visit the Web site at `http://www.alw.nih.gov/Security` for further suggestions.

Configuring a Server to Recognize VRML Files

To configure a UNIX Web server to recognize VRML files, you need to set up the MIME types as follows:

```
AddType      x-world/x-vrml   wrl
AddEncoding  gz      x-gzip
```

or

```
type=x-world/x-vrml  exts=wrl
enc=x-gzip           exts=gz
```

Your URL

If you're using a server maintained by an Internet service provider (ISP), your ISP can tell you the URL of your Web site. If you're maintaining your own server, you can determine your URL as follows:

- The first part of the URL denotes the protocol used by the server to transfer the files. Some options include *http*, *ftp*, and *Gopher*. The protocol identifier is followed by a colon and two slashes—for example: `http://`, `ftp://`, `gopher://`. Web content, including VRML scenes, is almost always served over HTTP.

- The second part is the name of the server—for example, `www.sgi.com`. The name doesn't have to start with "www"; it's just a convention.

- The third part is the path to your home page, which serves as the launch point for visitors to your site. The default home page is `index.html`, so your path will be shorter if you use that name for your home page. For example, the launch point for the Tenochtitlán site is

  `http://vrml.sgi.com/handbook`

The home page in this example has the name *index.html*. Consult the documentation for your HTTP server to understand the mapping between your server's local filesystem and this public-access pathname.

A VRML world needs a *.wrl* suffix, so it can't be named *index.html*. You'll probably want to make your home page an HTML page, with pointers linking it to your VRML worlds.

Organizing and Publishing Your Files

Before you publish your work on the Web, be sure to complete the following steps, described in the following sections:

1. Use relative addresses for files.

2. Use the correct MIME type suffix for each file.

3. Verify all URLs.

4. Add information nodes to your files if useful.

5. Compress the files.

The final section in this chapter lists ideas for ways to announce your new work on the Web.

Use Relative Addresses

Before you copy your files to the designated location on the server, be sure that your file specifications use relative addressing. In VRML, if a URL doesn't start with a protocol specifier (such as `http://`), the browser assumes the referenced file is relative to the URL of the main scene. Using relative addresses for anchor nodes, inlines, and texture files makes life easier because when you move your files, you'll need to change only the top pathname and the other directories will move with it.

Large VRML worlds, such as the example used in this book, will probably require a hierarchy of directories, as shown in Figure 9-1. The Aztec world contains two main subdirectories, one for 3D models and one for the HTML Web pages. The main VRML file is *Tenochtitlan.wrl* in the *aztec.city* directory. This subdirectory contains additional directories, including a *textures* directory, which holds the texture files.

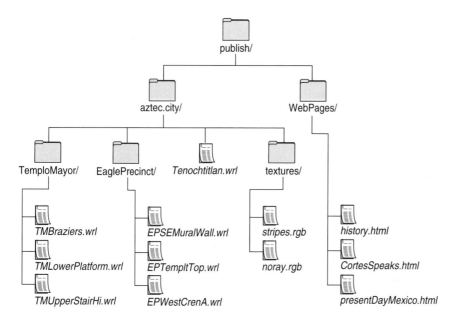

Figure 9-1 Organizing a set of files for a VRML world

How to Include a VRML World in an HTML File

Use the EMBED HTML tag to include a VRML world in an HTML file. Include the complete path to the VRML file, as well as the width and height in pixels for the viewport used to display the VRML world on the HTML page.

```
<EMBED SRC="VRML/book/orig/models/temple.demo.wrl" WIDTH=600
HEIGHT=512>
```

Note: At the time of publication, the World Wide Web Consortium (W3C) is working on a draft proposal for a new tag, <INSERT>, which will provide support for inserting any type of multimedia object into an HTML document. This tag will cover VRML files, Java applets, Microsoft Component Object Model (COM) objects (for example, OLE Controls and OLE Document embeddings), and a wide range of other media plug-ins. For the current status of this work, see http://www.w3.org/pub/WWW/TR.

Use MIME Type Extensions

Each document sent over the Web should have the appropriate MIME (Multipurpose Internet Mail Extensions) type file suffix, which identifies the kind of data in the file. The browser uses this suffix to identify the file type (image, movie, sound) and the format it's in (VRML, GIF, JPEG, MPEG, WAV) and to launch a helper application to view or play the document if necessary. Consult your browser documentation for information on how to configure MIME types on your local system.

Common MIME types and suffixes are

VRML (3D worlds)	.wrl
HTML (text)	.html
GIF (2D image)	.gif
JPEG (2D image)	.jpeg, .jpg, .jpe
PNG (2D image)	.png
AIFF (sound)	.aif, .aiff
AIFC (sound)	.aifc
AU (sound)	.au, .snd
Wave (sound)	.wav
MPEG (video)	.mpeg, .mpg, .mpe
Quicktime (video)	.qt, .mov, .moov
AVI (video)	.avi
ASCII Text	.txt
PostScript	.ps
JavaScript	.js, .ls, .mocha

Verify Remote URLs

If you reference remote URLs in your VRML file, it's a good idea to double-check each reference before final publication to ensure that it's correct and still active.

Add Information Nodes

Before you publish your work, you can add a title to your world, as well as credits and a copyright notice for your file, with the WorldInfo node, described below. Also, be sure to include a NavigationInfo node, which provides useful hints to browsers about default viewer type, speed, and headlight.

WorldInfo Node

The WorldInfo node lets you specify a title that browsers can display in their window border. The scene author, copyright information, and any other relevant information can be included in the *info* field of this node. For example:

```
WorldInfo {
    title "Aztec City of Tenochtitlan"
    info [ "created by Delle Maxwell" ]
}
```

The WorldInfo node is a global node that can appear anywhere in a VRML file.

NavigationInfo Node

The NavigationInfo node can be used as a child of any grouping node. It provides a hint to the browser about which interactive viewing method is most appropriate for your world. The choices all VRML browsers support are "WALK," "EXAMINE," "FLY," and "NONE." The *type* field of this node allows you to specify which viewer the browser should use by default. The following list describes the type of content usually associated with each of these modes:

- "WALK" mode is appropriate for immersive landscapes in which the viewer navigates through the scene with reference to a ground plane or terrain.

- "EXAMINE" mode is appropriate for inspecting objects, where the viewer tumbles and turns the model with reference to its center or point of interest.

- "FLY" mode is used to explore open expanses in which the viewer flies freely in any direction throughout the space.

- "NONE" indicates that no browser-specific navigational interface will be presented to move the viewer through the scene. Any navigation through the scene must be provided explicitly by the content author (for example, through the use of viewpoints and scripts).

The *speed* field lets you specify the rate at which the viewer normally travels through the world in meters per second. (The browser interprets what "normal" travel speed means.) The *avatarSize* field contains values used to describe the virtual presence of the viewer within the world, for purposes of collision detection and terrain following (see Chapter 11, "Node

Reference"). The *visibilityLimit* field sets the maximum distance the viewer is able to see.

The *headlight* field specifies whether the browser should turn on a headlight for the world. A headlight is a directional light that always points in the direction the user is looking. It's useful because it provides default lighting for worlds that do not contain explicit lighting. Setting this field to TRUE allows a browser to provide a user interface that controls the light. For example:

```
NavigationInfo {
   type        "WALK"
   speed       5.0
   headlight   TRUE
}
```

 If you specify your own lights, you might want to turn the browser headlight off.

Compress the Files

As described in Chapter 10, "Improving Performance," all files should be compressed if possible—uncompressing a file is almost always faster than transferring a larger file. Use the *gzip* utility to compress all VRML, HTML, text, and PostScript® files.

Textures should be compressed using JPEG (don't *gzip* a texture file). Be sure to use the suffix *.jpg* for JPEG files so the browser will know how to handle them.

At the time of publication, work on developing a binary VRML file format is underway. Consult `http://vrml.sgi.com/handbook` for more up-to-date information on this topic.

Announce Your Work on the Web

There are a number of places you can notify when your server is ready to greet the world. A few possibilities are

- Fill out the submission form at the Netscape site to have your site included in the Netscape *What's New?* page:

  `http://home.netscape.com/home/whats-new.html`

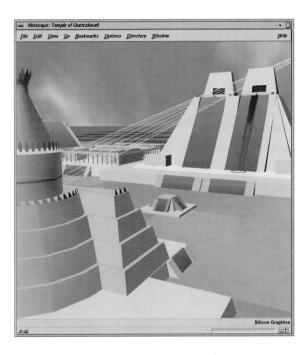

Plate 1 Light rays activated by clicking a sun icon. The distant models of Tenochtitlán temples use LOD nodes and color per vertex. (Plates 1 through 5, by Delle Maxwell, use the Cosmo™ Player plug-in browser from Silicon Graphics, Inc.)

Plate 2 Panoramic view of the ceremonial center at Tenochtitlán. The sky is a set of texture maps specified in a Background node.

Plates 1 and 2. http://vrml.sgi.com/handbook/Aztec

Plate 3 View of the spring at Tenochtitlán. The poem text is a texture map with a transparent background. Transparent blue polygons form the water of the spring. The eagle on the cactus is a texture that animates when the user clicks it.

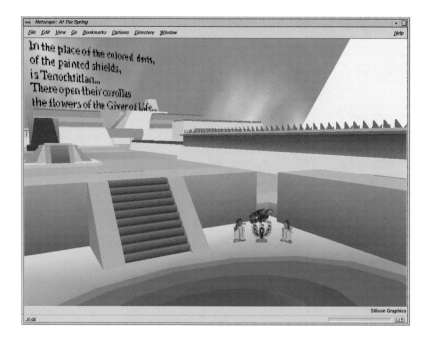

Plate 4 View of the sacrificial skull rack at Tenochtitlán. Clicking and dragging one of the skulls activates a line sensor that allows the user to slide the skull along the rack.

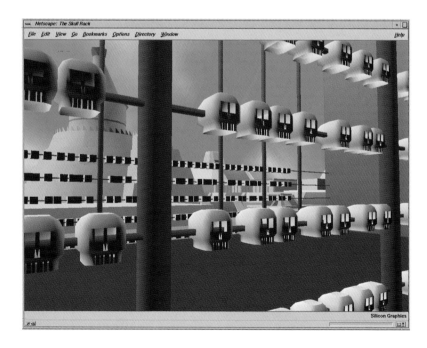

Plates 3 and 4. http://vrml.sgi.com/handbook/Aztec

Plate 5 Chacmool at the entrance to the Temple of Tlaloc at Tenochtitlán. One-component textures and vertex coloring are used throughout this scene. Clicking the chacmool brings up the HTML page shown below.

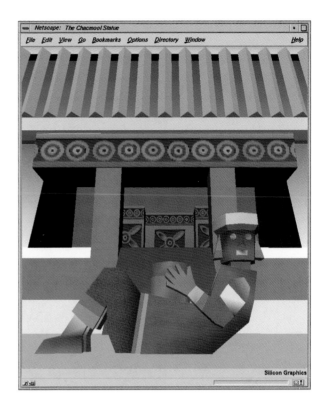

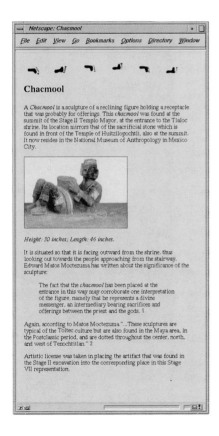

Plate 6 Background information about the chacmool statue. This HTML page is linked to the chacmool using an Anchor node. (From *Visions of the Aztec World* by David Carrasco and Eduardo Matos Moctezuma, University Press of Colorado, 1992. Reprinted by permission.)

Plates 5 and 6. http://vrml.sgi.com/handbook/Aztec

Plate 7 Using the default crease angle to show facets between polygons. See Chapter 8.

Plate 8 Using a crease angle of two radians to create smoother shading.

Plate 9 Using color per face.

Plate 10 Using color per vertex.

Plate 11 Using color per vertex and a one-component texture.

Plate 12 Using a three-component texture for the dinosaur's skin. The eye is a separate object that uses color per vertex.

Plates 7 through 12 by Sam Chen, Silicon Graphics, Inc.; data for model courtesy of Viewpoint DataLabs, International.

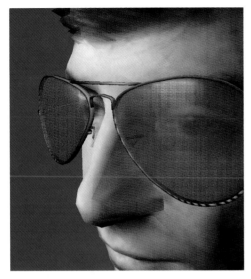

Plate 13 Shopping on the Web. The head is scanned in as a model and then texture mapped with the face image. Users can try on sunglasses in cyberspace, viewing themselves from different angles.

Plate 14 A virtual meeting space that provides a shared electronic whiteboard and facilities for video-conferencing.

Plates 13 and 14 courtesy of Advanced Applications and Technologies Department, British Telecommunications Laboratories.   http://virtualbusiness.labs.bt.com/vrml/portal/home

Plate 15 A model of the San Francisco Bay Area created as part of the Virtual San Francisco project developed by Planet 9 Studios. The orange boxes are hyperlinks to smaller neighborhoods.

Plate 16 A close-up view of the San Francisco neighborhood south of Market Street, created as part of the Virtual SOMA project developed by Planet 9 Studios. The building facades are texture mapped onto the models. Plates 15 and 16 show the WorldView™ browser from Intervista Software.

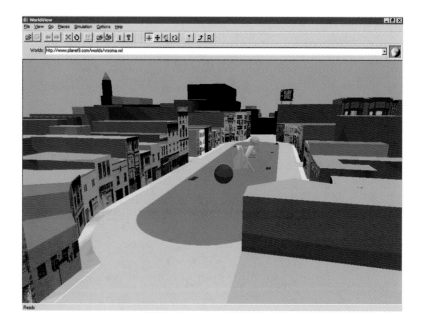

Plates 15 and 16. http://www.planet9.com

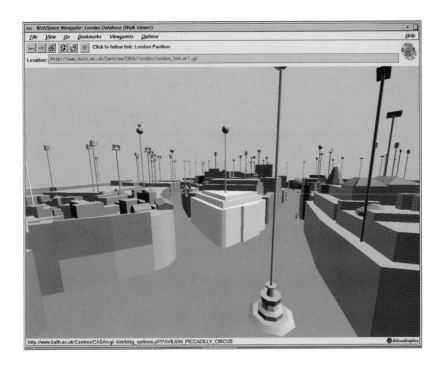

Plate 17 Detailed model of London used for analyzing the range of cellular radio signals. (Advanced Applications and Technologies Department, British Telecommunications Laboratories.)

Plate 18 Whimsical treatment of a 3D corporate landscape using 2D texture maps. The background of each texture map is transparent, producing a cutout effect and allowing the scene's ground and sky to show through. (© 1996, Paul S. Hoffman, Cognetics Corporation.)

Plate 17. http://virtualbusiness.labs.bt.com/vrml/portal/home
Plate 18. http://www.cognetics.com/vrml/agvrml.wrl

Plate 19 Architectural model created using the Lightscape Visualization System, which precalculates lighting effects using radiosity techniques. Because the lighting calculations are then "built in" to the objects' vertex colors, the resulting images can be displayed at interactive frame rates.
(© 1995, Lightscape Technologies, Inc.; data courtesy of A.J. Diamond, Donald Schmitt and Company, Toronto.)

Plate 20 A virtual castle with texture-mapped paintings and architectural details.
(Monika Fleischmann, Josef Speier, and Wolfgang Strauss.
© VisWiz, German National Research Center for Information Technology.)

Plate 19. http://www.lightscape.com
Plate 20. http://viswiz.gmd.de/VMSD/PAGES.en/projects.navi.html

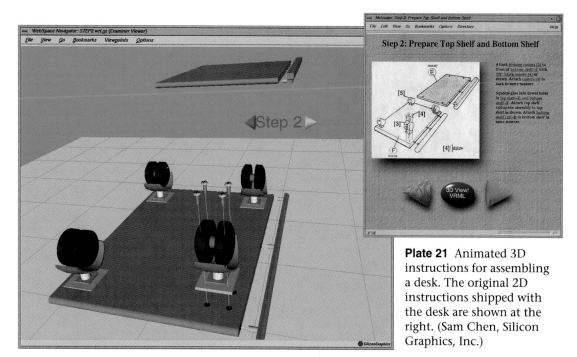

Plate 21 Animated 3D instructions for assembling a desk. The original 2D instructions shipped with the desk are shown at the right. (Sam Chen, Silicon Graphics, Inc.)

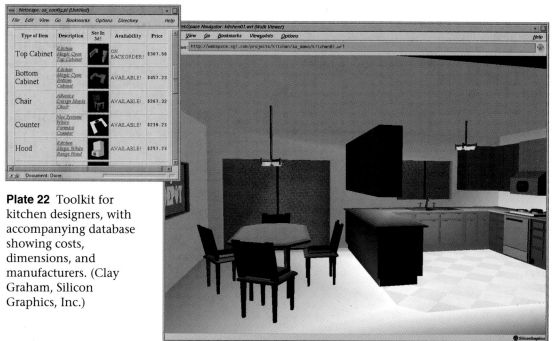

Plate 22 Toolkit for kitchen designers, with accompanying database showing costs, dimensions, and manufacturers. (Clay Graham, Silicon Graphics, Inc.)

Plate 21. http://vrml.sgi.com/Repository/SGI-Depot
Plate 22. http://vrml.sgi.com/projects/kitchen/sa_demo/index.html

Plate 23 Graphical representation of statistics on the number of visits to a Web site. (VRStat by Denis P. Leconte.)

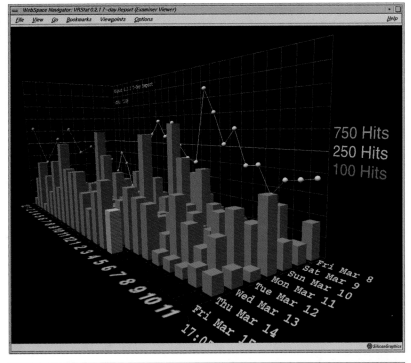

Plate 24 View into the interior of cytochrome P450, an enzyme that plays a key role in cancer research. (H. Vollhardt and J. Brickmann, Institute of Physical Chemistry, Technische Hochschule Darmstadt.)

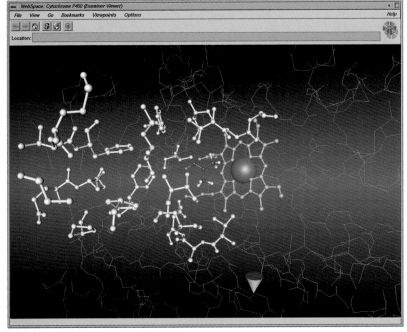

Plate 23. http://www.earthnews.com/personal/d.leconte/vrml/denis.html
Plate 24. http://www.pc.chemie.th-darmstadt.de/vrml

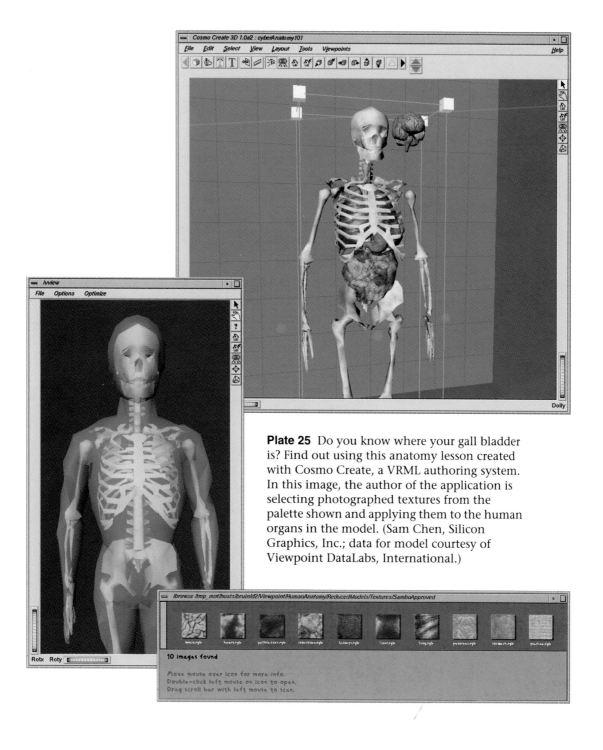

Plate 25 Do you know where your gall bladder is? Find out using this anatomy lesson created with Cosmo Create, a VRML authoring system. In this image, the author of the application is selecting photographed textures from the palette shown and applying them to the human organs in the model. (Sam Chen, Silicon Graphics, Inc.; data for model courtesy of Viewpoint DataLabs, International.)

Plate 26 Interactive educational fly-through of the solar system. Users can attach themselves to one of the orbiting moons and view Saturn from a new perspective. Dramatic sounds signal the user's approach to the Voyager satellite. (Sam Chen, Silicon Graphics, Inc.)

Plate 27 Global structure of the MBone, the multicast backbone that allows real-time video and audio streams to be sent across the Internet. MBone "tunnels" are drawn as arcs and contain links to information about the tunnel endpoints. Researchers use this visualization to track redundancies in the structure. (Tamara Munzner, K. Claffy, Bill Fenner, and Eric Hoffman.)

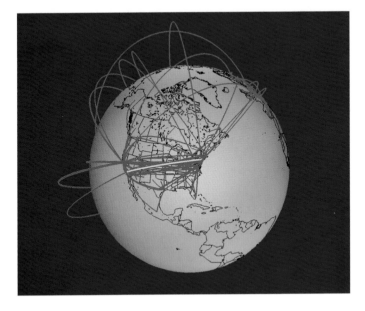

Plate 27. http://www.nlanr.net/Vis/Mbone

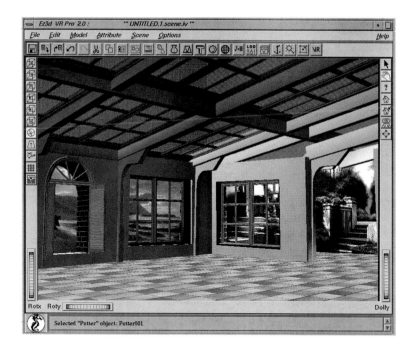

Plate 28 Elaborately textured world created with Ez3d™ VRML Author, an application based on Open Inventor™ that provides modeling, rendering, and VRML authoring tools. (© 1996 Radiance Software International.)

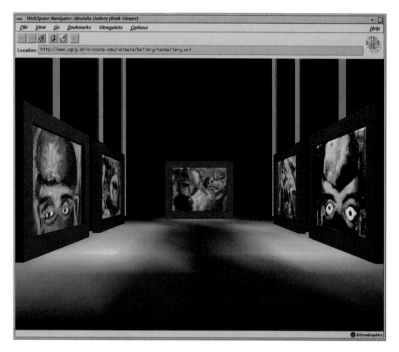

Plate 29 A virtual art gallery showing a series of paintings entitled *Dennet's Dream*. The dramatic gallery setting allows the user to perceive the works as wall-sized monoliths, preserving the sense of scale that is lost when the paintings are reproduced in a 2D format. (Matthew Lewis, Advanced Computing Center for the Arts and Design, Ohio State University.)

Plate 28. http://www.radiance.com/~radiance
Plate 29. http://www.cgrg.ohio-state.edu/~mlewis/Gallery/gallery.html

Plate 30 David Blair's metaphorical history of the Diaspora. This hypermedia project incorporates VRML, audio, video, hypertext, and the ability for users to make publicly visible additions to the document. The triangular object in the 3D scene is a navigation marker for following viewpoints.

Plate 31 The Out of Box Experience, a VRML-based, multimedia "welcome experience" for users of Silicon Graphics workstations. This scene shows the entry space, where users can customize their new systems. (Models by Construct Internet Design; color and textures by Rob Aguilar. Courtesy of Silicon Graphics, Inc.)

Plate 30. http://www.race.u-tokyo.ac.jp/~artist1

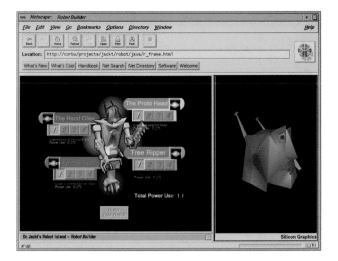

Plate 32 Build your own robot. Choose parts from the interface on the left and view the completed robot assembly on the right. The user interface was built using Java. The robot is VRML 2.0.

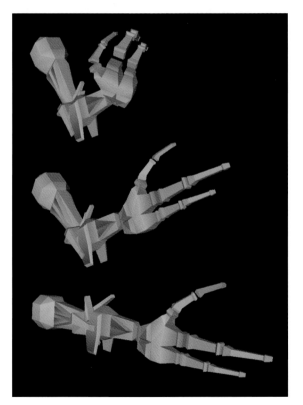

Plate 33 Three frames showing an animated robot arm. When activated by a touch sensor, the arm can rotate about the shoulder, elbow, wrist, and finger joints. The model illustrates extensive use of color per vertex. (Plates 32 and 33 by Clay Graham, Silicon Graphics, Inc.; from a game called Dr. Jackt's Robot Island.)

Plate 34 A view into PointWorld, where avatars can hold public, group, or one-on-one chat sessions. Users fill out cyberspace business cards with general information to share with other avatars. The CyberGate™ browser shown here includes extensions for multiuser interaction. (Black Sun Interactive, Inc.)

Plate 35 OnLive! Traveler™, a VRML browser with extensions for multiparticipant, real-time voice communications, community building, and socialization. In this image, three users are having a face-to-face conversation using their own voices lip-synched through their chosen avatars. Space by Tony Gascon, Ali Ebtekar, and Steve DiPaola. Avatars by Stasia McGehee. © OnLive!™ Technologies, 1996.

Plate 34. http://www.blacksun.com
Plate 35. http://www.onlive.com

- To add your site to the Yahoo database, follow the directions at this location:

    `http://www.yahoo.com/new`

- To add your site to the NCSA's *What's New* page, fill out the form at the following location:

    `http://www.ncsa.uiuc.edu/SDG/Software/Mosaic/Docs/`
    `    whats-new-form.html`

- Another good service is at this location:

    `http://www.submit-it.com/`

- If you're using an ISP server, the ISP may provide an index to its sites. Check with the system administrator of your server.

- Don't forget to include your new URL on your business card and in all of your conventional advertising.

Using the Common Gateway Interface (CGI)

The Common Gateway Interface (CGI) is a method for communicating between a browser and a server for processing user input through a script and generating output. The output of the script is then sent back to the user's browser and displayed.

The input for the script is obtained using a form written in HTML. The script is usually written in a simple programming language such as perl. A script can use the values filled into a form by the user to create a VRML file. The resulting file is then sent back to the user, who can view the new VRML world that has just been created "on the fly." The toolkit for kitchen designers, shown in Plate 22, uses CGI to process user input and create the specified kitchen.

HTML Form

The form for obtaining user input to the CGI script is written in standard HTML. Consult one of the references listed in "About This Book" for details on creating HTML forms. The form should use the POST method, which sends user data to the server using *stdin* (the standard input method for the operating system).

The ACTION attribute of the <FORM> tag should be the URL of the script that will process the input. This script is usually placed in the *cgi-bin* directory on the server.

Example 9-1 shows a form that allows the user to fill in values for the height, width, and depth of a box. The form is submitted to the script given in the ACTION attribute when the user clicks the *MakeVRML* button.

Example 9-1   Example of an HTML form

```
<HTML>
<HEAD>
<TITLE>Form for Creating a Box</TITLE>
</HEAD>
<BODY>
<FORM METHOD="POST"
 ACTION="/cgi-bin/mkbox.pl">
Cube:<p>
height:<INPUT TYPE="TEXT" NAME="heightCube" SIZE="3"
VALUE="4"><p>
width:<INPUT TYPE="TEXT" NAME="widthCube" SIZE="3" VALUE="6"><p>
depth:<INPUT TYPE="TEXT" NAME="depthCube" SIZE="3" VALUE="6"><p>
<INPUT TYPE="SUBMIT" NAME="MakeVRML" VALUE="MakeVRML!"></P>
</FORM>
</BODY>
</HTML>
```

Script

The Perl script shown in Example 9-2 takes the values supplied by the user and inserts them into the *size* field of a Box node.

Example 9-2   Script for generating a VRML scene containing a box

```perl
#!/usr/sbin/perl
read(STDIN, $buffer, $ENV{'CONTENT_LENGTH'});

@pairs = split(/&/, $buffer);
foreach $pair (@pairs)
{
    ($name, $value) = split(/=/, $pair);
    # Un-Webify plus signs and %-encoding
    $value =~ tr/+/ /;
    $value =~ s/%([a-fA-F0-9][a-fA-F0-9])/pack("C", hex($1))/eg;
    $form{$name} = $value;
}
```

```
print "Content-type: x-world/x-vrml\n\n";
print <<"EOT";
#VRML V2.0 utf8
Shape {
  appearance Appearance {
    material Material { }
  }
  geometry Box {
        size $form{'heightCube'} $form{'widthCube'}
        $form{'depthCube'}
  }
}
EOT
```

In this example, the script reads the values from *stdin* and then uses the following code to parse the input and split it into name/value pairs:

```
@pairs = split(/&/, $buffer);
foreach $pair (@pairs)
{
    ($name, $value) = split(/=/, $pair);
    # Un-Webify plus signs and %-encoding
    $value =~ tr/+/ /;
    $value =~ s/%([a-fA-F0-9][a-fA-F0-9])/pack("C", hex($1))/eg;
    $form{$name} = $value;
}
```

The script must identify the content type it is sending back to the browser. In perl, the syntax to identify VRML content is

```
print "Content-type: x-world/x-vrml\n\n";
```

(A content type of

```
print "Content-type: html/text\n\n";
```

would simply print the contents of the VRML file, not display it as a 3D scene.)

The VRML contents begin with the standard VRML header, followed by the VRML file, with variables inserted where user data will be supplied. In this example, user data is supplied for *heightCube*, *widthCube*, and *depthCube*.

Putting Form and Script Files on the Server

Be sure your Web server is configured to allow users to execute cgi-bin programs. Go to the following location for details on CGI:

```
http://hoohoo.ncsa.uiuc.edu/cgi
```

Your service provider may require you to obtain a special account before you can install cgi-bin scripts. Copy the script to the *cgi-bin* directory on the server. Copy the HTML form to the public directory where your other VRML and HTML Web files are located. You will also need a compiler or interpreter for whatever scripting language you choose to use.

Improving Performance

By this time, you may have spent weeks creating a complex and interesting 3D scene. You've refined the models until they're lifelike and perfected their colors and texturing. You've experimented with lighting, and now you're ready to share your creation with the world.

One problem: It takes ten minutes to download your scene. Another problem: Even on a high-powered PC, navigating through your scene is cumbersome and painful. You move the mouse and it seems to take minutes for the scene to catch up.

Figure 10-1   Large scenes take a long time to transmit

This chapter describes how to optimize your VRML files to decrease download time and increase rendering speed. Once you're familiar with the process, you should incorporate many of these tips in the initial planning and creation of your VRML scenes. If possible, view your world using a variety of browsers and see how performance and rendering vary on different platforms. Your authoring software may provide tools for implementing some of these optimizations. Others require human inspection and judgment and the creation of additional models for your scene. In all cases, knowledge of these techniques can help you create VRML worlds that are usable and easy to explore as well as visually compelling.

The chapter is divided into two major parts:

- Reducing file size (to speed up transmission time)
- Increasing rendering speed, with a goal of achieving a minimum frame rate of 10 frames per second, which is the frame rate required to simulate the visual continuity of moving through the real world

Reducing File Size

The larger the file, the more time required to transmit it over the World Wide Web. If it takes too long to fetch the data for your scene, many users lose patience and move on to another site. The moral of the story is: Reduce file size when you can. Techniques for making files smaller include the following:

- Instancing
- Using prototypes
- Using Text nodes
- Using space-efficient geometry nodes
- Relying on automatic normals
- Eliminating white space
- Rounding floating point numbers
- Compressing files

The following sections describe each of these techniques in more detail.

Use Instancing

If the same object is used more than once in the scene, it's most efficient to give the object a name the first time it's used (with DEF) and then refer to the object by name (with USE) in subsequent uses. For example, since the left and right temples at the base of the Great Temple are similar, they are defined and used in this manner. The lower-right temple ("LowerRightTemple") is represented by an LOD node that contains two inlined versions of the temple as well as a low-complexity child that is a simple box. Here is an example of defining the lower-right temple and then using that object for the lower-left temple with a simple translation.

Example 10-1   Using multiple instances of the same object

```
DEF LowerRightTemple Group {
  children LOD {
    center 897.65 26.22 -1111.12
    range [ 100, 200 ]
    level [
      Group {
        children Inline {
          url "TMLowerTemple.wrl"
          bboxCenter 897.65 26.22 -1111.12
          bboxSize    37.5  16.25    20
        }
      },
      Group {
        children Inline {
          url "TMLowerTemple2.wrl"
          bboxCenter  897.65  26.22 -1111.12
          bboxSize     37.71  16.28    20.81
        }
      },
      Transform {
        children Shape {
          appearance Appearance {
            material Material {
              diffuseColor    .8 .73 .54
            }
          }
          geometry Box {
            size    37.71 16.28 20.81
          }
        }
```

```
          translation    897.65 26.22 -1111.12
      }
    ]
  }
}
Transform {
  children USE LowerRightTemple
  translation   -195 0 0
  rotation 0 0 1  0
}
```

Use Prototypes

Prototyping objects that are used frequently with a few modifications is another way to reduce file size. As with DEF/USE, the object is defined once, and only the public interface that changes needs to be specified. In addition, because prototypes expose which parts of the scene hierarchy are changeable, the browser is free to optimize the parts that remain the same (see Chapter 4, "Building Objects," for more information).

Use the Text Node

Be sure to use the Text node for text. Some translators convert text to polygons, resulting in very large numbers of polygons for a simple string of text. Using the Text node reduces polygon count and allows the browser to optimize for rendering performance, using lower resolution for the text when it is far away.

Use Space-Efficient Geometry Nodes

Nodes such as the Box, Cone, Cylinder, Sphere, Extrusion, and ElevationGrid provide a compact way of describing objects with many polygons. Using these nodes saves on transmission time. (Some browsers provide optimizations for these shapes. On others, a simple IndexedFaceSet might render faster.)

Use Automatic Normals

Rely on automatic normal generation when possible instead of supplying your own normals for each shape.

Eliminate White Space

Eliminate unnecessary white space in the file. You can throw away leading tabs and spaces as well as newlines and commas to make your file smaller. However, the newlines, indentations, and commas improve readability, so don't go overboard here if you want anyone to inspect and understand your VRML source. When you compress a file with *gzip*, white space is automatically compacted (see "Compress Files," later in this section).

Round Floating Point Numbers

Round floating point numbers to fewer decimal places. This step requires that you be familiar with the scale used in your scene. If your scene encompasses thousands of meters, you can easily round the floating point numbers to one or two decimal places with little noticeable effect. (Some authoring systems allow you to specify the number of decimal places used, or you can run a script to round to the appropriate decimal place.) James Waldrop's DataFat Munger, an example of such a utility, can be found at the following location:

```
http://vrml.arc.org/vrmltools/datafat.html
```

Normal vectors and colors are always in the range of 0 to 1, so it's easy to round them.

Remove the leading 0 in numbers such as 0.7. Round to 0 when appropriate. For example, you can probably round 1.444×10^{-17} to 0 without any noticeable effect on your scene.

Compress Files

Use JPEG or PNG format for textures. GIF format is also acceptable to some browsers. JPEG is a lossy form of compression (that is, when the file is compressed originally, some information is lost), but it can achieve a compression in the range of 100 to one. Utilities for JPEG compression allow you to control the tradeoff between compression and image quality. This form of image compression is generally very effective and results in little noticeable degradation of the image.

Use MPEG format for movies and animated textures.

Finally, use the *gzip* utility to compress the VRML file, as well as any accompanying HTML files, before you publish them. It's faster to uncompress a file than to transfer a large file over the network. Most browsers automatically decompress files. Using gzip can result in 10- to 100-times reduction in file size. For information on gzip, check the following location:

```
http://crusty.er.usgs.gov/gzip.html
```

In the Aztec city example, the file *TemploMayor.wrl* is 132,447 bytes in uncompressed form and 20,503 bytes after using gzip. The texture file *speckle.rgb* is 49,664 bytes before compression and 6019 bytes in JPEG format.

Increasing Rendering Speed

Another major concern for scene authors is to ensure that users can navigate smoothly and continuously through the virtual world, with the scene rendering instantly on the screen as the user moves. A minimum frame (redraw) rate of 10 frames per second is required to make the VRML world feel interactive, with visual continuity that simulates moving through the real world.

This section describes many ways to author VRML scenes that render more efficiently. By using Inline, Anchor, and LOD nodes, polygon reduction, spatial scene organization, and a variety of other methods, you'll learn how to create scenes that browsers on many platforms can render efficiently. These are the basic techniques for increasing rendering speed:

- Simplify the scene.

- Divide the scene into chunks so that the browser can perform optimizations during rendering. Techniques include spatial organization within the VRML file, creating nested hierarchies of groups, and using Inline and Anchor nodes.

- Use nodes that facilitate browser optimization, including LOD nodes, performance LOD nodes (without explicit ranges), geometric primitives, and nodes with geometric hints fields.

- Use scripts effectively.

The following sections describe each of these techniques in more detail. Note that these are general guidelines, not absolute rules, since browsers perform different kinds of optimizations, and rendering libraries also have different characteristics.

Simplify the Scene

As a scene author, you'll constantly need to monitor the tradeoff between visual complexity and performance. Keep in mind that simplifying the scene results in faster rendering and a better experience for visitors to your world.

Reduce Polygon Count

The cold, harsh reality is that you have a limited polygon budget for your scene. Many PCs cannot handle scenes with more than about 2,000 polygons and maintain an acceptable interactive frame rate. To appeal to the widest audience, consider this limitation when designing and planning your VRML scene. Wherever possible, try to create models that are visually appealing yet economical in their use of polygons. Sometimes it's more important to convey the "idea" of the object, and less important to use a visually complex object. For example, chairs come in all styles. Do you need an ornate Windsor chair, or could a more streamlined model suffice? Simplifying models and textures in your scene may result in vast performance improvements. Many authoring packages provide tools for reducing the polygon count of an object.

Use Textures Instead of Polygons

Effective use of textures can be a relatively inexpensive way to add interest and detail to a scene. An image of a sign, textured onto the front of a building, will probably render much more quickly and with more fidelity than a model of the sign's typography that is constructed with hundreds of flat polygons.

Although large textures can degrade performance, adding a small texture to a flat polygon is often cheaper in terms of performance than drawing a large number of polygons. A tiled floor, for example, is an easy way to add visual interest to a scene. Figure 10-2 shows an example of using a small texture on a large surface, the roof of the Temple of Quetzalcoatl.

Use One-Component Textures

Try to keep textures as small as possible while still achieving their desired effect. It's often efficient to use a one-component texture (an intensity map) instead of a three-component texture (red-green-blue). Combining a one-component texture with the basic material color of an object can produce a very realistic surface (Example 10-2 and Figure 10-3).

Figure 10-2   Texturing a large surface with a small texture

Example 10-2   Combining a one-component texture with a material

```
Group {
  children DEF TlalocAltar Transform {
    children Group {
      children Shape {
        appearance Appearance {
          material Material {
            ambientIntensity    1.1
            diffuseColor        .26 .32 .21
            specularColor       .2  .11 .11
            shininess   .087
          }
```

Chapter 10: Improving Performance

```
texture ImageTexture {
  url "textures/SquareFloral.jpg"
  repeatS      TRUE
  repeatT      TRUE
}
textureTransform TextureTransform {
  translation 0 .3
  rotation    0
  scale       2.82 2.45
  center      .5 .2
}
}
geometry        IndexedFaceSet { ...
}
}
}
}
}
```

Figure 10-3   Combining a one-component texture with a material

Use Textures in LOD Nodes

For detailed textures, be sure to provide simplified versions of the texture that can be used in LOD nodes. Although this technique does not reduce transmission time or increase rendering speed, it improves the user's perception of speed since the user sees some texturing while waiting for the fully detailed texture to appear. The most complex model of an object would use the full texture, which you'll usually specify in the *url* field of the ImageTexture node (Example 10-3).

The medium complexity model of an object might use a simplified texture, specified in the *image* field of the PixelTexture node (Example 10-4). The texture supplied here should be very small—not more than 16 by 16 pixels.

The lowest complexity model would probably omit the texture entirely, relying instead on a single overall material color that represents the average color of the texture from afar.

Example 10-3   Using the ImageTexture node for the detailed texture

```
texture         ImageTexture {
  url "textures/sac.knife.jpg"
  repeatS       FALSE
  repeatT       FALSE
}
```

Example 10-4   Using the PixelTexture node for the simplified texture

```
texture PixelTexture {
  image 3 4 1 0x66 0x66 0x66 0x66 0x66
              0x66 0x22 0x22 0x22 0x66
              0x66 0x66
  repeatS        FALSE
  repeatT        FALSE
}
```

Figure 10-4 shows the detailed and simplified textures for the knife side by side.

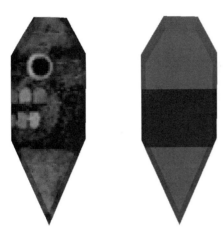

Figure 10-4   Using different textures in an LOD node

Textures should be no larger than 128 by 128 pixels. Keep textures as small as possible to maintain the desired effect.

Use Lights Sparingly

Lights are expensive in terms of performance. On most platforms, a VRML file should contain no more than two or three lights. Placing a directional light under a Transform node localizes the effects of the light. (Some browsers, however, support only global lights, so it's safest not to rely on local lighting.)

Some modeling packages provide "prelighting" solutions. This lighting involves assigning colors to the vertices of an object so that the colors are actually part of the object but give the appearance of light falling on it. Because the calculations are "hard-wired" into the object, the browser doesn't need to perform any additional lighting calculations, and you can include fewer lights in the scene. (Note, though, that these prelighting solutions can dramatically increase polygon count because they subdivide large polygons into very small polygons. You'll need to strike a balance between the savings realized from prelighting and the overhead that results from added fill time.) The Aztec city uses per-vertex lighting on the stairs of the temple, shown in Figure 10-5. Note that the tops of the stairs are lighter than the bottoms.

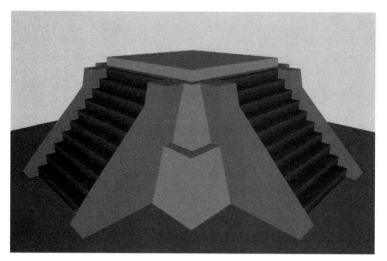

Figure 10-5   Temple stairs with per-vertex lighting

For faster rendering, limit the scope of the lights you use by making the ranges for point and spot lights as small as possible. Use a limited number of directional lights, especially if they are used at high levels of the scene hierarchy and thus affect large parts of the scene.

Use the Billboard Node

The Billboard node is an economical way to add realism to a scene. This node allows you to include 2D images in your scene and to rotate them so that they are always facing the camera. Because you don't need to include full 3D models of the objects, the file is much smaller without sacrificing realistic effects. The eagle landing on the cactus by the spring in the Tenochtitlán scene is an example of an animated Billboard node. This node's *axisOfRotation* field allows you to specify which axis the billboard children should be rotated around. Objects such as trees and the eagle animation are rotated around the *y* axis, since they have a vertical orientation. The helmet and headdress markers are also Billboard nodes. Their axis of rotation is specified as (0 0 0), which is a special case indicating that the object should always face the screen.

Example 10-5 shows a Billboard node for a tree from the Aztec world. The tree itself is shown in Figure 10-6.

Example 10-5 Using the Billboard node

```
Group {
  children Billboard {
    children DEF Tree Transform {
      children Group {
        children Shape {
          appearance Appearance {
            material Material {
              diffuseColor  1 1 1
              emissiveColor .19 .19 .19
            }
            texture ImageTexture {
              url   "textures/treeSquare.jpg"
            }
            textureTransform TextureTransform {
              rotation       1.57
              center         .5 .5
            }
          }
          geometry IndexedFaceSet {
            coord   Coordinate {
              point [ -1 -1 0,
                       1 -1 0,
                       1  1 0,
                      -1  1 0 ]
            }
            coordIndex      [ 3, 0, 1, -1, 3, 1, 2, -1 ]
            ccw       FALSE
            solid     FALSE
            creaseAngle    .5
          }
        }
      }
    }
    axisOfRotation     0 1 0 # billboard rotates about the y axis
  }
}
```

Use Fewer Nodes

Use as few nodes as possible to achieve the desired effect. For geometry nodes that contain a Color field (such as IndexedFaceSet), for example, you could create one Color node defining all the colors in your standard "palette" and then index into that node to select individual colors from it. Use the DEF/USE syntax to create multiple instances of the same Color node.

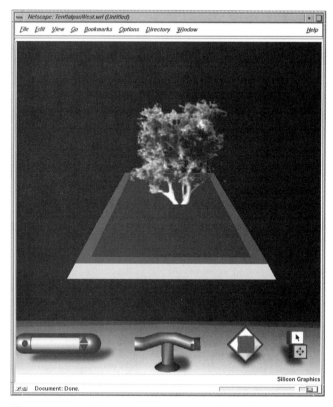

Figure 10-6   Using a Billboard node for a tree

Divide and Conquer

Dividing a large file into smaller chunks can greatly increase rendering speed, since it allows the browser to perform certain optimizations during rendering. Authoring techniques for dividing a large file into smaller pieces include the following:

- Creating a nested hierarchy of groups within groups
- Arranging objects spatially in the VRML file
- Using Inline nodes
- Using Anchor nodes

Create a Nested Hierarchy

The first step in structuring an efficient VRML file is to place each object in its own grouping node (usually a Group or a Transform). You may already have placed each object in its own group, since most modelers allow you to create objects individually.

Create hierarchies of objects by nesting groups of objects inside related groups. As described in Chapter 3, *nesting* refers to including a grouping node as a child of another grouping node. For example, the temple object consists of the sides, the staircases, the two top temples, and so on.

Note that an object can be composed of multiple shapes, and you don't need to put each shape under its own grouping node. Instead, shapes that make up a reasonably sized object should be grouped together under a common grouping node.

Example 10-6   Creating a hierarchy of grouped objects

```
Group {
  children Transform {
    children [
      Transform {
        children [
          Transform {
            children [
              Shape {
                 .
                #Inside of Tlaloc Shrine here
                 .
              }
            ]
            rotation       0 1 0  0
          },
          Transform {
            children [
              Shape {
                 .
                #Exterior facade of Tlaloc Shrine here
                 .
              }
            ]
            rotation       0 1 0 0
          }
        ]
      },
      Transform {
```

```
        children [
          Shape {
            .
            #Main Body of Tlaloc Shrine here
            .
          }
        ]
        rotation        0 1 0 0
      }
    ]
  }
}
```

A flat scene—that is, one with little nesting of groups—is much harder for a browser to optimize, since all objects are created equal. A hierarchical file is easier to optimize, since the browser can look at the top-level objects and, if they're not in view, can quickly ignore a large portion of the scene description that belongs to the containing group.

Arrange Objects Spatially

As you collect objects into groups, look at the objects in relation to each other. Are things close to each other in the scene close to each other in the VRML file? In other words, is the VRML file organized spatially? Buildings on the west side of the city should be grouped together. Objects on each face of an individual building should be together, and objects inside each building should be grouped according to their location. Organizing the VRML file spatially helps the browser move through the scene quickly, drawing only the parts that are visible. This is one of the key behind-the-scenes jobs performed by the browser, which uses a feature built into the Group and Transform nodes.

Each Transform and Group node has fields describing the bounding box for the objects contained in the group. A *bounding box* is the smallest rectangular solid that encloses the object, as described in Chapter 8, "Using Colors, Normals, and Textures." The Viewpoint node specifies an angle for the *field of view,* which, together with the *orientation* and *position* fields, determines how much of the scene is visible at a given time (Figure 10-7).

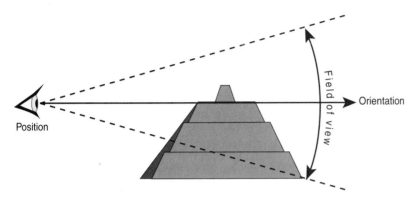

Figure 10-7   Field of view

The browser compares the bounding box specified in a grouping node to the current field of view; if the bounding box is outside the field of view, the browser simply ignores that branch of the VRML scene.

If a given Transform or Group node contains objects on opposites sides of the room (or worse—on opposite sides of the world), the browser won't be able to cut out part of the scene. *View culling* is the term used to describe this process of selecting objects to be discarded or ignored. If the north wall of the room is under one Transform, for example, and the south wall is under a different Transform, half of the scene can be culled at any given time depending on which wall the user is viewing.

Here's a detailed example of how you might model a room shaped like the letter *H*. At first, you might be tempted to create the walls as a single IndexedFaceSet. If you do, the browser tries to draw every polygon in the set since some portion of the room is always visible. It's far more efficient to break up the walls into several different sets based on location. For example, you might break them up into 14 indexed face sets, as shown in Figure 10-8.

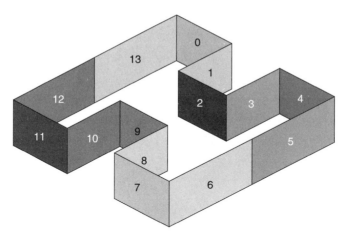

Figure 10-8 Dividing a large object into multiple smaller objects for culling

Group the indexed face sets as shown in Figure 10-9. When the walls are grouped in this fashion, the scene hierarchy can be culled at a high level (half the room can be culled with a single test). When you model the floor and ceiling for this room, you can group them with their associated walls.

In general, don't create large objects that span large scenes. If you have a large floor in your model, for example, break it up into several sections, putting each section under its own Transform or Group node to facilitate culling. If you do have large objects, avoid grouping other smaller objects with them.

The *bboxCenter* and *bboxSize* fields of the Transform and Group nodes are also useful when you have animated objects. Use these fields to specify the maximum size for the geometry that is animating (for example, the complete path of a bouncing ball). If the bounding box falls outside the field of view, the browser may not need to recalculate the animation.

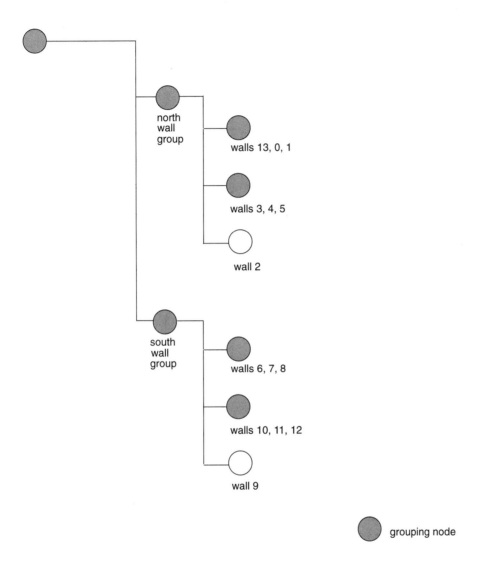

walls 13, 0, 1

walls 3, 4, 5

wall 2

walls 6, 7, 8

walls 10, 11, 12

wall 9

north wall group

south wall group

grouping node

Figure 10-9   Grouping objects spatially

Use Inline Nodes

When you create an Inline node, be sure to specify the bounding box size and center as well as the filename for the object.

```
Inline {
  url         "LowerPlatform.wrl"
  bboxSize    208 8.00 140.94
  bboxCenter  799.89 3.99 -775.53
}
```

One of the bottlenecks in performance occurs when a VRML file is initially loaded. If you include all the objects in the main file, the browser has to load all of them. However, if you use an Inline node, the browser does not immediately load the node. Instead, it goes to the specified URL to fetch the data, and in the meantime, displays a wireframe box (using the size of the bounding box you specify) where the object will eventually appear. While this is happening, the user can continue navigating through the scene.

In addition to using an inlined object's bounding box as a placeholder, browsers look at an object's bounding box to determine quickly if that object is in view. For example, as you stand at the West Gate of Tenochtitlán, the entire city is in view. The browser is going to have to do a lot of work to load all the objects, even in their simplest form. But as you move into the scene, you're closer to a few of the objects, and many objects are no longer visible because they're behind you or too far to your left or right.

The browser may do speedy calculations by looking at the current field of view and checking the Inline bounding boxes. If an object's bounding box is outside the current field of view, the browser does not need to fetch the data at the specified URL.

Nest Inline Nodes

You can nest Inline nodes too. The browser can check the parent bounding box and, if it's in view, can collect the data or can in turn check the bounding boxes of the child nodes contained by the parent node. If the parent's bounding box is not in view, the browser can then ignore that entire branch of the VRML file.

Example 10-7 Nesting Inline nodes

```
Group {
  children      [
    DEF TempleInside Transform {
      children  [
        DEF BowlsAndAltar Transform {
          children    [
            Inline {
              url "Bowls.wrl"
              bboxCenter     833.86 134.82 -1221.01
              bboxSize       9.16 .45 1.17
            },
            Inline {
              url "Altar.wrl"
              bboxCenter     833.85 132.3 -1221.5
              bboxSize       11.3    4.6    3
            }
          ]
        },
        Inline {
          url "Room.wrl"
          bboxCenter    833.5 135.01 -1222
          bboxSize      21.    10       12
        }
      ]
    }
  ]
}
```

The URLs of child nodes can be specified relative to their parent node. If a filename does not start with a protocol specifier (such as http:), the URL is considered to be relative to the parent file.

Use Anchor Nodes

Another way to limit the size of a scene is to create links using Anchor nodes for logically separate parts of the scene. This way, the browser doesn't need to load the extra data until the user requests it (by clicking the link). In the Aztec world, for example, one of the temples could contain a portal to a completely different world where the user could explore the three levels of Aztec cosmology—the celestial, the terrestrial, and the subterrestrial. The user would click the portal to enter this new world. Clicking a guided tour signpost would return the user to the "real" Tenochtitlán scene.

Example 10-8 Using the Anchor node

```
DEF Portal Anchor {
  children Group {
    children Shape {            # clickable geometry: green portal
      appearance Appearance {
        material Material {
          ambientIntensity .04
          diffuseColor     .03  .23 .09
          emissiveColor    .02  .1  .04
        }
      }
      geometry IndexedFaceSet {
        coord Coordinate {
          point    [ 798  4 -767,
                     798 55 -767,
                     802 48 -767,
                     802 55 -767,
                     802 55 -767,
                     802 55 -783.39,
                     802 48 -783.39,
                     800 55 -783.5,
                     798 55 -767,
                     798 55 -783.39,
                     798 48 -783.39
                   ]
        }
        coordIndex      [ 2, 1, 0, -1, 1, 2, 3, -1,
                          5, 4, 6, -1, 2, 6, 4, -1,
                          5, 7, 4, -1, 8, 4, 7, -1,
                          7, 9, 8, -1, 10, 0, 9, -1,
                          8, 9, 0, -1
                        ]
        ccw     FALSE
      }
    }
  }
  url "Cosmology.wrl#InTheBeginning"
  description "Portal to View Levels of Aztec Cosmology"
}
```

Let the Browser Do Its Job

Structuring the file correctly, as described earlier in this chapter, is one way to help the browser render the scene efficiently. Other techniques that give the browser control include liberal use of LOD nodes, use of geometric primitives such as spheres, cones, and cylinders, and use of the geometric hints fields provided by the ElevationGrid, Extrusion, and IndexedFaceSet nodes.

Combine LOD and Inline Nodes

The LOD node allows you to create alternative representations of the same object, with varying levels of detail. The children of an LOD node can be actual shapes, or they can be Inline nodes or grouping nodes. It's usually recommended that the last LOD child (the least complex version of the model) be a simple shape, not an Inline node, since many browsers display the least complex child before they go off to fetch the high-resolution inlined file.

The Temple of Huitzilopochtli contains an example of an LOD node containing three children. The first two children are Inline nodes, and the last child is the simplest geometry for the table, an indexed face set.

Example 10-9   Combining LOD and Inline nodes

```
DEF TableofHuitzil Group {
  children  LOD {
    center  0 5.5 0
    range   [ 45, 150 ]
    level   [
      DEF DetailTableSet Group {
        children Inline {
          url    "THSet.wrl"
          bboxCenter    0   5.5   0
          bboxSize      38 11   38
        }
      },
      DEF TableSet2 Group {
        children Inline {
          url "THSet.2.wrl"
          bboxCenter    0   5.5   0
          bboxSize      38 11   38
        }
      },
```

```
DEF SimplestTable Group {
  children Transform {
  children Shape {
    appearance Appearance {
      material Material {
        ambientIntensity  .32
        diffuseColor      .47 .42 .37
        specularColor     .1  .08 .04
        emissiveColor     .1  .09 .04
        shininess         .1
      }
    }
    geometry IndexedFaceSet {
      coord Coordinate {
        point [  -.39  1.55   .39,
                 -1    -1     1,
                  .39  1.55   .39,
                 1     -1     1,
                  .39  1.55  -.39,
                 1     -1    -1,
                 -.39  1.55  -.39,
                 -1    -1    -1
             ]
      }
      coordIndex    [ 0, 1, 3, 2, -1, 4, 5, 7,
                      6, -1, 6, 7, 1, 0, -1, 2,
                      3, 5, 4, -1, 6, 0, 2, 4, -1 ]
      creaseAngle   .5
      }
    }
    translation .02 4.31   .01
    rotation    0    0    1     0
    scale       19.05 4.31 19.05
  }
  }
  ]
  }
}
```

In some cases, when the object is very far away or when it consists only of
a very fine detail in the scene, it can be omitted entirely and you can simply
make the last LOD child an empty shape. The Temple of Quetzalcoatl uses
this technique for the feathery trim in several places. Here's one example.

Example 10-10 Using an empty shape for the last LOD child

```
DEF QZLowerFeathers Group {
  children [
    LOD {
      range        204.96
      center       800 72.5 -765.5
      level [
        Group {
          children [
            Inline {
              url "file:QZLowerFeathers.wrl"
              bboxSize     35  5       35
              bboxCenter 800 72.5 -765.5
            }
          ]
        },
        Group {
        }
      ]
    }
  ]
}
```

Many browsers provide optimizations for the box, cone, cylinder, and sphere primitives, so they are good choices for the geometry used in the last LOD child.

The "Performance" LOD

If you do not explicitly specify values in the *range* field of the LOD node, the browser chooses which level of the object to display at a given time. For convenience, LOD nodes without explicit ranges are referred to as *performance LODs*. Performance LODs allow you to tune your scene's richness to the capabilities of the hardware platform on which it is being run. When you nest LOD nodes, you can specify ranges for some of them and omit the ranges for others, leaving control to the browser when possible.

You could use a performance LOD, for example, for a city street full of building models. Each building has the following structure:

```
LOD {
  LOD {
    range [ near, far ]
    level [
      # A:  very detailed model { }
      # B:  moderately detailed model { }
    ]
  }
  # C: least detailed model
  Box { }
}
```

Because there are so many detailed models down the length of the street, it's impossible to render them all in real time. But you never want the street to disappear entirely, and you want the user to be able to walk down the street at a reasonable speed. Each building model consists of two LOD nodes: an outer performance LOD node without any explicit ranges, and an inner LOD node with *near* and *far* ranges for its two models.

The inner, ranged LOD will adapt each building to the level appropriate for its distance from the camera, choosing either A (the very detailed model) or B (the moderately detailed model). The outer, performance LOD allows the browser to adapt as many buildings as necessary to keep up with the scene dynamics. As the user starts to move down the street, many buildings degrade to simple blocks (C). When the user stops, the scene fills in completely with A and B as appropriate.

How Many LOD Models Do You Need?

Try to make at least three LOD versions of each model. Each level should contain roughly one-tenth the number of polygons of the previous level. As a rough guideline, here are suggestions for the ratio of levels of detail for the same object:

- 1,000 polygons, texture mapped. This model is handled well by computers with good polygon performance and hardware acceleration for texture mapping.

- 100 polygons, texture mapped. This model is handled well by computers with moderate polygon performance and no hardware acceleration for texture mapping.

- 10 or fewer polygons, not texture mapped. This model is handled well by computers with low polygon performance and no hardware acceleration for texture mapping.

As the browser moves closer to the object, the more complex LOD children pop into view. Try to make this transition as smooth as possible for the user.

In addition to the LOD node, you can use the *visibilityLimit* of the NavigationInfo node to simplify the scene. This field specifies the maximum distance that is visible to the user, and browsers can clip the view beyond this distance.

Simple Geometry

Use the simple VRML geometry nodes (Box, Cone, Cylinder, Sphere, Text) instead of indexed face sets when the results are acceptable to you. Many browsers provide their own LOD representations of these prefabricated shapes, as well as for Extrusion and ElevationGrid nodes.

Geometry Hints

The ElevationGrid, Extrusion, and IndexedFaceSet nodes have fields that provide hints to the browser about the geometry and enable the browser to perform certain optimizations, such as backface culling and one-sided lighting.

First, all three nodes have a *solid* field, which indicates whether the shape encloses a volume. By default, this field is TRUE and should be changed only for nonsolid shapes.

The *solid* field is very important because most of the objects in the real world are solid objects—they are composed of closed surfaces, and you can't view them from the inside. When an object is solid, the browser can throw away any polygon whose normal points away from the viewer. This process of eliminating the back-facing surfaces of an object is termed *backface culling*. If your scene contains mainly solid objects, you want to convey that information to the browser, since you can cut its work in half if it knows to render only the front-facing surfaces of the objects in the scene. Browsers can also use this information to turn off two-sided lighting, since this hint indicates that the back-facing surfaces can never be seen (and thus don't need to be lit).

The ElevationGrid, Extrusion, and IndexedFaceSet nodes also all have a *ccw* field that specifies whether the vertices are specified in counterclockwise order or not. By default, this field is TRUE and should be changed only for shapes whose vertices are not ordered in a counterclockwise direction.

Most VRML authors use a modeler to create their objects, and modelers usually produce vertices in a consistent order (check your modeler documentation). If you're creating objects manually or using objects created by different modelers, be sure the vertices for all the objects in the scene are ordered consistently. If you find that pieces of your object appear black, vertices for those faces may be specified in the wrong order.

A third field that provides a hint to the browser is the *convex* field, found in the Extrusion and IndexedFaceSet nodes. In general, it is less work for the browser to render polygons it knows are convex. Consult the documentation for specific browsers for details on how they use this information to optimize rendering.

Turn Off Collision Detection and Use Collision Proxies

By default, surfaces in a VRML world are impenetrable. The browser prevents users from navigating through them. Most of the time, that's the way you want things to be. However, collision detection takes a lot of processing power. You may therefore wish to use a Collision grouping node, which lets you control collision detection on its child nodes, for either of two purposes: turning off collision detection on certain pieces of geometry and setting up *collision proxies*.

Turn Off Collision Detection

One way to reduce the cost of detecting collisions is to set up collision detection only for those objects that a user is likely to try to navigate through. For instance, if you expect users to be "walking" along a floor, it may be a good idea to put the room's ceiling inside a Collision node with the *collide* field set to FALSE. The walls and floor should probably be outside the Collision node so that collisions with them are detected, as would be expected.

If you insert a Collision node with its *collide* field set to FALSE, collision detection stops at that point in the scene hierarchy. The child nodes of that Collision node are not checked for collision.

When handled properly, collision detection can provide a variety of creative opportunities. You could, for instance, leave collision detection on in most of your world but turn it off for a waterfall. Users would then be able to walk through the waterfall into a cave behind it. Another possibility: you could combine collision detection with a Sound node to create a thudding or crashing noise when the user runs into something. You could even determine which direction the user came from and have objects fall over in the appropriate direction when the user runs into them.

The Collision node generates an outgoing event called *collideTime* that gives the time of collision. You can route that information to a script for processing.

The maximum distance at which a collision is detected is specified as the first value in the *avatarSize* field of the NavigationInfo node.

Use Collision Proxies

Determining whether the viewer has collided with an object is a computationally intensive process. To improve the speed of this process for a complicated shape, you can specify a stand-in for that shape in the Collision node's *proxy* field. The proxy is a simpler piece of geometry than the original shape and occupies roughly the same space; it is used in collision testing instead of the original shape because it more efficient for testing collisions. A box or a sphere is a good shape to use as a proxy for more complex shapes.

For instance, a proxy for the chacmool model might consist of a box completely surrounding the model, as shown in Example 10-11.

Example 10-11 Using a collision proxy

```
DEF PositionOnTemple Transform {
  children [
    Collision {
      collide TRUE
      proxy Shape { geometry Box { size 4.3 2.51 1.16 } }
        children [
          Inline {
            url "Chacmool.wrl"
          }
        ]
      }
    }
  ]
  translation 763.88 124.07 -1196.75
}
```

Now, any time a user brushes up against the chacmool, the browser has to check for collision only against the surfaces of the surrounding box rather than against each of the small polygons that make up the chacmool model.

The node given in the *proxy* field is usually either a Shape node or a grouping node containing Shape nodes. The geometry inside the Shape nodes should be either a geometry primitive (browsers may be optimized to check for collision against boxes and spheres) or a simple indexed face set. Note that you can't specify a geometry node directly in the *proxy* field.

Note: Lines and points can't be used as proxies because they have no thickness. If you want to collide with an object composed of indexed line sets (a chain-link fence, for example), use a proxy for collision.

Example 10-12 is an example of how the Aztec world uses a ramp as a proxy for the steps to the Great Temple.

Example 10-12 Using a ramp as a proxy for a staircase

```
DEF RampCollide Transform {
  children [
    Collision {
      collide TRUE
      proxy Shape {
        geometry IndexedFaceSet {
          coord  Coordinate {
            point [ -21.99 124 -87.45,
                    -21.99  18  -4.64,
                     21.99  18  -4.64,
                     21.99 124 -87.45,
                     21.99 124 -90.45,
                    -21.9  124 -90.45
            ]
          }
          coordIndex [ 3, 0, 2, -1, 1, 2, 0, -1,
                       3, 4, 5, -1, 5, 0, 3, -1
          ]
        }
      }
    }
    children [
      DEF HiResStair Transform {
        children [
          Shape {
            appearance Appearance {
```

```
                material Material {
                    ambientIntensity .08
                    diffuseColor    .1 .1 .1
                    emissiveColor   .1 .1 .1
                }
            }
            geometry
                IndexedFaceSet { }
        }
    ]
  }
 ]
}
]
}
```

Try to provide one proxy for each reasonably sized object in the scene. If you insert a Collision node with a proxy in it, that proxy is used for the collision detection test. Regardless of whether the proxy is hit or not, the child nodes of that Collision node are ignored during collision detection. It is thus a waste of effort to nest proxies (unless you have wiring that's turning collision detection on and off and the proxies might be used in some cases).

There's an art to determining a useful proxy. Proxies should be as simple as possible while maintaining the same basic shape as the underlying geometry. You have to make artistic decisions about where you want the user to be able to easily pass through and where you don't. For instance, if you're creating two closely spaced pillars, you may want to use a flat rectangle in front of them as a collision proxy (to prevent users from squeezing between them). On the other hand, if you don't want the pillars to get in the way, you might want to turn off collision detection entirely. There's usually no need to set up collision detection with small objects. Unless you want to give users the feeling of a tight, cramped space, for instance, there's no need to check for collisions with a light bulb hanging from the ceiling.

You may want to use the same node as a proxy and as actual geometry in the scene. For example, you could create a room with walls, furniture, and a light. (Figure 10-10 shows the scene hierarchy for this world.) Then, you could add a collision node at the top of the scene that uses the walls as a proxy for collision testing for the entire room. Figure 10-11 shows how this scene would look, with multiple instances of the walls, first as the proxy, and then as the actual geometry in the room.

It's a good idea to use a collision proxy with a billboard node, to prevent unwanted collisions. For example, if the user approaches the billboard and then turns in place, a collision might occur. If you're using a billboard to simulate a tree, for instance, you might use a cylinder as a collision proxy for the tree trunk.

Figure 10-10   A simple world

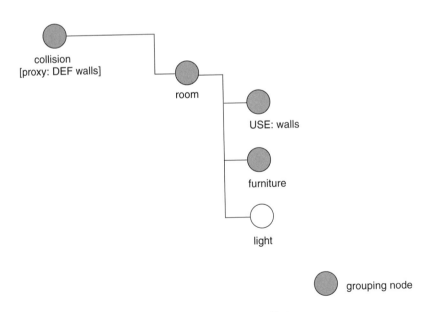

Figure 10-11   Reusing scene geometry as a collision proxy

Use Scripts Efficiently

Scripts can also improve rendering performance. Use proximity sensors and scripts to activate expensive items such as animations, lights, and sounds so that they occur only when the user is close enough to appreciate them.

Since it takes some time to load the interpreter for the scripting language and time to run the script itself, each script should do a reasonable amount of work. Scripts that send events are easy for the browser to optimize, whereas scripts that modify individual nodes directly (and require pointers to specific nodes) are harder to optimize.

Specify Wiring at the Lowest Level

In your script, specify routes at the lowest levels of the scene hierarchy. Specifying routes at the child level allows the browser to optimize parent groupings that are not changing.

Make Things Invisible

A VisibilitySensor node can be used to speed up a script when the objects that the script controls aren't visible to the user. There are many details of animation, such as moving a character's legs, which are unnecessary if the user isn't watching. Of course, in the case of such animation, you still want to translate the character through space; he or she shouldn't stop dead just because nobody's looking. But you don't need to go through the full animation walk-cycle if nobody can see it.

> Recall that you can also turn off animations by specifying a bounding box in the Transform or Group node that contains the geometry for the animation. That technique gives the browser control over when the animation actually occurs. The VisibilitySensor provides you with a more explicit means of specifying when the animation should be turned on or off.

Chapter 11

Node Reference

The following sections list all node types in alphabetical order, beginning on page 264. Each node description begins with the file format syntax for the node, listing default values for each field. A comment for each field indicates the field type and which fields are exposed fields. (See Chapter 12, "Field Reference," for a description of each field type.)

Each exposed field has an associated *set_* incoming event and a *_changed* outgoing event. For example, the Transform node's *rotation* field has an implicit *set_rotation* **eventIn** and a *rotation_changed* **eventOut**. (For brevity, the "set_" and "_changed" parts of the event names for an exposed field's events can be omitted.)

Since they are not part of the node syntax, events are listed in a separate section within each node description.

Some nodes are grouping nodes that can contain other grouping nodes or child nodes, shown in Figure 11-1. Figure 11-2 shows other rules for node usage (some nodes, such as the Material node, can be used only in specified fields of other nodes).

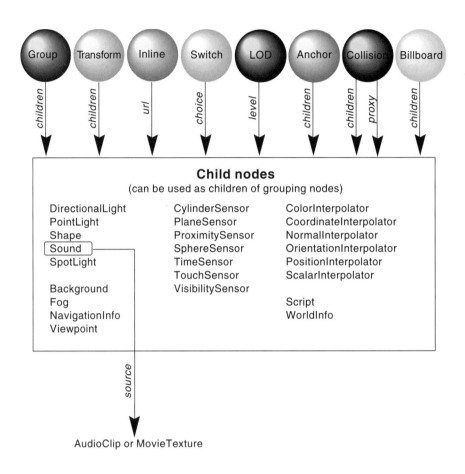

Figure 11-1 Grouping nodes and child nodes

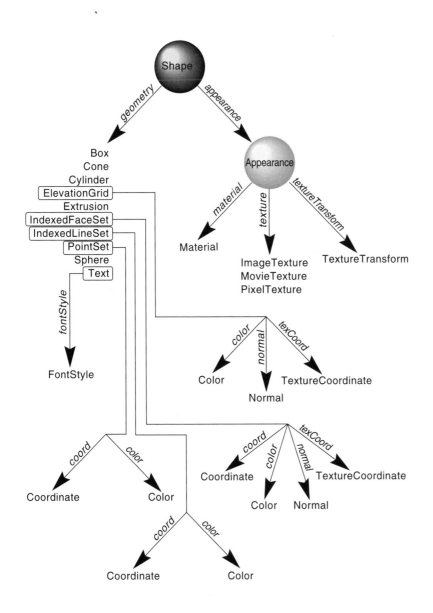

Figure 11-2   Nodes used within fields of other nodes

Suggested Structure of a VRML File

There are only a few basic rules for structuring a VRML file. Here are some general guidelines to get you started.

- A VRML file starts with the following header (required):

  ```
  #VRML 2.0 utf8
  ```

- Global nodes such as WorldInfo can be placed anywhere in the file; usually they appear at the beginning of the file.

- Prototypes are usually placed at the beginning of the file. A prototype must be defined before you can create an instance of the prototyped type.

- The scene hierarchy usually comes next in the file. Most scene hierarchies have one node as a root node, but that's not required; a scene hierarchy is allowed to have any number of nodes as top-level nodes.

- Scripts and interpolators can be placed anywhere in the file. Often, they are placed after the scene hierarchy.

- Routes must appear after the nodes and fields they refer to. Often, they are placed after the scene hierarchy, for easy reference.

- Time sensors can appear either before or after the scene hierarchy.

Rules for Names

When you use DEF to name a node, and when you create new node types, fields, and events, keep these naming rules in mind:

- Names can't begin with a digit (0 through 9).

- Names can't contain any of these characters:

  - non-printable ASCII characters (that is, characters with ASCII values of 0x0 through 0x20)

  - double (") or single (') quotes

  - sharp sign (#)

  - plus (+)

  - comma (,)

- – minus (–)
- – period (.)
- – square brackets ([])
- – backslash (\)
- – curly braces ({})
- VRML is case-sensitive; "Sphere" is different from "sphere" and "BEGIN" is different from "begin."

Anchor

```
Anchor {
  children     [ ]        # exposed field MFNode
  description  ""         # exposed field SFString
  parameter    [ ]        # exposed field MFString
  url          [ ]        # exposed field MFString
  bboxCenter   0  0  0    # SFVec3f
  bboxSize    -1 -1 -1    # SFVec3f
}
```

Fields

children
objects in the scene that contain hyperlinks to other files (specified in the *url* field). In most browsers, clicking one of the children loads the file specified in the *url* field.

description
a user-friendly prompt that the browser can display in place of the URL or in addition to it.

parameter
additional information for the VRML or HTML browser. This information is a string in the form *keyword=value*. For example, some browsers allow you to specify a frame in an HTML document as a link. The *parameter* field would be as follows:

```
parameter [ "target=name_of_frame" ]
```

url
specifies the URL of the file to load. If multiple URLs are specified, they are listed in descending order of preference. The browser loads the first file in the list that it finds.

bboxCenter
center of the bounding box that surrounds the Anchor node's children.

bboxSize
dimensions in *x*, *y*, and *z* of the bounding box that surrounds the Anchor node's children.

Events

addChildren   **eventIn**   **MFNode**

adds the specified node to the Anchor node's list of children. If the node is already in the Anchor node's *children* field, it is ignored.

removeChildren   **eventIn**   **MFNode**

removes the specified node from the Anchor node's list of children. If the node is not in the Anchor's node's *children* field, it is ignored.

Description

The Anchor grouping node fetches the specified file over the network when the user chooses any of its children. If the file is a VRML world, that world is loaded and displayed, replacing the world of which the Anchor is a part. If another type of document is fetched, it is up to the browser to determine how to handle that data.

Exactly how a user "chooses" a child of the Anchor is up to the VRML browser. Usually, clicking one of the Anchor's children with the mouse results in the new scene replacing the current scene. An Anchor with an empty URL ("") does nothing when its children are chosen.

Viewpoints

An Anchor can be used to take the viewer to a particular viewpoint in a virtual world by specifying a URL ending with "#viewpointName", where "viewpointName" is the name of a viewpoint defined in the world. For example:

```
Anchor {
  url      [ "Tenochtitlan.wrl#entryView" ]
  children [ Box { } ]
}
```

specifies an anchor that puts the viewer in the "Tenochtitlan" world looking from the viewpoint named "entryView" when the Box is chosen.

If no world is specified, then the current scene is implied. For example:

```
Anchor {
  url       "#AtTheTop"
  children  [ Sphere { } ]
}
```

takes the viewer to the "AtTheTop" viewpoint in the current world when the Sphere is chosen.

Bounding Box

The *bboxCenter* and *bboxSize* fields are optionally used to specify the maximum bounding box for the objects in this grouping node. The browser uses this bounding box for optimizations to determine whether the group needs to be drawn. The bounding box must be large enough to completely contain all the children in the group, including the effects of all sounds and lights that are children in this group. If the size of this group changes over time because its children are animating, the bounding box should be large enough to contain all possible animations of the group.

Appearance

```
Appearance {
  material          NULL  # exposed field SFNode
  texture           NULL  # exposed field SFNode
  textureTransform  NULL  # exposed field SFNode
}
```

Fields

material   contains a Material node.

texture   contains an ImageTexture, MovieTexture, or
                    PixelTexture node.

textureTransform contains a TextureTransform node. If the *texture* field is
                    NULL, *textureTransform* has no effect.

Description

The Appearance node occurs only within the *appearance* field of a Shape
node. The value for any of the fields in this node can be NULL. However, if
a field contains anything, it must contain a specific type of node, as
described above.

If *material* is NULL, the geometry associated with the Appearance node is
not lit—all lights are ignored during rendering of that geometry. If *material*
contains a default (empty) Material node, however, the geometry is lit using
the default Material node values. That is, specifying

```
appearance  Appearance { }
```

inside a Shape node results in no lighting, while specifying

```
appearance  Appearance { material  Material { } }
```

inside a Shape node results in lighting based on default material values.

AudioClip

```
AudioClip {
  description  ""      # exposed field SFString
  loop         FALSE   # exposed field SFBool
  pitch        1.0     # exposed field SFFloat
  startTime    0       # exposed field SFTime
  stopTime     0       # exposed field SFTime
  url          [ ]     # exposed field MFString
}
```

Fields

description   a text description of the sound, which the browser can display in addition to or instead of playing the sound.

loop   specifies whether the sound is repeated when it finishes playing.

pitch   a multiplier for the pitch of the sound clip (for instance, 2.0 means double the frequency, which also means playing twice as fast). Only positive values are valid.

startTime   the time when the sound should start playing. While a sound is playing, *set_startTime* events are ignored.

stopTime   the time when the sound should stop playing. The value of *stopTime* is ignored if it's less than or equal to *startTime*.

url   specifies the URL of the file to load. If multiple URLs are specified here, they are listed in order of preference. The browser loads the highest-preference file that's in a format it can interpret. The browser may play a lower-preference file while loading a higher-preference one.

Events

duration_changed **eventOut   SFTime**
                  the length of time the sound takes to play from beginning to end with *pitch* set to 1.0. Usually only sent out when the browser switches from playing one sound source to playing another.

isActive   **eventOut   SFBool**
indicates whether the sound is currently playing or not.
Sent with value TRUE when a sound starts playing, and
with value FALSE when it stops.

Description

The AudioClip node provides information on where to obtain a prerecorded
sound file and how to play it back. An AudioClip node can appear only in
the *source* field of a Sound node.

Sound files can theoretically be in any sound format, but for widest
compatibility, provide at least one URL for a WAVE file in PCM format.

If *loop* is TRUE, the sound plays forever, or until *stopTime* is reached. If *loop*
is FALSE, the sound plays through once, stopping either at the end of the
sound or when *stopTime* is reached, whichever comes first. The length of the
sound is determined by the sound file and is not specified in the VRML file.

Background

```
Background {
    groundColor   [ ]              # exposed field MFColor
    groundAngle   [ ]              # exposed field MFFloat
    skyColor      [ 0 0 0 ]        # exposed field MFColor
    skyAngle      [ ]              # exposed field MFFloat
    frontUrl      [ ]              # exposed field MFString
    backUrl       [ ]              # exposed field MFString
    rightUrl      [ ]              # exposed field MFString
    leftUrl       [ ]              # exposed field MFString
    topUrl        [ ]              # exposed field MFString
    bottomUrl     [ ]              # exposed field MFString
}
```

Fields

groundColor   RGB values to be used as ground colors. The first value listed is the color seen when looking straight down; there should be one more *groundColor* value than there are *groundAngle* values.

groundAngle   floating point values that indicate the cutoff angle, in radians, for each ground color. The implicit initial value of this field is 0 radians (straight down). The last value in the list indicates the elevation angle of the horizon, where the ground color ramp and the sky color ramp meet; from the final *groundAngle* value up to π radians (straight up), the sky color shows through. If *groundColor* is left empty, no ground colors are used.

skyColor   RGB values to be used as sky colors. The first value listed is the color seen when looking straight up; there should be one more *skyColor* value than there are *skyAngle* values.

skyAngle   floating point values that indicate the cutoff angle, in radians, for each sky color. This field implicitly starts at 0 radians (straight up) and implicitly ends at π radians (straight down); if the final value given is less than π, then the final *skyColor* is used to fill the rest of the sky sphere (from the final *skyAngle* value down to π radians).

frontUrl, backUrl, rightUrl, leftUrl, topUrl, bottomUrl

> six images, each of which is mapped onto a face of a cube. This cube forms a panorama surrounding the geometry in the world and usually contains distant features such as mountains, skyscrapers, or clouds.

Events

set_bind   **eventIn   SFBool**

> specifying TRUE for this event binds this Background node to the browser's viewer, making it the active Background node for the file.

isBound   **eventOut   SFBool**

> indicates whether this is the active Background node (TRUE) or whether it is inactive (FALSE).

Description

The Background node is used to specify a color-ramp backdrop that simulates ground and sky, as well as a panorama that is placed behind all geometry in the scene and in front of the ground and sky.

The first Background node in the VRML file is used as the initial background. Subsequent Background nodes in the file aren't displayed until they receive *set_bind* events.

The background is not affected by translations or scales in the scene hierarchy. Rotations in the hierarchy rotate the background as any other geometric object. Ground colors, sky colors, and panoramic images do not translate with respect to the user, though they do rotate with respect to the user. That is, the user can never get any closer to the background but can turn to examine all sides of the panorama cube and can look up and down to see the concentric rings of ground and sky (if visible).

Ground and Sky Colors

The ground and sky backdrop conceptually consists of a sphere with an infinite radius, painted with a smooth gradation of ground colors (starting with a circle straight downward and rising in concentric bands up to the horizon) and a separate gradation of sky colors (starting with a circle straight upward and falling in concentric bands down to the horizon). Some browsers may implement the backdrop as a cube painted in concentric square rings instead of as a sphere.

Specifying Both Panorama and Ground/Sky Planes

Transparency values in the panorama images allow the *groundColor* and *skyColor* to show through. Often, the *topUrl* and *bottomUrl* images are not specified, to allow sky and ground to show. The other four images may depict mountains or other distant scenery. By default, there is no panorama.

Binding

Background nodes are bindable nodes, so the browser maintains a stack of Background nodes. The top Background node on the stack is the currently active one. To push a Background node onto the top of the stack, send a TRUE value to the *set_bind* incoming event of the Background node in question. The newly bound background colors and panorama replace the previously bound ones. A FALSE value for *set_bind* pops the Background node from the stack and displays the next Background node in the stack, or a default-valued Background node if the stack is empty.

Fog does not affect Background nodes. When you bind a Fog node, if the background is visible and a different color from the fog you should bind a new Background as well. When you unbind the fog, unbind the background.

See Also

"Binding the Browser to a Node" on page 157; Chapter 8, "Using Colors, Normals, and Textures"; "Fog" on page 299.

Billboard

```
Billboard {
  children          [ ]       # exposed field MFNode
  axisOfRotation    0  1  0   # exposed field SFVec3f
  bboxCenter        0  0  0   # SFVec3f
  bboxSize         -1 -1 -1   # SFVec3f
}
```

Fields

children
any grouping or child node. All children are affected by the Billboard node's local coordinate system.

axisOfRotation
specifies an axis to use to perform the rotation. This axis is defined in the local coordinates of the Billboard node. The default is useful for objects such as images of trees and lamps positioned on a level surface. When an object is oriented at an angle—for example, on the slope of a mountain—then you can set the *axisOfRotation* to an appropriate angle.

bboxCenter
center of the bounding box that surrounds the children of the Billboard node.

bboxSize
dimensions in *x*, *y*, and *z* of the bounding box that surrounds the children of the Billboard node.

Events

addChildren
eventIn   MFNode
adds the specified node to the Billboard node's list of children. If the node is already in the Billboard node's *children* field, it is ignored.

removeChildren
eventIn   MFNode
removes the specified node from the Billboard node's list of children. If the node is not in the Billboard node's *children* field, it is ignored.

Description

The Billboard node is a grouping node that modifies its coordinate system so that its local *z* axis rotates around *axisOfRotation* to point at the viewer. The modified coordinate system applies to all the node's children, so you can billboard any geometry.

Setting the *axisOfRotation* to (0 0 0) allows the node's children to rotate freely (around any axis) to face the viewer. This setting is useful for screen-aligned objects such as text and icons.

For other values of *axisOfRotation*, the node's children can rotate only around the given axis. If the viewer looks along that axis—for example, if the *axisOfRotation* is set to (0 1 0) and the viewer flies over the object—then the object is likely to spin wildly as the viewer passes directly over the axis.

See Also

Chapter 10, "Improving Performance."

Box

```
Box {
  size  2 2 2  # SFVec3f
}
```

Field

size   *x*, *y*, and *z* extents of the box's width, height, and depth

Description

The Box is a geometry node that represents a rectangular solid centered at (0, 0, 0) in the local coordinate system, whose faces are aligned with the local coordinate axes. By default, the box measures 2 units in each dimension, from −1 to +1.

The Box may be invisible from the inside, depending on the browser. Don't place the user inside a Box; if you want the user to see the inside of a piece of geometry, use an indexed face set with *solid* set to FALSE.

Box: Default Texture Mapping

Textures are applied individually to each face of the box. The entire texture goes on each face. On the front, back, right, and left sides of the box, the texture is applied right side up. On the top, the texture appears right side up when the top of the box is tilted toward the user. On the bottom, the texture appears right side up when the top of the box is tilted toward the −z axis (Figure 11-3).

Figure 11-3   Default texture mapping for a box

Collision

```
Collision {
  children     [ ]        # exposed field MFNode
  collide      TRUE       # exposed field SFBool
  proxy        NULL       # SFNode
  bboxCenter   0  0  0    # SFVec3f
  bboxSize    -1 -1 -1    # SFVec3f
}
```

Fields

children   object or objects that are checked for collision. If a proxy object is supplied, the proxy is checked for collision in place of the children.

collide   for the children of this node, specifies whether collision detection should be on (TRUE) or off (FALSE).

proxy   alternate object to be checked for collision, in place of the children of this node.

bboxCenter   center of the bounding box that surrounds the children of the Collision node.

bboxSize   dimensions in *x*, *y*, and *z* of the bounding box that surrounds the children of the Collision node.

Events

addChildren   **eventIn   MFNode**
                    adds the specified node to the Collision node's list of children. If the node is already in the Collision node's *children* field, it is ignored.

removeChildren   **eventIn   MFNode**
                    removes the specified node from the Collision node's list of children. If the node is not in the Collision node's *children* field, it is ignored.

collideTime   **eventOut   SFTime**
                    specifies the time when the user intersects the Collision node's children or proxy.

Description

The Collision grouping node allows you to turn off collision detection for certain objects in the scene or to supply a simpler proxy object to speed up collision detection.

Collision Detection in a Scene

By default, all objects in the scene are collidable. If there are no Collision nodes specified in a scene, browsers check for user collision during navigation. For example, collision detection can keep users from walking through walls in a building or can limit the user to navigating certain restricted regions of the scene. What happens when the user navigates into a collidable object is defined by the browser. For example, when the user runs into an object, the browser may have the user bounce off the object or simply come to a stop.

Collision Proxies

Since collision detection for arbitrarily complex geometry is computationally expensive, one method of increasing performance is to define an alternate geometry, a proxy, for colliding against. The collision proxy, defined in the *proxy* field, is any valid VRML group or child node. During collision detection, only the geometry in the proxy is used; all the Collision node's children, as well as nongeometric nodes in the proxy, are completely ignored. A proxy can be as crude as a simple bounding box or sphere or can be more detailed, such as the convex hull of the children.

Colliding with Invisible Geometry

If the *children* field is empty, *collide* is TRUE, and a proxy is specified, then collision detection is done against the proxy even though nothing is displayed. This is a way of colliding against "invisible" geometry.

Nesting Collision Nodes

Proxies and children can include nested Collision nodes. Each level of the Collision is evaluated normally.

If a child Collision node detects a collision and issues a *collision* eventOut, all parent Collision nodes of that child also issue a *collision* eventOut, with the same *collideTime* as that of the child Collision node.

If the value of the *collide* field is FALSE, collision detection is not performed with the children, proxy, or any Collision nodes that are descendants of this node. If the root node of a scene is a Collision node with the *collide* field set to FALSE, collision detection is disabled for the entire scene, regardless of whether descendant Collision nodes have set the *collide* field to TRUE.

See Also

"NavigationInfo" on page 317 (*avatarSize* field); Chapter 10, "Improving Performance."

Color

```
Color {
  color  [ ]  # exposed field MFColor
}
```

Field

color   RGB values, to be applied to each face or vertex of an
                           object

Description

This node defines a set of RGB colors to be used in the *color* field of an
IndexedFaceSet, IndexedLineSet, PointSet, or ElevationGrid node.

Color nodes are used to specify multiple colors for a single piece of
geometry, such as a different color for each face or each vertex of an
IndexedFaceSet. A Material node is used to specify the overall material
parameters of a lit geometry. If both a Material and a Color node are
specified for a geometry, the colors replace the diffuse component of the
material.

Textures take precedence over colors. If both a Texture and a Color node are
specified for a piece of geometry, the Color node is ignored.

See Also

Chapter 8, "Using Colors, Normals, and Textures."

ColorInterpolator

```
ColorInterpolator {
  key        [ ]  # exposed field MFFloat
  keyValue   [ ]  # exposed field MFColor
}
```

Fields

key
a list of keyframe times, each represented as a fraction of the total animation time (a floating point number, usually from 0 to 1, inclusive)

keyValue
a list of RGB color values, one for each keyframe, to interpolate among

Events

set_fraction **eventIn** **SFFloat**
the fraction of the animation that's been completed

value_changed **eventOut** **SFColor**
the color value corresponding to the given point in the animation

Description

The ColorInterpolator node allows you to perform keyframe animation on a color value. To set up the interpolator, choose color values for specific moments in the animation (preferably including the beginning and ending values), and list those values in the *keyValue* field. List the corresponding fractions (one for each key color value) in the *key* field. For instance, to change a color value from red at the start of the animation, to green halfway through, to blue at the end, use this interpolator:

```
ColorInterpolator {
  key        [ 0, .5, 1 ]
  keyValue   [ 1 0 0, 0 1 0, 0 0 1 ]
}
```

Color interpolators are generally sent *set_fraction* events from time sensors and generally send outgoing values to fields of a Material node. Since time sensors send out fraction values from 0 to 1, interpolators usually have all *key* values within that range; however, *key* values are not restricted to any particular range.

See Also

"Engines" in Chapter 6; "TimeSensor" on page 356.

Cone

```
Cone {
  bottomRadius  1      # SFFloat
  height        2      # SFFloat
  side          TRUE   # SFBool
  bottom        TRUE   # SFBool
}
```

Fields

bottomRadius   radius of the cone's base

height   height of the cone

side   specifies whether the side of the cone is visible (TRUE)
                   or invisible (FALSE)

bottom   specifies whether the bottom of the cone is visible
                   (TRUE) or invisible (FALSE)

Description

The Cone is a geometry node that represents a simple cone whose central axis is aligned with the local y axis. By default, the cone is centered at (0, 0, 0) and has a default size of –1 to +1 in all three dimensions.

The Cone may be invisible from the inside, depending on the browser. Don't place the user inside a Cone; if you want the user to see the inside of a piece of geometry, use an indexed face set with *solid* set to FALSE.

Cone: Default Texture Mapping

When a texture is applied to the side of a cone, it wraps counterclockwise (from above) starting at the back of the cone. The texture has a vertical seam at the back where it intersects the *yz* plane. For the bottom, a circle is cut out of the texture square and applied to the cone's base circle. The texture appears right side up when the top of the cone is rotated toward the –*z* axis (Figure 11-4).

Figure 11-4   Default texture mapping for a cone

Coordinate

```
Coordinate {
  point   [ ]   # exposed field MFVec3f
}
```

Field

point   specifies the x, y, and z coordinates of the geometry

Description

A Coordinate node specifies a set of 3D coordinates to be used in the *coord* field of vertex-based geometry nodes such as the IndexedFaceSet, IndexedLineSet, and PointSet nodes.

CoordinateInterpolator

```
CoordinateInterpolator {
  key        [ ]  # exposed field MFFloat
  keyValue   [ ]  # exposed field MFVec3f
}
```

Fields

key   a list of keyframe times, each represented as a fraction of
                     the total animation time (a floating point number from
                     0 to 1, inclusive)

keyValue   a list of sets of vertex locations, one set for each
                     keyframe, to interpolate among

Events

set_fraction   **eventIn**   **SFFloat**
                     the fraction of the animation that's been completed

value_changed   **eventOut**   **MFVec3f**
                     a set of vertex locations corresponding to the given
                     point in the animation

Description

The CoordinateInterpolator node allows you to perform keyframe
animation on a set of vertices. As a result, it contains more numbers in the
keyValue field than most interpolators.

To set up the interpolator, pose the animated vertices for specific moments
in the animation (preferably including the beginning and ending values).
For each keyframe, list the coordinates for all the vertices in the *keyValue*
field. List the corresponding fractions (one for each set of vertex locations)
in the *key* field.

For instance, to change a right triangle to a different right triangle halfway
through the animation and end up with an isosceles triangle, you can use
this interpolator:

```
CoordinateInterpolator {
  key        [ 0, .5, 1 ]
  keyValue   [ 0 0 0, 1 0 0, 0 1 0,   # initial set of vertices
               0 0 0, 1 0 0, 1 1 0,   # second set of vertices
               0 0 0, 2 0 0, 1 1 0    # final set of vertices
             ]
}
```

Coordinate interpolators are generally sent *set_fraction* events from time sensors and generally send outgoing values to the *point* field of a Coordinate node in an indexed face set. Since time sensors send out fraction values from 0 to 1, interpolators usually have all *key* values within that range; however, *key* values are not restricted to any particular range.

See Also

"Engines" in Chapter 6; "TimeSensor" on page 356.

Cylinder

```
Cylinder {
  radius  1      # SFFloat
  height  2      # SFFloat
  side    TRUE   # SFBool
  top     TRUE   # SFBool
  bottom  TRUE   # SFBool
}
```

Fields

radius	specifies the radius of the cylinder
height	specifies the height of the cylinder
side	specifies whether the side of the cylinder is visible (TRUE) or invisible (FALSE)
top	specifies whether the top ($y = +1$) of the cylinder is visible (TRUE) or invisible (FALSE)
bottom	specifies whether the bottom ($y = -1$) of the cylinder is visible (TRUE) or invisible (FALSE)

Description

The Cylinder is a geometry node that represents a simple capped cylinder centered around the y axis. By default, the cylinder is centered at (0, 0, 0) and has a default size of -1 to $+1$ in all three dimensions. You can use the *radius* and *height* fields to create a cylinder with a different size.

The Cylinder may be invisible from the inside, depending on the browser. Don't place the user inside a Cylinder; if you want the user to see the inside of a piece of geometry, use an indexed face set with *solid* set to FALSE.

Cylinder: Default Texture Mapping

When a texture is applied to a cylinder, it is applied differently to the sides, top, and bottom. On the sides, the texture wraps counterclockwise (from above) starting at the back of the cylinder. The texture has a vertical seam at the back, intersecting the yz plane. For the top and bottom, a circle is cut out of the texture square and applied to the top or bottom circle. The top texture appears right side up when the top of the cylinder is tilted toward the $+z$ axis, and the bottom texture appears right side up when the top of the cylinder is tilted toward the $-z$ axis (Figure 11-5).

Figure 11-5   Default texture mapping for a cylinder

CylinderSensor

```
CylinderSensor {
  minAngle    0          # exposed field SFFloat
  maxAngle    -1         # exposed field SFFloat
  enabled     TRUE       # exposed field SFBool
  diskAngle   0.262      # exposed field SFFloat
  offset      0          # exposed field SFFloat
  autoOffset  TRUE       # exposed field SFBool
}
```

Fields

minAngle   the smallest angle that a *rotation* event can contain. (Any smaller number of radians is changed to *minAngle*.)

maxAngle   the largest angle that a *rotation* event can contain. (Any larger number of radians is changed to *maxAngle*.)

enabled   indicates whether the sensor is currently paying attention to pointing device events. To turn off the sensor, send it a *set_enabled* event with value FALSE.

diskAngle   determines whether the sensor behaves like a conceptual cylinder or like a conceptual disk. If the user clicks near the axis of the cylinder, the sensor behaves like a disk; otherwise it acts like a cylinder.

offset   indicates how many radians to rotate the associated geometry from its initial orientation, each time the user begins a new drag.

autoOffset   indicates whether to keep track of the current orientation between drags (TRUE) by saving the current orientation in *offset* at the end of a drag. If *autoOffset* is FALSE, dragged geometry resets to its initial orientation each time the user begins a new drag.

Events

isActive   **eventOut**   **SFBool**
indicates whether the user is dragging geometry associated with the sensor.

trackPoint_changed **eventOut**   **SFVec3f**
the unclamped point on the conceptual cylinder's surface that the user is pointing to at any given moment during a drag.

rotation_changed   **eventOut**   **SFRotation**
the conceptual cylinder's current orientation at any given moment during a drag.

Description

The CylinderSensor node interprets 2D dragging input (such as a user dragging with a mouse) as a rotation in 3D space around the *y* axis. It can behave in two different ways, like a conceptual cylinder or like a conceptual flat disk, depending on where the user clicks (in relation to the local *y* axis of the sensor).

When the user presses the pointing device button while pointing to any of the sensor's sibling geometry, the browser generates a conceptual cylinder around the *y* axis of the sensor's local coordinate system. The cylinder's proportions are determined by *diskAngle*; you can think of *diskAngle* as the angle at the vertex of a cone inside the conceptual cylinder, with the flat disk of the cone corresponding to the top surface of the cylinder.

If the user is pointing to the upper or lower flat faces of the cylinder, dragging motion is interpreted as rotating a flat disk (as if the user were rotating a record on a turntable or turning a vehicle's steering wheel). If the user is pointing to the curved sides of the cylinder, dragging motion is interpreted as rotating that cylinder. If you're interested only in a particular range of rotation values, you can set *minAngle* and *maxAngle* to clamp *rotation* events to that range. If *minAngle* is greater than *maxAngle*, rotation events are not clamped.

If you want geometry to stay rotated after the user has rotated it, leave *autoOffset* set to TRUE. If you want the geometry's rotation to reset with each new drag, set *autoOffset* to FALSE.

Other pointing device sensors don't generate events while a cylinder sensor is active (that is, while the user is dragging the sensor's sibling geometry).

DirectionalLight

```
DirectionalLight {
    on                  TRUE     # exposed field SFBool
    intensity           1        # exposed field SFFloat
    ambientIntensity    0        # exposed field SFFloat
    color               1 1  1   # exposed field SFColor
    direction           0 0 -1   # exposed field SFVec3f
}
```

Fields

on	indicates whether the light is turned on or not. A light that's turned off has no effect on other objects.
intensity	brightness of the light.
ambientIntensity	a value that's multiplied by the *intensity* of the light to determine the amount it adds to a world's ambient lighting.
color	color of the light.
direction	direction the light points toward, as a vector from the origin to the point given in this field.

Description

A DirectionalLight node defines a directional light source that illuminates along rays parallel to a given 3D vector. Note that the *direction* field indicates the direction the light is pointing toward, not the direction the light is coming from.

A directional light illuminates all sibling objects (that is, all objects that are children of the light's parent grouping node) and all of those objects' descendants. It has no effect on objects outside its parent grouping node.

Note that some browsers on some systems may not be able to light different objects in different ways; on such a browser, a directional light may light everything in your world, not just siblings. For maximum cross-browser compatibility, it's therefore best to put directional lights at the top level of your world so that they affect all objects.

ElevationGrid

```
ElevationGrid {
  xDimension       0      # SFInt32
  xSpacing         0.0    # SFFloat
  zDimension       0      # SFInt32
  zSpacing         0.0    # SFFloat
  height           [ ]    # MFFloat
  color            NULL   # exposed field SFNode
  colorPerVertex   TRUE   # SFBool
  normal           NULL   # exposed field SFNode
  normalPerVertex  TRUE   # SFBool
  texCoord         NULL   # exposed field SFNode
  ccw              TRUE   # SFBool
  solid            TRUE   # SFBool
  creaseAngle      0      # SFFloat
}
```

Fields

xDimension   the number of vertices in the *x* direction. Must be greater than 1.

xSpacing   the distance between vertices in the *x* direction. Can't be a negative number.

zDimension   the number of vertices in the *z* direction. Must be greater than 1.

zSpacing   the distance between vertices in the *z* direction. Can't be a negative number.

height   a list of heights, one for each vertex of the grid, in row-major order.

color   may contain a Color node, if you wish to provide colors for each quadrilateral or each vertex (rather than for the entire elevation grid at once, using a Material node).

colorPerVertex   indicates whether you've provided one color per vertex (TRUE) or one per quadrilateral (FALSE). Ignored if the *color* field is NULL. If you specify a Color node, you must provide at least (*xDimension* − 1) × (*zDimension* − 1) colors if *colorPerVertex* is FALSE, and at least *xDimension* × *zDimension* colors if *colorPerVertex* is TRUE.

normal	may contain a Normal node, if you wish to explicitly specify normals for the elevation grid. If no normals are specified, the browser generates normals automatically.
normalPerVertex	indicates whether you've provided one normal per vertex (TRUE) or one per quadrilateral (FALSE). Ignored if the *normal* field is NULL.
texCoord	may contain a TextureCoordinate node to explicitly map a texture onto the elevation grid.
ccw	default ElevationGrid normals have a positive *y* component in order to make the faces of the grid face up. If *ccw* is set to FALSE, the fronts of the faces face down (toward –*y*).
solid	indicates whether the back faces (the underside of the grid if *ccw* is TRUE) are invisible or not; leave this at its default value of TRUE unless you expect users to see the underside of the terrain.
creaseAngle	the angle at which to make the edge between two adjacent faces look smooth (as opposed to faceted).

Event

set_height	eventIn	MFFloat
	allows you to set the values for the *height* array.	

Description

The ElevationGrid node creates a rectangular grid of varying height, especially useful in modeling terrain. The model is specified primarily by a list of height values that describe the height of the surface above each point of the grid.

The *xDimension* and *zDimension* fields define the number of grid points in the *z* and *x* directions, respectively, defining a grid made up of (*xDimension* – 1) × (*zDimension* – 1) rectangles.

The *height* field is a list of floating point values representing the height above the grid (in other words, the *y* value) for each vertex of the geometry. The height values for the first row are stored first (in order), then those for the second row, and so on.

The vertex locations for the elevation grid are defined by the *height* field and the *xSpacing* and *zSpacing* fields. The vertex corresponding to grid point (i, j) is placed at $(xSpacing \times i, height[i + xDimension \times j], zSpacing \times j)$ in the local coordinate space, where $0 <= i < xDimension$ and $0 <= j < zDimension$.

ElevationGrid: Default Texture Mapping

The default texture coordinates range from [0,0] at the first vertex to [1,1] at the last vertex. The *s* texture coordinate is aligned with the *x* axis and the *t* texture coordinate with the *z* axis.

See Also

"Terrain Modeling with the ElevationGrid Node" on page 107.

Extrusion

```
Extrusion {
   spine          [ 0 0 0, 0 1 0 ]   # MFVec3f
   crossSection   [   1   1,    1 -1,
                     -1 -1,  -1   1,
                      1   1 ]          # MFVec2f
   scale          [ 1 1 ]             # MFVec2f
   orientation    [ 0 0 1  0 ]        # MFRotation
   beginCap       TRUE                # SFBool
   endCap         TRUE                # SFBool
   ccw            TRUE                # SFBool
   solid          TRUE                # SFBool
   convex         TRUE                # SFBool
   creaseAngle    0                   # SFFloat
}
```

Fields

spine

the piecewise linear 3D path along which the cross-section is extruded, described as a series of vertices in the local coordinate system.

crossSection

a piecewise linear 2D path, described as a series of vertices in the *xz* plane, that's extruded through space.

scale

a series of scaling factors, each of which indicates the scaling in *x* and *z* directions of the *crossSection* curve at the corresponding joint of the *spine*. If only one value is given, it applies at all joints.

orientation

a series of rotations, each of which indicates the orientation of the *crossSection* curve at the corresponding joint of the *spine*. If only one value is given, it applies at all joints.

beginCap

indicates whether or not to place a planar capping polygon at the starting end of the extrusion.

endCap

indicates whether or not to place a planar capping polygon at the other end of the extrusion.

ccw

indicates whether the vertices of the cross-section are listed in counterclockwise order or not when viewed from above (that is, from the +*y* axis).

solid	indicates whether the back faces of the gometry (the inner surface of the extrusion) are invisible (TRUE) or visible (FALSE). If the user can never see the inside of the extrusion, leave this set to TRUE.
convex	indicates whether all faces in the shape are convex. If your cross-section isn't convex and you have *beginCap* or *endCap* set to TRUE, set this to FALSE.
creaseAngle	the angle at which to make the edge between two adjacent faces look smooth (as opposed to faceted).

Events

set_spine	eventIn	MFVec3f
	sets the value of the *spine* path.	
set_crossSection	eventIn	MFVec2f
	sets the value of the *crossSection* path.	
set_scale	eventIn	MFVec2f
	sets the value of the *scale* field.	
set_orientation	eventIn	MFRotation
	sets the value of the *orientation* field.	

Description

The Extrusion node provides a compact format for describing a wide variety of shapes: those which can be constructed by sweeping out a path through space with a 2D cross-section.

The *crossSection* field describes a 2D path in the *xz* plane that's scaled, extruded through space, and twisted by the other curves. A copy of the cross-section is placed at each joint of the *spine* path, scaled and rotated by appropriate values from the *scale* and *orientation* fields; then corresponding vertices of the cross-section at adjacent joints are connected to form the sides of the object. If *beginCap* or *endCap* is specified, the appropriate flat polygonal caps are added at the ends of the extrusion.

An extrusion automatically generates its own normals.

Extrusion: Default Texture Mapping

The default texture mapping is to map textures like the label on a soup can: the coordinates range in the *s* direction from 0 to 1 along the *crossSection* curve and in the *t* direction from 0 to 1 along the spine. When the *crossSection* is closed, the texture has a seam that follows the line traced by the *crossSection* curve's start/end point as it travels along the spine. If the *beginCap* and/or *endCap* exist, textures map onto them in a planar fashion. For the caps, the textures' *s* and *t* directions correspond to the *x* and *z* directions in which the *crossSection* coordinates are defined.

See Also

"Extrusions" on page 109.

Fog

```
Fog {
  fogType          "LINEAR"   # exposed field SFString
                              #   "LINEAR", "EXPONENTIAL"
  visibilityRange  0          # exposed field SFFloat
  color            1 1 1      # exposed field SFColor
}
```

Fields

fogType   the rate at which fog thickens as distance from the
                    viewer increases

visibilityRange   the maximum distance at which a user can see anything
                    through the fog; a value of 0 or less means no fog

color   the color of the fog

Events

set_bind   **eventIn**   **SFBool**
             makes this Fog node the current one

isBound   **eventOut** **SFBool**
             indicates when the node becomes bound or unbound

Description

The Fog node defines a region of decreased visibility, to simulate fog,
smoke, or smog. The browser blends the fog's color with the color of
rendered objects, increasing the thickness of the fog the further away an
object is. At distance *visibilityRange* and beyond, all objects are totally
obscured by the fog.

To fade objects out smoothly as they approach the far clipping plane,
combine Fog with the *visibilityLimit* field of the NavigationInfo node.

Binding

Fog nodes are bindable nodes, so the browser maintains a stack of Fog
nodes. The top Fog node on the stack is the currently active one. To push a
Fog node onto the top of the stack, send a TRUE value to the *set_bind*
incoming event of the Fog node in question. The newly bound fog values
replace the previously bound ones. A FALSE value for *set_bind* pops the Fog
node from the stack and displays the next Fog node in the stack, or a

default-valued Fog node (which turns off fog by setting *visibilityRange* to 0) if the stack is empty.

The Background node is unaffected by the Fog node; if the background is visible from where the user is, it shows through regardless of fog. For best results, when you bind a Fog node also bind a Background node that's the same color as the Fog node. When you unbind the Fog node you can unbind the Background node to return to the previous background.

See Also

"Binding the Browser to a Node" on page 157; "Background" on page 270.

FontStyle

```
FontStyle {
  size          1.0         # SFFloat
  family        "SERIF"     # SFString
                            #   "SERIF", "SANS", "TYPEWRITER"
  style         "PLAIN"     # SFString  "PLAIN", "BOLD",
                            #   "ITALIC", "BOLD ITALIC"
  horizontal    TRUE        # SFBool
  leftToRight   TRUE        # SFBool
  topToBottom   TRUE        # SFBool
  language      ""          # SFString
  justify       [ "BEGIN" ] # MFString  "BEGIN", "MIDDLE",
                            #   "END", "FIRST"
  spacing       1.0         # SFFloat
}
```

Fields

size
the height of each line of horizontal text, or the width of each line of vertical text.

family
indicates whether the text should be in a serif font, a sans-serif font, or a typewriter-like fixed-width font. The browser chooses a specific font to be used in each of those categories; for example, a browser might use Times Roman for the serif font, Helvetica for the sans-serif font, and Courier for the typewriter font. An empty string ("") indicates a serif font.

style
indicates whether the text should be in a roman ("PLAIN"), bold, italic, or bold italic typeface. An empty string ("") indicates roman.

horizontal
indicates the major direction of the text—that is, whether the text reads horizontally (TRUE) or vertically (FALSE).

leftToRight
indicates whether the text reads left-to-right (TRUE) or right-to-left (FALSE). For horizontal text, this indicates whether each character should be to the left or the right of the previous one, while for vertical text it indicates whether each line of text should be to the left or the right of the previous one.

topToBottom	indicates whether the text reads top-to-bottom (TRUE) or bottom-to-top (FALSE). For horizontal text, this indicates whether each line of text should be above or below the last; for vertical text, it indicates whether each character should be above or below the last.
language	the language to use—the same UTF-8 string can appear differently depending on what language it's in. Specified as a two-character language code (such as `"en"` for English, `"jp"` for Japanese, `"sc"` for Swedish), followed optionally by an underscore and a two-character territory code (such as `TW` for Taiwan or `CN` for China) for languages that are different in different regions. An empty string (`""`) indicates that the user's language bindings should be used.
justify	the first string value indicates whether to line up the beginnings of the lines of text, to center each line of text, or to line up the ends. For left-to-right horizontal text, for instance, `"BEGIN"` indicates left-justified text, `"MIDDLE"` indicates centered text, and `"END"` indicates right-justified text. The second string value indicates how to align the block of text in the minor direction. If no value is specified for the second string, minor alignment defaults to `"FIRST"`.
spacing	determines the distance, in lines, between consecutive lines of text. A value of 1, for instance, means single-spaced text; each line is placed *size* units away from the previous line. A value of 2 means double-spaced text, equivalent to placing a blank line between adjacent lines.

Description

The FontStyle node occurs only in the *fontStyle* field of the Text node. It defines the size, font family, and style of the text font, as well as the direction and spacing of the text strings and any language-specific rendering techniques that must be used for non-English text.

Text is considered to have a major direction of advance and a minor direction of advance, corresponding to the value of the *horizontal* field. The first value in the *justify* field indicates how to individually justify each line of text in the major direction. For instance, if the first value in the *justify* field is `"BEGIN"`, then the beginnings of the text lines are aligned with each other. The second string in the *justify* field indicates how to align the entire set of text strings in the minor direction. For instance, if *horizontal* is TRUE and the second value in the *justify* field is "MIDDLE", then the individual lines are first justified according to the first string in *justify*, and the entire block of text is then centered vertically (that is, in the minor direction) across the *x* axis.

If *horizontal* is TRUE and the minor (second) alignment string in *justify* is "FIRST", the *x* axis is used as a baseline for the first line of text in the block. In all other cases, a value of "FIRST" (for either major or minor alignment) is identical to "BEGIN".

The alignment of individual characters (within a given line) along the minor axis is defined by the baseline. In horizontal text, the baseline is always below the text; all characters in a given horizontal line of text rest on the baseline. In vertical text, the baseline depends on the value of *leftToRight*: if *leftToRight* is TRUE, the baseline is along the left edge of each line of text, while if *leftToRight* is FALSE, the baseline is along the right edge of each line of text.

Horizontal text is positioned on the +*x* side of the *y* axis when *leftToRight* is TRUE and the first *justify* string is "BEGIN". Horizontal text is positioned on the −*x* side of the *y* axis when *leftToRight* is TRUE and the first *justify* string is "END". When the first *justify* value is "MIDDLE" and horizontal is TRUE, each string is centered across the *y* axis. The minor *justify* value for horizontal text determines placement of the block of text relative to the *x* axis.

For vertical text, the major *justify* value determines text placement in relation to the *x* axis and the minor *justify* value determines text placement in relation to the *y* axis.

The format used for the *language* field is based on the POSIX locale specification and the RFC 1766. The values for the language tag are based on the ISO 639 standard. The values for the territory tag are based on the ISO 3166 country code. For more details on these standards, consult these references:

```
http://www.chemie.fu-berlin.de/diverse/doc/ISO_639.html

http://www.chemie.fu-berlin.de/diverse/doc/ISO_3166.html
```

Group

```
Group {
  bboxCenter  0  0  0   # SFVec3f
  bboxSize   -1 -1 -1   # SFVec3f
  children    [ ]        # exposed field MFNode
}
```

Fields

bboxCenter	center of the bounding box that surrounds the children of this group.
bboxSize	dimensions in *x*, *y*, and *z* of the bounding box that surrounds the children of this group.
children	group or child nodes.

Events

addChildren	**eventIn**	**MFNode**
	adds the specified node to this group's list of children. If the node is already in the Group's list of children, it is ignored.	
removeChildren	**eventIn**	**MFNode**
	removes the specified node from the group's list of children. If the node is not in the Group's list of children, it is ignored.	

Description

A Group node is a lightweight grouping node that can contain any number of children. It is equivalent to a Transform node without the transformation fields.

The *bboxCenter* and *bboxSize* fields are optionally used to specify the maximum bounding box for the objects in this group. The browser uses this bounding box for optimizations to determine whether the group needs to be drawn. The bounding box must be large enough to completely contain all the children in the group, including the effects of all sounds, lights, and fog nodes that are children in this group. If the size of this Group changes over time because its children are animating, the bounding box should be large enough to contain all possible animations of the group.

ImageTexture

```
ImageTexture {
  url       [ ]    # exposed field MFString
  repeatS   TRUE   # SFBool
  repeatT   TRUE   # SFBool
}
```

Fields

url
specifies the URL of the texture file. If multiple URLs are specified, they are listed in descending order of preference. The browser loads the first file in the list that it finds. Textures can be in JPEG or PNG format. (In addition, some browsers support the GIF format.) To turn off texturing, specify this field with no values: [ ].

repeatS
specifies whether the texture wraps in the *s* direction, if needed, to fill the shape. TRUE specifies to repeat the texture. FALSE specifies to clamp the texture coordinates, repeating the last row of pixels to fill the shape.

repeatT
specifies whether the texture wraps in the *t* direction, if needed, to fill the shape. TRUE specifies to repeat the texture. FALSE specifies to clamp the texture coordinates, repeating the last row of pixels to fill the shape.

Description

The ImageTexture node specifies a texture map and parameters for applying that map to geometry. The texture map is a two-dimensional image that extends from 0 to 1 in the horizontal (*s*) and vertical (*t*) directions.

Texture images may be one-component (gray-scale), two-component (gray-scale plus transparency), three-component (full RGB color), or four-component (full RGB color plus transparency). The texture image modifies the diffuse color and transparency of an object's material (specified in a Material node). Lighting calculations use the rest of the object's material properties (with the modified diffuse color) to produce the final image.

The texture image modifies the diffuse color and transparency depending on how many components are in the image, as follows:

One-component texture:
> Diffuse color is multiplied by the intensity values in the texture image.

Two-component texture:
> Diffuse color is multiplied by the intensity values in the texture image. Material transparency is multiplied by transparency values in texture image.

Three-component texture:
> RGB colors in the texture image replace the material's diffuse color.

Four-component texture:
> RGB colors in the texture image replace the material's diffuse color. Transparency values in the texture image replace the material's transparency.

See Also

Chapter 8, "Using Colors, Normals, and Textures"; "PixelTexture" on page 325.

IndexedFaceSet

```
IndexedFaceSet {
    coord               NULL    # exposed field SFNode
    coordIndex          [ ]     # MFInt32
    texCoord            NULL    # exposed field SFNode
    texCoordIndex       [ ]     # MFInt32
    color               NULL    # exposed field SFNode
    colorIndex          [ ]     # MFInt32
    colorPerVertex      TRUE    # SFBool
    normal              NULL    # exposed field SFNode
    normalIndex         [ ]     # MFInt32
    normalPerVertex     TRUE    # SFBool
    ccw                 TRUE    # SFBool
    solid               TRUE    # SFBool
    convex              TRUE    # SFBool
    creaseAngle         0       # SFFloat
}
```

Fields

coord contains a Coordinate node listing the vertices of the indexed face set.

coordIndex a list of polygons, each specified as a series of indices into the Coordinate node.

texCoord may contain a TextureCoordinate node to explicitly map a texture onto the indexed face set.

texCoordIndex a list of indices into the TextureCoordinate node.

color may contain a Color node listing colors to use when coloring per-vertex or per-face.

colorIndex a list of indices into the Color node.

colorPerVertex if there's a Color node in the *color* field, indicates whether to assign one color to every vertex (TRUE) or one to every face (FALSE).

normal may contain a Normal node, if you wish to explicitly specify normals.

normalIndex a list of indices into the Normal node.

normalPerVertex indicates whether you've provided one normal per vertex (TRUE) or one per face (FALSE). Ignored if the *normal* field is NULL.

ccw	indicates whether each face's vertices are listed in counterclockwise (TRUE) or clockwise (FALSE) order when viewed from the front.
solid	indicates whether the user can see the backs of any of the faces or not.
convex	indicates whether all faces are convex; if they are, some browsers can perform certain optimizations.
creaseAngle	angle at which to make the edge between two adjacent faces look smooth (as opposed to faceted).

Events

set_colorIndex	**eventIn**	**MFInt32**
	sets the *colorIndex* field's values.	
set_coordIndex	**eventIn**	**MFInt32**
	sets the *coordIndex* field's values.	
set_normalIndex	**eventIn**	**MFInt32**
	sets the *normalIndex* field's values.	
set_texCoordIndex	**eventIn**	**MFInt32**
	sets the *texCoordIndex* field's values.	

Description

An IndexedFaceSet node represents a 3D shape formed by constructing faces (polygons) from vertices located at the given coordinates (specified by a Coordinate node). An indexed face set specifies its polygonal faces as lists of indices in its *coordIndex* field. An index of –1 indicates that the current face has ended and the next one is about to begin. An indexed face set can appear only in the *geometry* field of a Shape node (see "Shape" on page 342).

Explicit texture coordinates (as defined by a TextureCoordinate node) may be bound to vertices of an indexed shape by using the indices in the *textureCoordIndex* field. As with all vertex-based shapes, if there is a current texture but no texture coordinates are specified, a default texture coordinate mapping is calculated using the bounding box of the shape. The longest dimension of the bounding box defines the *s* (horizontal) texture coordinates, and the next longest defines the *t* (vertical) texture coordinates. The value of the *s* coordinate ranges from 0 to 1, from one end of the bounding box to the other. The *t* coordinate ranges between 0 and the ratio of the second greatest dimension of the bounding box to the greatest dimension.

IndexedLineSet

```
IndexedLineSet {
  coord           NULL   # exposed field SFNode
  coordIndex      [ ]    # MFInt32
  color           NULL   # exposed field SFNode
  colorIndex      [ ]    # MFInt32
  colorPerVertex  TRUE   # SFBool
}
```

Fields

coord	contains a Coordinate node listing the vertices to use
coordIndex	a list of indices into the Coordinate node, indicating which vertices to connect and in what order
color	may contain a Color node listing colors to use when coloring per-vertex or per-segment
colorIndex	a list of indices into the Color node
colorPerVertex	if there's a Color node in the *color* field, indicates whether to assign one color to every vertex (TRUE) or one to every polyline (FALSE)

Events

set_colorIndex	**eventIn**	**MFInt32**
	sets the *colorIndex* field's values	
set_coordIndex	**eventIn**	**MFInt32**
	sets the *coordIndex* field's values	

Description

An IndexedLineSet node describes a 3D shape formed by constructing a series of line segments from vertices located at the given coordinates. The indices in the *coordIndex* field specify the segments. An index of −1 indicates that the current connected series has ended and the next one is about to begin.

An indexed line set can appear only in the *geometry* field of a Shape node (see "Shape" on page 342).

Line sets are unaffected by lights and can't be textured. They are not tested for collisions.

Inline

```
Inline {
  url           [ ]       # exposed field MFString
  bboxCenter   0  0  0    # SFVec3f
  bboxSize    -1 -1 -1    # SFVec3f
}
```

Fields

url   specifies the URL of a valid VRML file that contains a
                grouping or child node. If multiple URLs are specified,
                they are listed in descending order of preference. A
                browser may display a URL for a lower-preference file
                while it is obtaining, or if it is unable to obtain, the
                higher-preference file.

bboxCenter   center of the bounding box that surrounds the children
                of this group.

bboxSize   dimensions in *x*, *y*, and *z* of the bounding box that
                surrounds the children of this group. The default value
                indicates no bounding box.

Description

The Inline node is a lightweight grouping node that reads its children from
anywhere on the World Wide Web. Reading the children can be delayed
until the Inline is actually displayed. An Inline with an empty *url* field does
nothing.

The *bboxCenter* and *bboxSize* fields are optionally used to specify the object-
space bounding box for the Inline's children. The browser uses this
bounding box to quickly determine whether the contents of the bounding
box are visible.

LOD

```
LOD {
  range    [ ]    # MFFloat
  center   0 0 0  # SFVec3f
  level    [ ]    # exposed field MFNode
}
```

Fields

range
ideal distances for displaying each level of detail. Values should be in ascending order, from shortest range to longest range.

center
center of the LOD children (used for calculating distances).

level
nodes that represent the same object or objects at varying levels of detail, from highest detail to lowest.

Description

The LOD (level of detail) node is used to allow browsers to switch between various representations of objects automatically.

The level of the object displayed is based on the distance between the object and the user. This distance is calculated from the viewpoint, transformed into the local coordinate space of the LOD node (including any scaling transformations), to the *center* point of the LOD. If the distance is less than the first value in the *range* field, then the first level of the LOD is drawn. If the distance is between the first and second values in the *range* field, the second level is drawn, and so on.

If there are *n* values in the range field, the LOD should have (*n*+1) nodes in its *level* field. Specifying too few levels results in the last level being used repeatedly for the lowest levels of detail. If too many levels are specified, the extra levels are ignored.

You should set LOD ranges so that the transitions from one level of detail to the next are barely noticeable. Browsers may adjust which level of detail is displayed to maintain interactive frame rates and may display a simpler level of detail while a higher level of detail (contained in an Inline node, for example) is fetched. Don't use LOD nodes to emulate simple behaviors, because the results are undefined. For example, using an LOD node to make a door appear to open when the user approaches probably will not work in all browsers. Use a ProximitySensor instead.

All nodes under an LOD node continue to receive and send events, regardless of which LOD level is active.

Performance LOD Node

If you do not specify any values in the *range* field, this indicates that the browser can decide which child to draw to optimize rendering performance. For best results, specify ranges only where necessary, and nest LOD nodes with and without ranges. See Chapter 10, "Improving Performance."

Material

```
Material {
  diffuseColor      0.8 0.8 0.8   # exposed field SFColor
  ambientIntensity  0.2           # exposed field SFFloat
  specularColor     0   0   0     # exposed field SFColor
  emissiveColor     0   0   0     # exposed field SFColor
  shininess         0.2           # exposed field SFFloat
  transparency      0             # exposed field SFFloat
}
```

Fields

diffuseColor specifies the diffuse color, which reflects all light sources depending on the angle of the surface with respect to the light source. The more directly the surface faces the light, the more diffuse light is reflected.

ambientIntensity specifies how much ambient light from light sources this surface should reflect. Ambient light is omnidirectional and depends only on the number of light sources, not on their positions with respect to the surface. Ambient color is calculated as *ambientIntensity * diffuseColor.*

specularColor specifies the color of an object's highlights.

emissiveColor specifies the light produced by a glowing object. Emissive color is useful for displaying radiosity-based models (where the light energy of the room is computed explicitly) or for displaying scientific data. This color field is used when all other colors are black (0 0 0).

shininess degree of shininess of an object's surface, ranging from 0.0 for a diffuse surface with no shininess to 1.0 for a highly polished surface.

transparency degree of transparency of an object, ranging from 0.0 for a completely opaque surface to 1.0 for a completely clear surface.

Description

The Material node defines surface material properties for associated geometry nodes. The fields in the Material node determine the way light reflects off an object to create color. Field values for this node range from 0.0 to 1.0.

The *specularColor* and *shininess* determine the specular highlights—for example, the shiny spots on an apple. When the angle from the light to the surface is close to the angle from the surface to the viewer, the *specularColor* is added to the diffuse color calculation. Lower shininess values produce soft glows, while higher values result in sharper, smaller highlights.

Note that some low-end rendering systems may not support the full range of materials. For example, some systems do not support partial transparency, and some do not support both diffuse and emissive colored objects in the same world.

MovieTexture

```
MovieTexture {
    url         [ ]       # exposed field MFString
    speed       1         # exposed field SFFloat
    loop        FALSE     # exposed field SFBool
    startTime   0         # exposed field SFTime
    stopTime    0         # exposed field SFTime
    repeatS     TRUE      # SFBool
    repeatT     TRUE      # SFBool
}
```

Fields

url
specifies the URL of the movie file. If multiple URLs are specified, they are listed in descending order of preference. The browser loads the first file in the list that it finds. Movies can be in MPEG1-Systems (audio and video) or MPEG1-Video (video-only) format.

speed
specifies the rate at which a movie should be played. A value of 1 is normal speed. A value of 2 indicates to play the movie twice as fast. A negative value indicates to play the movie backwards (this feature may not work for streaming movies or for large movie files). *set_speed* events are ignored while a movie is playing.

loop
specifies whether the movie is repeated when it finishes playing.

startTime
specifies the time when the movie should start playing. While a movie is playing, *set_startTime* events are ignored.

stopTime
specifies the time when the movie should stop playing. The value of *stopTime* is ignored if it's less than or equal to *startTime*.

repeatS
specifies whether the texture wraps in the *s* direction, if needed, to fill the shape. TRUE specifies to repeat the texture. FALSE specifies to clamp the texture coordinates, repeating the last row of pixels to fill the shape.

repeatT	specifies whether the texture wraps in the *t* direction, if needed, to fill the shape. TRUE specifies to repeat the texture. FALSE specifies to clamp the texture coordinates, repeating the last row of pixels to fill the shape.

Events

duration_changed	**eventOut** **SFFloat** duration of the movie, in seconds. This value is sent as soon as the movie is loaded. A value of –1 implies that the movie has not yet loaded.
isActive	**eventOut** **SFBool** indicates whether the movie is currently playing. This event is sent with value TRUE when a movie starts playing and with value FALSE when it stops.

Description

The MovieTexture node specifies an animated movie texture map and parameters for controlling the movie and the texture mapping. The texture map is a two-dimensional image that extends from 0 to 1 in the horizontal (*s*) and vertical (*t*) directions.

Movie textures are either referenced by the Appearance node's *texture* field (as a movie texture) or by the Sound node's *source* field (as an audio source only).

Playing the Movie

If the value of *speed* is positive and the MovieTexture is inactive when the movie is first loaded, the movie begins playing at frame 0. If the value of *speed* is negative when the movie is first loaded, the movie begins playing at the last frame.

If speed equals 0, a MovieTexture will always display frame 0.

When a MovieTexture becomes inactive, the frame corresponding to the time at which the MovieTexture became inactive remains as the current texture on the object.

NavigationInfo

```
NavigationInfo {
  avatarSize         [ 0.25, 1.6, 0.75 ]   # exposed field MFFloat
  headlight          TRUE                  # exposed field SFBool
  speed              1.0                   # exposed field SFFloat
  type               "WALK"                # exposed field MFString
                                           #    "WALK", "EXAMINE",
                                           #    "FLY", "NONE"
  visibilityLimit    0.0                   # exposed field SFFloat
}
```

Fields

avatarSize   specifies parameters to be used in determining the viewpoint dimensions for the purpose of collision detection and terrain following if the viewer type allows these. The transformation hierarchy scales the *avatarSize*; translations and rotations have no effect on *avatarSize*. Some browsers may require additional values in this field.

The first value in this field is the allowable distance between the user's position and any collision geometry (as specified by a Collision node) before a collision is detected.

The second value is the height above the terrain the viewpoint should be maintained.

The third value is the height of the tallest object over which the viewpoint can "step." This allows staircases to be built with dimensions that can be ascended by all browsers.

headlight   specifies whether a browser should turn on a headlight. A headlight is a directional light that always points in the direction the user is looking. Scenes that use precomputed lighting (for example, radiosity solutions) can turn the headlight off. The headlight has intensity 1, color 1 1 1, ambientIntensity 0.0, and direction 0 0 –1.

speed   sets the rate at which the viewer travels through a scene, in meters per second. Since viewers may provide mechanisms to travel faster or slower, this is the default or average speed of the viewer. In an examiner viewer, this field affects only panning and dollying; it does not affect rotation speed. The transformation hierarchy scales the speed; translations and rotations have no effect on speed.

type specifies a navigation paradigm. Types are `"WALK"`, `"EXAMINE"`, `"FLY"`, and `"NONE"`. This field is multivalued so that you can specify fallback types if a browser doesn't understand a given type. Browser-specific types can also be specified in this field. They should end in a unique suffix to prevent conflicts. Strings are case-sensitive.

visibilityLimit sets the farthest distance the user is able to see. The browser may clip all objects beyond this limit, fade them into the background, or ignore this field. A value of 0.0 (the default) indicates an infinite visibility limit. This value is scaled by the current transformation hierarchy (including the Viewpoint).

Events

set_bind **eventIn   SFBool**
specifying TRUE for this event binds this NavigationInfo node to the browser's viewer, making it the active NavigationInfo node for the file.

isBound **eventOut   SFBool**
indicates whether this is the active NavigationInfo node (TRUE) or whether it is inactive (FALSE).

Description

The NavigationInfo node contains information describing the physical characteristics of the viewer and viewing model.

The first NavigationInfo node in the VRML file is used as the initial NavigationInfo node. Subsequent NavigationInfo nodes in the file are ignored until they receive *set_bind* events. The current NavigationInfo node is considered to be a child of the current Viewpoint, regardless of where it is initially located in the file. Whenever the current Viewpoint or the current NavigationInfo node changes, the current NavigationInfo node is reparented to the current Viewpoint node. Changing the *scale* field of the Viewpoint affects the NavigationInfo node's *speed*, *avatarSize*, and

visibilityLimit fields, which are all scaled by the current transformation
hierarchy.

Type of Navigation

A walk viewer is used for exploring a virtual world and has some notion of
gravity. A fly viewer is similar to a walk viewer, except that it has no notion
of gravity. Both walk and fly viewers have some notion of "up," however.
An examiner viewer is typically used to view individual objects and often
provides the ability to spin the object and move it closer or farther away.
The "NONE" option removes all viewer controls. The user navigates using
only controls provided in the scene, such as guided tours. Browsers can also
supply additional viewer types.

NavigationInfo Binding

NavigationInfo nodes are bindable nodes, and the browser maintains a
stack of NavigationInfo nodes. The top NavigationInfo node on the stack is
the currently active one. To push a NavigationInfo node onto the top of the
stack, send a TRUE value to the *set_bind* incoming event of the desired
NavigationInfo node. Once active, the NavigationInfo node is then bound
to the browser's view. A FALSE value for *set_bind* pops the NavigationInfo
node from the stack and unbinds it from the browser. The next
NavigationInfo node in the stack becomes the current NavigationInfo
node, or a default-valued NavigationInfo node is used if the stack is empty.

See Also

"Collision" on page 277.

Normal

```
Normal {
  vector   [ ]   # exposed field MFVec3f
}
```

Field

vector   unit-length normal vectors

Description

This node defines a set of 3D surface normal vectors to be used in the *normal* field of some geometry nodes (IndexedFaceSet, ElevationGrid). Normals should be unit-length.

If no normals are specified, most browsers can generate default normals for the specified geometry.

NormalInterpolator

```
NormalInterpolator {
  key        [ ]   # exposed field MFFloat
  keyValue   [ ]   # exposed field MFVec3f
}
```

Fields

key

a list of keyframe times, each represented as a fraction of the total animation time (a floating point number from 0 to 1, inclusive)

keyValue

a list of sets of normal values, one set for each keyframe, to interpolate among

Events

set_fraction

eventIn   SFFloat
the fraction of the animation that's been completed

value_changed

eventOut   MFVec3f
a set of normalized normal values corresponding to the given point in the animation

Description

The NormalInterpolator node allows you to perform keyframe animation on a set of normals. To set up the interpolator, choose a set of normals for each of several specific moments in the animation (preferably including the beginning and ending of the animation), and list those normals in the keyValue field. List the corresponding fractions (one for each set of normals) in the key field.

For instance, to change a set of normals to simulate a moving light (such as the sun moving across the sky), you can use this interpolator:

```
NormalInterpolator {
  key      [ 0, .5, 1 ]
  keyValue [ .894 .447 0, 0 1 0, 0 0 1, #initial set of normals
             .928 .371 0, 0 1 0, 0 0 1, #second set of normals
             .957 .287 0, 0 1 0, 0 0 1  #final set of normals
           ]
}
```

Normal interpolators are generally sent *set_fraction* events from time sensors, and generally send outgoing values to the *vector* field of a Normal node in an indexed face set. Since time sensors send out fraction values from 0 to 1, interpolators usually have all *key* values within that range; however, *key* values are not restricted to any particular range.

See Also

"Engines" in Chapter 6; "TimeSensor" on page 356.

OrientationInterpolator

```
OrientationInterpolator {
  key        [ ]  # exposed field MFFloat
  keyValue   [ ]  # exposed field MFRotation
}
```

Fields

key	a list of keyframe times, each represented as a fraction of the total animation time (a floating point number from 0 to 1, inclusive)
keyValue	a list of orientation values, one for each keyframe, to interpolate among

Events

set_fraction   **eventIn**   **SFFloat**
the fraction of the animation that's been completed

value_changed   **eventOut**   **SFRotation**
the orientation value corresponding to the given point in the animation

Description

The OrientationInterpolator node allows you to perform keyframe animation on a rotation value. To set up the interpolator, choose orientations for specific moments in the animation (preferably including the beginning and ending values), and list those values in the *keyValue* field. List the corresponding fractions (one for each key orientation value) in the *key* field.

For instance, to start with an object in its default orientation, then rotate it a quarter turn around the *y* axis, then a half turn in the other direction around the *y* axis, you can use this interpolator:

```
OrientationInterpolator {
  key      [ 0, .5, 1 ]
  keyValue [ 0 1 0  0, 0 1 0  1.57, 0 1 0  -1.57]
}
```

Note that these orientations aren't cumulative. Each key value should be a rotation relative to the initial orientation, not an additional amount to rotate from the current orientation.

Also note that each rotation should be within π radians (180 degrees) of the last, to avoid rotating in the wrong direction.

Orientation interpolators generally receive *set_fraction* events from time sensors, and generally send outgoing values to the *rotation* field of a Transform or the *orientation* field of a Viewpoint node. Since time sensors send out fraction values from 0 to 1, interpolators usually have all *key* values within that range; however, *key* values are not restricted to any particular range.

See Also

"Engines" in Chapter 6; "TimeSensor" on page 356.

PixelTexture

```
PixelTexture {
  image    0 0 0  # exposed field SFImage
  repeatS  TRUE   # SFBool
  repeatT  TRUE   # SFBool
}
```

Fields

image   2D texture map, in the form of an SFImage (see
                   Chapter 12, "Field Reference").

repeatS   specifies whether the texture wraps in the *s* direction, if
                   needed, to fill the shape. TRUE specifies to repeat the
                   texture. FALSE specifies to clamp the texture
                   coordinates, repeating the last row of pixels to fill the
                   shape.

repeatT   specifies whether the texture wraps in the *t* direction, if
                   needed, to fill the shape. TRUE specifies to repeat the
                   texture. FALSE specifies to clamp the texture
                   coordinates, repeating the last row of pixels to fill the
                   shape.

Description

The PixelTexture node defines a 2D image-based texture map as an explicit
array of pixel values and parameters controlling tiling repetition of the
texture.

Texture images can be one-component (gray-scale), two-component (gray-
scale plus transparency), three-component (full RGB color), or four-
component (full RGB color plus transparency). The texture image modifies
the diffuse color and transparency of an object's material (specified in a
Material node). Lighting calculations use the rest of the object's material
properties (with the modified diffuse color) to produce the final image.

The texture image modifies the diffuse color and transparency depending on how many components are in the image, as follows:

One-component texture:

Diffuse color is multiplied by the intensity values in the texture image.

Two-component texture:

Diffuse color is multiplied by the intensity values in the texture image. Material transparency is multiplied by transparency values in texture image.

Three-component texture:

RGB colors in the texture image replace the material's diffuse color.

Four-component texture:

RGB colors in the texture image replace the material's diffuse color. Transparency values in the texture image replace the material's transparency.

See Also

Chapter 8, "Using Colors, Normals, and Textures"; "ImageTexture" on page 305; SFImage in Chapter 12, "Field Reference," for details on how to specify a pixel texture.

PlaneSensor

```
PlaneSensor {
  minPosition   0  0      # exposed field SFVec2f
  maxPosition  -1 -1      # exposed field SFVec2f
  enabled       TRUE      # exposed field SFBool
  offset        0  0  0   # exposed field SFVec3f
  autoOffset    TRUE      # exposed field SFBool
}
```

Fields

minPosition constrains *translation* events to be above and to the right of this point in the *xy* plane.

maxPosition constrains *translation* events to be below and to the left of this point in the *xy* plane.

enabled indicates whether the sensor is currently paying attention to pointing device events. To turn off the sensor, send it a *set_enabled* event with value FALSE.

offset indicates how far to translate the associated geometry from its initial position, each time the user begins a new drag.

autoOffset indicates whether to keep track of the current position between drags (TRUE) by saving the current location in *offset* at the end of a drag. If *autoOffset* is FALSE, dragged geometry resets to its initial position each time the user begins a new drag.

Events

isActive **eventOut** **SFBool**
indicates whether the pointing device currently has its button held down. This event is only sent when the button is pressed or released, not during the drag.

trackPoint_changed **eventOut** **SFVec3f**
the actual point in the *xy* plane that the user is pointing to at any given moment during a drag; ignores *minPosition* and *maxPosition*.

translation_changed **eventOut** **SFVec3f**
the clamped point in the *xy* plane that the user is pointing to at any given moment during a drag.

Description

The PlaneSensor node interprets dragging motion (such as a user dragging with a mouse) as a translation in the sensor's local *xy* plane whenever the user clicks and drags while pointing to any of the sensor's sibling geometry.

If you're interested only in a particular range of translation values, you can set *minPosition* and *maxPosition* to clamp *translation_changed* events to a rectangle in the plane with corners at those positions. If the *x* component of *minPosition* is greater than the *x* component of *maxPosition*, or the minimum *y* is greater than the maximum *y*, translations aren't clamped in that direction. If either minimum component is equal to the corresponding maximum component, translations are constrained in that dimension, resulting in interpreting dragging motion as a translation in one dimension, turning the plane sensor into a line sensor.

If you want geometry to stay translated after the user has moved it, leave *autoOffset* set to TRUE. If you want the geometry's position to reset with each new drag, set *autoOffset* to FALSE.

Other pointing device sensors don't generate events while a plane sensor is active (that is, while the user is dragging the sensor's sibling geometry).

PointLight

```
PointLight {
  on                TRUE    # exposed field SFBool
  intensity         1       # exposed field SFFloat
  ambientIntensity  0       # exposed field SFFloat
  color             1 1 1   # exposed field SFColor
  location          0 0 0   # exposed field SFVec3f
  radius            100     # exposed field SFFloat
  attenuation       1 0 0   # exposed field SFVec3f
}
```

Fields

on   indicates whether the light is turned on or not.

intensity   brightness of the light at its source.

ambientIntensity degree to which the light contributes to the world's ambient lighting.

color   color of the light.

location   location of the light in the local coordinate system.

radius   indicates how far away from the light an object can be and still be lit.

attenuation   degree of attenuation to use, if any. The first number in this field is for constant attenuation, the second for linear attenuation over a distance, and the third for quadratic attenuation (based on the square of the distance). Quadratic attenuation is the most realistic of the three, but also by far the slowest.

Description

A PointLight node defines a point light source at a fixed 3D location. A point source illuminates equally in all directions; that is, it's *omnidirectional*.

Light sources are affected by the current transformation.

PointSet

```
PointSet {
  coord   NULL  # exposed field SFNode
  color   NULL  # exposed field SFNode
}
```

Fields

coord   contains a Coordinate node listing the vertices to be
                   used by the point set

color   contains a Color node listing the colors to be used by
                   the point set, one color for each point

Description

A PointSet node represents an unconnected collection of points in 3D
space. A point set can appear only in the *geometry* field of a Shape node (see
"Shape" on page 342).

A point set can be used to represent airport landing lights, stars, or sparks.
Point sets are unaffected by lights and can't be textured. They are not tested
for collisions.

The Color node (if any) contained in the *color* field must contain at least as
many colors as there are points in the Coordinate node in the *coord* field.
Each color is assigned to the corresponding point—the first color listed is
applied to the first point listed, and so on.

PositionInterpolator

```
PositionInterpolator {
  key        [ ]   # exposed field MFFloat
  keyValue   [ ]   # exposed field MFVec3f
}
```

Fields

key　　　　　　　a list of keyframe times, each represented as a fraction of
　　　　　　　　　the total animation time (a floating point number from
　　　　　　　　　0 to 1, inclusive)

keyValue　　　　a list of locations in 3D space, one for each keyframe, to
　　　　　　　　　interpolate among

Events

set_fraction　　**eventIn**　　　　**SFFloat**
　　　　　　　　　the fraction of the animation that's been completed

value_changed　**eventOut**　　　**SFVec3f**
　　　　　　　　　the location value corresponding to the given point in
　　　　　　　　　the animation

Description

The PositionInterpolator node allows you to perform keyframe animation
on a location in 3D space. To set up the interpolator, choose position values
for specific moments in the animation (preferably including the beginning
and ending values), and list those values in the *keyValue* field. List the
corresponding fractions (one for each key color value) in the *key* field. For
instance, to move an object from the origin to a point some distance up the
y axis, ending up back at the origin, use this interpolator:

```
PositionInterpolator {
  key       [ 0, .5, 1 ]
  keyValue  [ 0 0 0, 0 10 0, 0 0 0 ]
}
```

Note that these translations aren't cumulative. Each key value should be the
actual position at the given time, not an additional amount to translate
from the current position.

Position interpolators generally receive *set_fraction* events from time sensors, and generally send outgoing values to the *translation* field of a Transform node. Since time sensors send out fraction values from 0 to 1, interpolators usually have all *key* values within that range; however, *key* values are not restricted to any particular range.

See Also

"Engines" in Chapter 6; "TimeSensor" on page 356.

ProximitySensor

```
ProximitySensor {
  center   0 0 0  # exposed field SFVec3f
  size     0 0 0  # exposed field SFVec3f
  enabled  TRUE   # exposed field SFBool
}
```

Fields

center   the center of the region in which the sensor detects user
                    motion.

size   the extents, along each axis, of the region around the
                    defined *center* in which the sensor detects user motion.

enabled   indicates whether the sensor is currently paying
                    attention to user motion. To turn off the sensor, send it
                    a *set_enabled* event with value FALSE.

Events

isActive   **eventOut**   **SFBool**
                    indicates whether the user has entered the region
                    (TRUE) or has left the region (FALSE).

position_changed **eventOut**   **SFVec3f**
                    the user's current position, updated whenever the user
                    moves into or within the region.

orientation_changed **eventOut**   **SFRotation**
                    the user's current orientation, updated whenever the
                    user moves into or within the region.

enterTime   **eventOut**   **SFTime**
                    the exact time at which the user enters the region.

exitTime   **eventOut**   **SFTime**
                    the exact time at which the user exits the region.

Description

The ProximitySensor node generates events whenever the user moves into,
out of, or within a box-shaped region. The region is defined by a *center* field
and a *size* field (like that of the Box node) giving the extents of the region
along each axis. Note that the extent in each direction is split evenly across
the center; for instance, if *size* is 4 4 4, the box-shaped region extends 2

units in each direction (left, right, forward, back, up, and down) from the center, not 4 units.

Note that user "motion" is determined relative to the sensor's coordinate system, not relative to the sensor's *center* field. If you move the sensor by changing its *center*, no user motion is detected; if you move the sensor by changing a parent transform, the sensor sends events as if the user had moved. Also, the motion of the user can be due to a variety of causes, such as viewpoint binding; *position_changed* and *orientation_changed* don't necessarily mean the user is navigating through the scene using a GUI.

Multiple proximity sensors generate events at the same time if the regions they are sensing overlap; each proximity sensor behaves independently of all others. A single proximity sensor USEd in multiple places detects user motion in the region defined by the union of all the box-shaped regions of the sensor instances; that is, it generates events if the user moves near any of its locations.

A proximity sensor that surrounds the entire world has an *enterTime* equal to the time that the user entered the world. Such a sensor can be used to start animations as soon as a world is loaded.

A proximity sensor with a *size* field set to 0 0 0 generates no events; that's equivalent to setting the *enabled* field to FALSE.

ScalarInterpolator

```
ScalarInterpolator {
  key         [ ]   # exposed field MFFloat
  keyValue    [ ]   # exposed field MFFloat
}
```

Fields

key   a list of keyframe times, each represented as a fraction of
                        the total animation time (a floating point number from
                        0 to 1, inclusive)

keyValue   a list of floating point values, one for each keyframe, to
                        interpolate among

Events

set_fraction   **eventIn**   **SFFloat**
                        the fraction of the animation that's been completed

value_changed   **eventOut**   **SFFloat**
                        the floating point value corresponding to the given
                        point in the animation

Description

The ScalarInterpolator node allows you to perform keyframe animation on
a single floating point value. To set up the interpolator, choose floating
point values for specific moments in the animation (preferably including
the beginning and ending values), and list those values in the *keyValue* field.
List the corresponding fractions (one for each key floating point value) in
the *key* field. For instance, to make a light's intensity decrease slowly until
halfway through the animation and then drop to zero during the second
half of the animation, you might use this interpolator:

```
ScalarInterpolator {
  key      [ 0, .5, 1 ]
  keyValue [ 1, .8, 0 ]
}
```

Scalar interpolators are generally sent *set_fraction* events from time sensors, and generally send outgoing values to fields that contain a single floating point value, like *intensity* or *radius*. Since time sensors send out fraction values from 0 to 1, interpolators usually have all *key* values within that range; however, *key* values are not restricted to any particular range.

See Also

"Engines" in Chapter 6; "TimeSensor" on page 356.

Script

```
Script {
  url              [ ]     # exposed field MFString
  mustEvaluate   FALSE   # SFBool
  directOutput   FALSE   # SFBool

  # And any number of:
  eventIn    eventTypeName eventName
  field      fieldTypeName fieldName initialValue
  eventOut   eventTypeName eventName
}
```

Fields

url	either the URL of a script to execute or the text of the script itself. May contain multiple values; the browser executes the first script in a language it understands.
mustEvaluate	indicates whether the browser must send events to the script even if it's not awaiting output from the script. If FALSE, the browser can sometimes improve performance by not sending events to the script until another node needs events sent out by the script. Should be left at FALSE unless the script does something that the browser can't detect (such as accessing the network).
directOutput	indicates whether the script is allowed to change the scene hierarchy directly and establish or remove routes dynamically, or whether the script can only communicate with the world by way of events. Should be left at FALSE if not needed, to allow browsers to optimize.

You can also include as many custom fields as you want; however, you can't include exposed fields.

Events

There are no events built into the Script node, but you can include as many as you want, of any varieties.

Description

A Script node contains a program called a *script*, written in a supported programming or scripting language such as JavaScript or Java. Scripts can receive events, process the information in the events, and produce outgoing events based on the results.

When a Script node receives an incoming event, it passes that event's value and timestamp to a function or method that has the same name as the incoming event. Functions can send the outgoing events specified in the Script node by assigning values to variables with the same names as those events. An outgoing event sent by a script has the same timestamp as the incoming event that set off the function that sent the outgoing event.

If a script sends multiple events with the same timestamp to another node, the type of the other node may determine what order the events are processed in. In general, this processing order tends to be the order you're mostly likely to want. For instance, if your script sends a *set_position* event and a *set_bind* event with the same timestamp to a Viewpoint node, the browser sets the viewpoint's new position before binding it. Most of the time, you're best off ignoring timestamps.

Some scripting languages (including both JavaScript and Java) define certain function or method names to have special purposes. If you provide a function called **initialize()**, for instance, it gets called as soon as the world is loaded, before any events are sent. The **shutdown()** function, if you define one, is called when the world is deleted (such as when the user clicks an Anchor that links to another world). The **eventsProcessed()** function is called after one or more **eventIn** functions have completed; it's up to the browser whether to call the function after each **eventIn** function or whether to wait until after all currently pending incoming events have been processed.

Instead of sending events to other nodes, you can access other nodes' events directly by placing the nodes in SFNode or MFNode fields of the Script node. For instance, instead of sending a *set_whichChoice* event through a ROUTE to a Switch node, you could do this:

```
DEF MY_SWITCH Switch {
  whichChoice -1
  ...
}
Script {
  field SFNode directNode   USE MY_SWITCH
  eventIn SFBool activate
```

```
directOutput  TRUE
url
  "javascript:
    function activate(value) {
      if (value == true)
        directNode.whichChoice = 0;
    }"
}
```

Note that if you want to access another node's fields directly or use the functions that add or remove routes, you have to set the Script node's *directOutput* field to TRUE.

The location of the Script node in the scene graph has no effect on its operation. For example, if a Script node is a child of a Switch node with *whichChoice* set to –1, the Script continues to receive and send events.

Browser API

Here are the details of function parameters and return values for the browser script interface, also called the browser API. All VRML scripting languages support some form of these functions; the functions are represented here with a C-like syntax.

```
SFString getName( );
SFString getVersion( );
```

The **getName()** and **getVersion()** functions return the name and version of the browser currently in use. These values are not guaranteed to be unique or to adhere to any particular format, and are for information only. If the information is unavailable these functions return empty strings.

```
SFFloat getCurrentSpeed( );
```

The **getCurrentSpeed()** function returns the speed at which the viewpoint is currently moving, in meters per second. If speed of motion is not meaningful in the current navigation type, or if the speed cannot be determined for some other reason, the function returns 0.0.

```
SFFloat getCurrentFrameRate( );
```

The **getCurrentFrameRate()** function returns the current frame rate in frames per second. Some browsers may not support this function; if frame rate isn't supported, or can't be determined, the function returns 0.0.

```
SFString getWorldURL( );
```

The **getWorldURL()** function returns the URL for the currently loaded world.

```
void replaceWorld( MFNode nodes );
```

The **replaceWorld()** function replaces the current world with the world represented by the passed nodes. This function usually doesn't return, since the world containing the running script is being replaced.

```
void loadURL( MFString url, MFString parameter );
```

The **loadURL()** function loads the world specified by *url*, using the given parameters. (These parameters are as described in "Anchor" on page 264.) This function returns immediately but if the URL is loaded into the current browser window or frame (for instance, if there is no TARGET parameter to redirect it to another frame), then the browser eventually replaces the current world with the new world.

```
void setDescription( SFString description );
```

The **setDescription()** function sets a description string to *description*; this function can be used with **loadURL()** to prototype an Anchor node. Different browsers display description strings in different ways. To clear the current description, send an empty string.

```
MFNode createVrmlFromString( SFString vrmlSyntax );
```

The **createVrmlFromString()** function takes a string consisting of a VRML scene description, parses the nodes contained in the string, and returns the corresponding VRML scene as an MFNode value.

```
void createVrmlFromURL( MFString url, SFNode node,
                        SFString event );
```

The **createVrmlFromURL()** function instructs the browser to load a VRML scene description from the given URL or URLs, but not to replace the current scene with the new scene. After the new scene is loaded, the nodes in the new scene are sent to an MFNode incoming event in the node specified by *node*. The *event* string contains the name of the MFNode incoming event in *node*.

```
void addRoute( SFNode fromNode, SFString fromEventOut,
               SFNode toNode, SFString toEventIn );
void deleteRoute( SFNode fromNode, SFString fromEventOut,
                  SFNode toNode, SFString toEventIn );
```

These functions respectively add and delete a route between the given event names in the given nodes.

See Also

Chapter 7, "Scripting"; Appendix B, "Java Notes and Examples"

Shape

```
Shape {
  appearance   NULL   # exposed field SFNode
  geometry     NULL   # exposed field SFNode
}
```

Fields

appearance   contains an Appearance node

geometry   contains a geometry node (for example, Box, Cone, IndexedFaceSet or PointSet)

Description

The specified appearance nodes, if any, are applied to the specified geometry node.

Sound

```
Sound {
    source      NULL    # exposed field SFNode
    intensity   1       # exposed field SFFloat
    priority    0       # exposed field SFFloat
    location    0 0 0   # exposed field SFVec3f
    direction   0 0 1   # exposed field SFVec3f
    minFront    1       # exposed field SFFloat
    maxFront    10      # exposed field SFFloat
    minBack     1       # exposed field SFFloat
    maxBack     10      # exposed field SFFloat
    spatialize  TRUE    # SFBool
}
```

Fields

source
an AudioClip or MovieTexture node containing the URL of a sound file to play; if not specified, the Sound node emits no sound.

intensity
adjusts the volume of the sound source; an intensity of 0 is silence and an intensity of 1 is the full volume as recorded in the sound file.

priority
a hint to the browser about how important this sound is. Should be left at 0 for background sounds, and set to 1 for short single-event sounds that you want to make sure are played.

location
the location of the sound source in 3D space.

direction
specifies a primary sound-emission direction as "front" and provides a vector to define the major axis of the audible-sound ellipsoids.

minFront
the distance along the *direction* vector at which the inner (full-intensity) ellipsoid ends.

maxFront
the distance along the *direction* vector at which the outer (audible) ellipsoid ends.

minBack	the distance in the direction opposite the *direction* vector at which the inner (full-intensity) ellipsoid ends.
maxBack	the distance in the direction opposite the *direction* vector at which the outer (audible) ellipsoid ends.
spatialize	indicates whether the sound should be played as if it's at a particular point in space (TRUE), or whether it should sound like ambient background sound (FALSE).

Description

This node defines parameters for a sound source, located at a specific 3D location, which emits sound primarily in a given direction but can be heard anywhere within an ellipsoidal space. The ellipsoidal region of audibility is defined by the *location* field (giving one focus of the ellipsoid) and the *maxBack* and *maxFront* fields (defining, with the *direction* vector, the two ends of the ellipsoid's major axis). The ellipsoid has a circular cross-section.

The *minBack* and *minFront* fields define a smaller ellipsoid inside the larger one, also with a circular cross-section and a focus at *location*. Anywhere inside the inner ellipsoid, the sound is at full volume; anywhere between the inner and outer ellipsoids, the volume decreases as a function of distance from the inner ellipsoid's surface, reaching complete inaudibility just outside the outer ellipsoid.

Browsers may limit the maximum number of sounds that can be played simultaneously.

A sound can be heard only while it is part of the traversed scene; sound nodes inside LOD nodes or Switch nodes are muted when they're not part of the current active child.

See Also

"Sound" in Chapter 5; "AudioClip" on page 268; "MovieTexture" on page 315.

Sphere

```
Sphere {
  radius  1  # SFFloat
}
```

Field

radius   radius of the sphere

Description

The Sphere is a geometry node that represents a sphere. By default, the sphere is centered at the origin and has a radius of 1.

Spheres generate their own normals.

Default Texture Mapping

When a texture is applied to a sphere, the texture covers the entire surface, wrapping counterclockwise from the back of the sphere (Figure 11-6). The texture has a seam at the back on the *yz* plane.

Figure 11-6   Default texture mapping for a sphere

The Sphere may be invisible from the inside, depending on the browser. Don't place the user inside a Sphere; if you want the user to see the inside of a piece of geometry, use an indexed face set with *solid* set to FALSE.

SphereSensor

```
SphereSensor {
  enabled      TRUE       # exposed field SFBool
  offset       0 1 0  0   # exposed field SFRotation
  autoOffset   TRUE       # exposed field SFBool
}
```

Fields

enabled   indicates whether the sensor is currently paying attention to pointing device events. To turn off the sensor, send it a *set_enabled* event with value FALSE.

offset   indicates how much to rotate the associated geometry from its initial orientation, each time the user begins a new drag.

autoOffset   indicates whether to keep track of the current orientation between drags (TRUE) by saving the current orientation in *offset* at the end of a drag. If *autoOffset* is FALSE, dragged geometry resets to its initial orientation each time the user begins a new drag.

Events

isActive   **eventOut**   **SFBool**
indicates whether the user is dragging geometry associated with the sensor.

trackPoint_changed **eventOut**   **SFVec3f**
the unclamped point on the conceptual sphere's surface that the user is pointing to at any given moment during a drag.

rotation_changed   **eventOut**   **SFRotation**
the conceptual sphere's current orientation at any given moment during a drag.

Description

The SphereSensor node interprets 2D dragging input (such as a user dragging with a mouse) as a rotation in 3D space around the local origin. When the user presses the pointing-device button while pointing to any of the sensor's sibling geometry, the browser generates a conceptual sphere, with radius given by the distance of the clicked point from the origin.

Subsequent dragging motion is interpreted as rotating that sphere, like rolling a ball in place. Unlike the motion of the other pointing device sensors, the rotation of a sphere sensor is always unclamped.

If you want geometry to stay rotated after the user has rotated it, leave *autoOffset* set to TRUE. If you want the geometry's rotation to reset with each new drag, set *autoOffset* to FALSE.

Other pointing device sensors don't generate events while a sphere sensor is active (that is, while the user is dragging the sensor's sibling geometry).

SpotLight

```
SpotLight {
    on                  TRUE        # exposed field SFBool
    intensity           1           # exposed field SFFloat
    ambientIntensity    0           # exposed field SFFloat
    color               1   1   1   # exposed field SFColor
    location            0   0   0   # exposed field SFVec3f
    direction           0   0  -1   # exposed field SFVec3f
    beamWidth           1.570796    # exposed field SFFloat
    cutOffAngle         0.785398    # exposed field SFFloat
    radius              100         # exposed field SFFloat
    attenuation         1   0   0   # exposed field SFVec3f
}
```

Fields

on	indicates whether the light is turned on or not.
intensity	brightness of the light at its source.
ambientIntensity	degree to which the light contributes to the world's ambient lighting.
color	color of the light.
location	light's location in the local coordinate system.
direction	axis of the cone of light.
beamWidth	angle subtended by the main cone of light (in radians). Light intensity falls off outside of that angle.
cutOffAngle	angle beyond which nothing is lit.
radius	indicates how far away from the light an object can be and still be lit (assuming the object is within the cone of the spotlight).
attenuation	degree of attenuation to use, if any. The first number in this field is for constant attenuation, the second for linear attenuation over a distance, and the third for quadratic attenuation (based on the square of the distance). Quadratic attenuation is the most realistic of the three, but also by far the slowest.

Description

A SpotLight node defines two cones of light: one with vertex angle equal to *beamWidth* and with height *radius*, inside of which the light is at maximum intensity, and another coaxial light-cone with vertex angle equal to *cutOffAngle*. Light intensity drops off from the surface of the inner cone to the surface of the outer cone, where it reaches zero.

Switch

```
Switch {
  whichChoice   -1    # exposed field SFInt32
  choice        [ ]   # exposed field MFNode
}
```

Fields

whichChoice   specifies the index of the active child. The first child in the *choice* field has an index of 0. If the value of *whichChoice* is less than zero or greater than the number of indices in the *choice* field, nothing is chosen.

choice   children of this grouping node. Each child has an index, beginning with 0 for the first child.

Description

The Switch grouping node activates zero or one of its children (which are specified in the *choice* field). Nonactive children are ignored. However, all nodes under a Switch node respond to events, regardless of whether they are active or nonactive.

Text

```
Text {
    string      [ ]    # exposed field MFString
    fontStyle   NULL   # exposed field SFNode
    maxExtent   0.0    # exposed field SFFloat
    length      [ ]    # exposed field MFFloat
}
```

Fields

string
the text string or strings to display, in UTF-8 encoding (a superset of ASCII).

fontStyle
contains a FontStyle node that describes how the text should be drawn.

maxExtent
the maximum extent in the major direction of any line of text in this node; must be greater than or equal to 0. The major direction is horizontal if the FontStyle node's *horizontal* field is TRUE, vertical otherwise. A value of 0 means the strings can be of any length.

length
the desired extent for each individual text string. A value of 0 for a string means the string can be of any length.

Description

The Text node draws one or more text strings in the specified style. If you provide more than one string, each string is drawn on a separate line, with space between lines determined by the FontStyle node.

The browser determines how far each string extends, in local coordinates, in the major direction (determined by the FontStyle node's *horizontal* field). If the longest string extends further than *maxExtent* units, it's scaled down to be only *maxExtent* units long; all the other strings are scaled by the same amount.

Each string also has a corresponding *length* value, indicating how long you'd like the string to be. The browser stretches or compresses each string to the desired length. Missing values are treated as zeroes.

A Text node doesn't perform collision detection.

Text: Default Texture Mapping

When a texture is applied to text, the origin of the texture is placed, by default, at the origin of the first text string. The texture is scaled equally in both s and t dimensions, to make the font height correspond to 1 unit. s increases to the right, and t increases upward.

See Also

"FontStyle" on page 301.

TextureCoordinate

```
TextureCoordinate {
  point  [ ]  # exposed field MFVec2f
}
```

Field

point   texture coordinates in the form (*s t*) to be mapped to the
                           vertices of an IndexedFaceSet or ElevationGrid

Description

This node defines a set of 2D coordinates to map textures to the vertices of
some geometry nodes. It is used in the *texCoord* field of the IndexedFaceSet
and ElevationGrid nodes.

Texture map parameter values range from 0 to 1 across the texture image.
The horizontal coordinate, *s*, is specified first, followed by the vertical
coordinate, *t*.

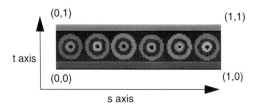

Figure 11-7   Texture coordinates

TextureCoordinate values, specified in the point field, can range from
–infinity to *+infinity*. If the texture map is repeated in a given direction (*s* or
t), a texture coordinate *c* is mapped into a texture map that has *n* pixels in
the given direction as follows:

location = (*c* – floor(*c*)) * *n*

If the texture is not repeated, c is clipped to the range of 0 to 1 as follows:

location = max (0, min(1, *c*)) * *n*

See Also

Chapter 8, "Using Colors, Normals, and Textures."

TextureTransform

```
TextureTransform {
  translation  0 0  # exposed field SFVec2f
  rotation     0    # exposed field SFFloat
  scale        1 1  # exposed field SFVec2f
  center       0 0  # exposed field SFVec2f
}
```

Fields

translation   specifies a translation.

rotation   specifies a rotation in radians about the center of the object, as defined in the *center* field.

scale   specifies a scale about the center of the object, as defined in the *center* field. The scale can be nonuniform.

center   specifies an arbitrary center point for the scale and rotation.

Description

The TextureTransform node defines a 2D transformation that is applied to texture coordinates. This node is used only in the *textureTransform* field of the Appearance node and affects the way textures are applied to the surfaces of the associated geometry node. The order of operations within this node is scale, rotation, translation.

See Also

"TextureCoordinate" on page 354; Chapter 8, "Using Colors, Normals, and Textures."

TimeSensor

```
TimeSensor {
  cycleInterval  1      # exposed field SFTime
  enabled        TRUE   # exposed field SFBool
  loop           FALSE  # exposed field SFBool
  startTime      0      # exposed field SFTime
  stopTime       0      # exposed field SFTime
}
```

Fields

cycleInterval the length of each cycle, in seconds. Must be greater than zero.

enabled if TRUE, time-related events are generated if other conditions (involving the current time and the other field values) are met. If FALSE, time-related events aren't generated under any conditions. The *set_* events for the exposed fields are processed, and the *_changed* events generated, whether *enabled* is TRUE or FALSE.

loop indicates whether the time sensor should repeat indefinitely (until *stopTime* is reached), or should stop after one cycle.

startTime the time at which to start generating events (an absolute time, in seconds since January 1, 1970).

stopTime the time at which to stop generating events (an absolute time, in seconds since January 1, 1970). Ignored if less than or equal to *startTime*.

Events

isActive **eventOut   SFBool**
indicates whether the time sensor is currently running. Sends TRUE when the time sensor starts running and FALSE when it stops; doesn't send values at any other time.

cycleTime **eventOut   SFTime**
the current time, sent at the start of each cycle.

| *fraction_changed* | **eventOut** | **SFFloat** |

the fraction of the current cycle that has completed, from 0 (start of cycle) to 1 (end of cycle).

| *time* | **eventOut** | **SFTime** |

the current time, in seconds since 12 midnight GMT January 1, 1970.

Description

A TimeSensor node generates events as time passes. It can be used to run animations (usually in conjunction with an interpolator); to cause a single action to occur (such as setting off an alarm) at a specified time; or to generate events at regular time intervals.

Usually, a time sensor's *startTime* field is set by a time event routed from another sensor or a script, in response to user action. The time sensor does nothing until the time specified by *startTime*; at that time, it generates an *isActive* TRUE event and begins generating *time*, *fraction_changed*, and *cycleTime* events.

The *time* events always have value equal to the current time. The other time-related events are generated in patterns called cycles. If *loop* is FALSE, a time sensor runs for only one cycle of length *cycleInterval* (or until *stopTime* is reached, if that occurs before the end of the first cycle). If *loop* is TRUE, the time sensor continues to run indefinitely, unless stopped by *stopTime* occurring or *enabled* being set to FALSE. At the beginning of each cycle, the sensor sends out a *fraction_changed* event with value 0, and a *cycleTime* event with value equal to the current time. For the duration of the cycle, every time the browser allows the sensor to generate an event (usually once per rendered frame), the *fraction_changed* values increase from 0 up to 1, indicating the fraction of the current cycle that has elapsed. At *fraction_changed* 1, the cycle ends and the next cycle begins.

A *cycleTime* event is generated only at the start of a cycle. To generate a one-time event such as an alarm, set *startTime* to the desired time and leave *loop* set to FALSE; the sensor then generates a single *cycleTime* event at *startTime*.

TimeSensors ignore *set_cycleInterval* and *set_startTime* events while they are actively generating time-related events. The *cycleInterval* and *startTime* fields are not changed, and *cycleInterval_changed* and *startTime_changed* outgoing events are not generated. If you want to restart an active time sensor, send it a *set_stopTime* event with value equal to the current time (which causes the TimeSensor to become inactive) and then send it a *set_startTime* event (setting it to the desired starting time).

If an active time sensor receives a *set_stopTime* event with a value less than the current time but greater than *startTime*, it sets *stopTime* to the given value but behaves as if the *stopTime* requested is the current time, and sends the final events. If an active time sensor receives a *set_stopTime* event with value less than or equal to that of *startTime*, the sensor ignores the event.

Setting the *loop* field to TRUE makes the time sensor start generating events at *startTime* and continue generating events forever, or until *stopTime* occurs (if *stopTime* is greater than *startTime*). To make a time sensor activate as soon as the browser loads the world, set *loop* to TRUE and leave *stopTime* and *startTime* at their default values (or set them to any values for which *stopTime* is less than or equal to *startTime*).

If you change *loop* from TRUE to FALSE while a time sensor is running, the sensor doesn't stop running until it completes the current cycle, or until *stopTime* is reached, whichever comes first.

Time sensors aren't guaranteed to generate time-related events with any particular frequency, but most browsers generate these events once per rendered frame of animation.

See Also

Chapter 6, "Animation and User Interaction"; interpolator nodes.

TouchSensor

```
TouchSensor {
  enabled TRUE  # exposed field SFBool
}
```

Field

enabled   indicates whether the sensor is currently paying
                          attention to pointing device input

Events

isOver   **eventOut**   **SFBool**
                  indicates whether the pointing device is currently
                  pointing to the sensor's sibling geometry (regardless of
                  whether the button is currently pressed)

isActive   **eventOut**   **SFBool**
                  indicates whether the pointing device button is
                  currently pressed

hitPoint_changed **eventOut**   **SFVec3f**
                  the location on the surface of the sibling geometry at
                  which the button was most recently released

hitNormal_changed **eventOut**   **SFVec3f**
                  the normal at the point given by *hitPoint_changed*

hitTexCoord_changed
                  eventOut   **SFVec2f**
                  the texture coordinate at the point given by
                  hitPoint_changed; can be used to turn a texture into an
                  interactive image map

touchTime   **eventOut**   **SFTime**
                  the time at which a click of the pointing device button
                  completes

Description

A TouchSensor node generates events based on input from a pointing
device (most commonly a mouse). These events indicate whether the user
is pointing to certain geometry as well as where and when the user clicks
the pointing device button.

The geometry that the touch sensor monitors is the sensor's sibling geometry—all geometry nodes that are descendants of the sensor's parent grouping node.

When the pointing device isn't pointing to the sensor's sibling geometry and the user moves the pointing device so that it does point to the sibling geometry, the sensor generates an *isOver* event with value TRUE. When the pointing device is pointing to the sibling geometry and the user moves the pointing device so that it no longer points to the geometry, the sensor sends an *isOver* FALSE event.

When the user moves the pointing device from one point on the geometry to another, the sensor sends a set of events indicating what the device is pointing to: *hitPoint_changed*, *hitNormal_changed*, and *hitTexCoord_changed*, indicating respectively where on the geometry the user is pointing, what the normal is at that point, and what the texture coordinate is at that point.

When the user presses the pointing device button (while pointing to the relevant geometry), the sensor sends an *isActive* TRUE event. When the user releases the button, whether or not still pointing to the geometry, the sensor sends an *isActive* FALSE event.

If the user presses the mouse button while pointing to the geometry, then releases it while still (or again) pointing to the geometry, the sensor sends a *touchTime* event indicating the time the button was released. You can use this event to mimic the behavior of many common user-interface items (those which don't perform an action until the user clicks and releases the pointing device button).

Other pointing device sensors don't generate events while a touch sensor is active (that is, while the pointing device button is pressed).

See Also

CylinderSensor, PlaneSensor, and SphereSensor nodes (the drag sensors).

Transform

```
Transform {
  bboxCenter       0  0  0       # SFVec3f
  bboxSize        -1 -1 -1       # SFVec3f
  translation      0  0  0       # exposed field SFVec3f
  rotation         0  0  1   0   # exposed field SFRotation
  scale            1  1  1       # exposed field SFVec3f
  scaleOrientation 0  0  1   0   # exposed field SFRotation
  center           0  0  0       # exposed field SFVec3f
  children        [ ]            # exposed field MFNode
}
```

Fields

bboxCenter	center of the bounding box that surrounds the children of this Transform.
bboxSize	dimensions in *x*, *y*, and *z* of the bounding box that surrounds the children of this Transform. The default value indicates no bounding box.
translation	specifies a translation vector.
rotation	specifies a rotation in terms of an axis and an angle, in radians.
scale	specifies a scale, which can be nonuniform.
scaleOrientation	specifies the rotational orientation for the scale operation.
center	specifies the origin for the scale and rotation operations.
children	group or child nodes, which are affected by the transformations specified in this node.

Events

addChildren	**eventIn** **MFNode** adds the specified node to this group's list of children. If the node is already in the Transform's list of children, it is ignored.
removeChildren	**eventIn** **MFNode** removes the specified node from the group's list of children. If the node is not in the Transform's list of children, it is ignored.

Description

A Transform is a grouping node that defines a coordinate system for its children that is relative to the coordinate systems of its parents.

The *bboxCenter* and *bboxSize* fields are optionally used to specify the maximum bounding box for the objects in this Transform. The browser uses this bounding box for optimizations to determine whether the group needs to be drawn. The bounding box must be large enough to completely contain all the children in the group, including the effects of all sounds, lights, and fog nodes that are children in this Transform. If the size of this Transform changes over time because its children are animating, the bounding box should be large enough to contain all possible animations of the Transform. The bounding box should be only the union of the Transform's children's bounding boxes; it should not include the Transform's transformation.

The *translation, rotation, scale, scaleOrientation*, and *center* fields define a geometric 3D transformation that is performed in the following order:

1. A scale about an arbitrary point. (The scale can be nonuniform.)

2. A rotation about an arbitrary point and axis.

3. A translation.

Viewpoint

```
Viewpoint {
  position     0 0 10      # exposed field SFVec3f
  orientation  0 0 1  0    # exposed field SFRotation
  fieldOfView  0.785398    # exposed field SFFloat
  description  ""          # SFString
  jump         TRUE        # exposed field SFBool
}
```

Fields

position specifies the relative location of the Viewpoint node in the local coordinate system.

orientation specifies a rotation relative to the default orientation. The default orientation has the user looking down the −*z* axis with +*x* to the right and +*y* straight up. Note that the single orientation rotation (which is a rotation about an arbitrary axis) is sufficient to completely specify any combination of view direction and "up" vector (that is, you can't include two *orientation* fields for one Viewpoint node). Viewpoint position and orientation are affected by the transformation hierarchy.

fieldOfView specifies a preferred field of view from this Viewpoint, in radians. A smaller field of view corresponds to a telephoto lens on a camera. A larger field of view corresponds to a wide-angle lens on a camera. The field of view should be greater than zero and smaller than π; the default value corresponds to a 45-degree field of view.

description identifies viewpoints that are to be made publicly accessible through a viewpoints menu or other device. If no description is given, this Viewpoint never appears in a brower's GUI. When the user selects a viewpoint's description in a GUI, the browser either animates to the new position or jumps directly there. Once the new position is reached, both the *isBound* and *bindTime* events are sent.

jump indicates whether the browser should teleport the viewer to the new viewpoint's location at the moment a viewpoint is bound or unbound (TRUE), or leave the viewer at its current location. If *jump* is TRUE, the move to the new location is instantaneous and the viewer is not considered to pass through any of the space between the former location and the new location. Note that if you unbind a Viewpoint whose *jump* field is TRUE, the viewer teleports to the location of the next Viewpoint on the stack.

Events

set_bind   **eventIn**   **SFBool**
sending a value of TRUE for this event binds this Viewpoint node to the browser, making it the active Viewpoint node for the file.

bindTime   **eventOut**   **SFTime**
time at which the Viewpoint is bound. This field is useful for starting an animation or script when a given Viewpoint becomes active.

isBound   **eventOut**   **SFBool**
this event sends a value of TRUE when a browser goes to a named Viewpoint and binds to it.

Description

The Viewpoint node defines a specific location in a local coordinate system from which the user can view the scene.

Initial Viewpoint

A viewpoint can be placed in a VRML world to specify the initial location of the viewer when that world is entered. The URL syntax `".../scene.wrl#GreatTemple"` specifies that the user's initial view when entering the *scene.wrl* world should be the first viewpoint in file *scene.wrl* that appears as `DEF GreatTemple Viewpoint {...}`.

Binding

Viewpoint nodes are bindable nodes, and the browser maintains a stack of Viewpoint nodes. The top Viewpoint node on the stack is the currently active one. To push a Viewpoint onto the top of the stack, send a TRUE value to the *set_bind* **eventIn** of the specific Viewpoint. Once active, the Viewpoint is then bound to the browser's view. All subsequent changes (for example, animations) to the viewpoint automatically change the user's view. A FALSE value for *set_bind* pops the Viewpoint node from the stack and unbinds it from the browser.

You can automatically move the user's view through the world by binding the user to a viewpoint and then animating that viewpoint.

VisibilitySensor

```
VisibilitySensor {
  center    0 0 0  # exposed field SFVec3f
  size      0 0 0  # exposed field SFVec3f
  enabled   TRUE   # exposed field SFBool
}
```

Fields

center   center of the bounding box that activates and
            deactivates this sensor.

size   dimensions in *x*, *y*, and *z* of the bounding box that
            activates and deactivates this sensor.

enabled   specifies whether the VisibilitySensor is active. If this
            field is FALSE, the sensor does not send output events. If
            TRUE, the sensor detects changes to the visibility status
            of the bounding box specified and sends events through
            the *isActive* outgoing event.

Events

isActive   **eventOut   SFBool**
             indicates whether any portion of the bounding box
             affects the rendered view. A value of TRUE for this field
             indicates that the bounding box is in view. A value of
             FALSE for this field indicates that the bounding box is
             not currently in view.

enterTime **eventOut   SFTime**
             the time when an *isActive* TRUE event is generated.

exitTime   **eventOut   SFTime**
             the time when an *isActive* FALSE event is generated.

Description

The VisibilitySensor node detects when the user can see a specific object or
area. When the area is visible, the sensor can activate a behavior or
animation. When the area is not in view, the sensor can deactivate the
behavior or animation to improve performance.

The VisibilitySensor checks whether the given bounding box is in view as the user navigates the world. It outputs a TRUE *isActive* event when any portion of the box enters the field of view, and a FALSE *isActive* event when the box completely exits the field of view. The VisibilitySensor does not detect occlusion by other objects. It compares the bounding box to the field of view regardless of other geometry in the world.

The bounding box specified by VisibilitySensor is affected by the current transformation.

WorldInfo

```
WorldInfo {
  title  ""   # SFString
  info   [ ]  # MFString
}
```

Fields

title   title for the world, which browsers can display in their
                     window border.

info   other information about the world, such as author,
                     copyright, and public domain information.

Description

The WorldInfo node contains information about the world. It has no effect
on the visual appearance or behavior of the world and is strictly for
documentation purposes.

Chapter 12

Field Reference

There are two general types of fields: fields that can contain only a single value (where a value may be a single number, a set of numbers defining a vector or color, or even a set of numbers that define an image), and fields that can contain multiple values. Single-valued field types have names that begin with "SF"; multiple-valued field types have names that begin with "MF." Note that a single value may contain more than one number; for instance, 1 0 0 is a single SFColor *value*, representing the color red, even though it contains three numbers.

In your VRML files, express a multiple-valued field as a series of single values separated by commas or white space, with the entire list enclosed in square brackets. If a multiple-valued field contains no values, use only the square brackets ("[ ]"), with no values between them. If the field contains exactly one value, you may omit the brackets and use just the value. For example, both of the following are valid ways to describe a multiple-valued field containing the single integer value 1:

```
1
[ 1 ]
```

This chapter describes each of the field types. Single-valued types are given in alphabetical order; multiple-valued types are listed with the corresponding single-valued types.

The same types are used for events as for fields. Each event type has an associated initial value, as specified in the type description. That value is returned when a script attempts to read the value of an outgoing event that hasn't yet been sent.

SFBool

An SFBool field contains a single Boolean value. The words TRUE and FALSE (with no quotation marks or other punctuation) are the only valid values for an SFBool field.

The initial value of an SFBool outgoing event is FALSE.

Note: The common programming shortcut of using 1 and 0 to correspond to true and false values, respectively, doesn't work in VRML.

SFColor and MFColor

An SFColor field is a single-valued field containing a color. An SFColor value is the same as an RGB value: a set of three floating point numbers, with each number between 0.0 and 1.0, inclusive, representing respectively the amounts of red, green, and blue that make up the color.

An MFColor field is a multiple-valued field that contains any number of these RGB color values. For example:

```
[ 1.0 0.0 0.0, 0 1 0, 0 0 1 ]
```

represents the three colors red, green, and blue.

The initial value of an SFColor outgoing event is (0 0 0). The initial value of an MFColor outgoing event is [ ].

SFFloat and MFFloat

An SFFloat field contains one single-precision floating point number, in ANSI C floating point format. An MFFloat field contains zero or more such floating point numbers.

The initial value of an SFFloat outgoing event is 0.0. The initial value of an MFFloat outgoing event is [ ].

SFImage

An SFImage field contains an uncompressed 2D color or gray-scale image.

An SFImage value consists of two integers representing the width and height of the image, then a third integer indicating the number of components in the image (from 1 to 4), followed by *width × height* hexadecimal numbers separated by white space. Each hexadecimal number represents a single pixel of the image.

The number of components in the image indicates whether the image is in shades of gray or in color, and whether it includes transparent or translucent pixels.

A one-component image uses a one-byte hexadecimal number for each pixel to represent the intensity of that pixel. For example, 0xFF is full intensity (white), while 0x00 is no intensity (black).

A two-component image uses two bytes per pixel, with intensity given in the first byte and degree of transparency in the second byte. A value of 0xFF for the transparency byte indicates total transparency, while 0x00 indicates completely opaque. So the number 0x40C0 indicates one-quarter intensity (dark gray) and three-quarters transparent.

Each pixel in a three-component image is represented by three bytes, one each for the red, green, and blue components of that pixel's color (so 0xFF0000 is red).

Four-component images put a transparency byte after the red, green, and blue values (so 0x0000FF80 is half-transparent blue). As with a two-component image, 0xFF is fully transparent and 0x00 is fully opaque.

Note: For readability, it's best to write out all the bytes of the hexadecimal number for each pixel even if that means writing several leading zeroes. However, writing out each number in full isn't actually required; if you wish, you can give a blue three-component pixel as 0xFF instead of 0x0000FF.

Pixels are specified from left to right, bottom to top. The first hexadecimal number describes the lower-left pixel of the image, and the last one describes the upper-right pixel.

For example,

```
1 2 1 0xFF 0x00
```

is a one-pixel wide by two-pixel high gray-scale image, with the bottom pixel white and the top pixel black. And

```
2 4 3 0xFF0000 0x00FF00 0 0 0 0 0xFFFFFF 0xFFFF00
```

is a two-pixel wide by four-pixel high RGB image, with the bottom-left pixel red, the bottom-right pixel green, the two middle rows of pixels black, the top-left pixel white, and the top-right pixel yellow.

This field type is found only in the PixelTexture node, though you can of course use it in any Script node or prototype.

The initial value of an SFImage outgoing event is (0 0 0).

SFInt32 and MFInt32

An SFInt32 field contains a single 32-bit integer. An SFInt32 value consists of an integer in decimal or hexadecimal (beginning with "0x") format.

An MFInt32 field is a multiple-valued field that contains any number of these integer values, separated by commas or white space. For example:

```
[ 17, -0xE20, -518820 ]
```

The initial value of an SFInt32 outgoing event is 0. The initial value of an MFInt32 outgoing event is [ ].

SFNode and MFNode

An SFNode field contains a single node, written in standard node syntax. An MFNode field contains any number of nodes. For example:

```
[ Transform { translation 1 0 0 },
  DEF PANDORA Box { },
  USE PANDORA ]
```

An SFNode field may contain the keyword NULL instead of a node, to indicate that it contains nothing.

Note that the *children* field of a group or transform is simply an MFNode field listing a set of nodes.

Also note that putting an SFNode field in a Script node gives that node's script direct access to the node listed in the SFNode field, without the need for a ROUTE statement. See Chapter 7 for details.

The initial value of an SFNode outgoing event is NULL. The initial value of an MFNode outgoing event is [ ].

SFRotation and MFRotation

An SFRotation field specifies an arbitrary rotation around an arbitrary axis. An SFRotation value consists of four floating point numbers separated by white space. The first three numbers represent an axis of rotation (a vector from the origin to the given point); the final number indicates how far to rotate about that axis, in radians. For example, a π-radian (180-degree) rotation about the y axis could be indicated as:

```
0 1 0 3.1416
```

An MFRotation field contains any number of these rotation values.

Note that rotations of viewpoints are rotations away from the default viewpoint orientation, which is looking along the $-z$ axis from the point (0, 0, 10).

The initial value of an SFRotation outgoing event is (0 0 1 0). The initial value of an MFRotation outgoing event is [ ].

SFString and MFString

An SFString field contains a sequence of characters (a string) in the UTF-8 character encoding. (UTF-8 is a superset of ASCII, so you can put an ASCII string in an SFString field.) An SFString value consists of a sequence of UTF-8 *octets* surrounded by double quotation marks. Any character (including newlines and the "#" character) may appear within the quotes. To include a double-quote character within the string, precede it with a backslash. To include a backslash in the string, type two consecutive backslashes. For example, these are valid SFString values:

```
"One, Two, Three, 123."
"He asked, \"Who is #1?\""
```

An MFString field contains zero or more string values, each in the same format as an SFString value.

The initial value of an SFString outgoing event is "". The initial value of an MFRotation outgoing event is [ ].

SFTime and MFTime

An SFTime field contains a single time value. Each time value is a double-precision floating point number in ANSI C floating point format, representing the number of seconds elapsed since January 1, 1970, at midnight GMT (also known as "the *Epoch*").

An MFTime field contains any number of time values.

The initial value of an SFTime outgoing event is –1. The initial value of an MFTime outgoing event is [ ].

SFVec2f and MFVec2f

An SFVec2f field defines a 2D vector. An SFVec2f value is a pair of floating point values separated by white space.

An MFVec2f field is a multiple-valued field that contains any number of such 2D vector values. For example:

```
[ 0 0, 1.2 3.4, 98.6 -4e1 ]
```

The initial value of an SFVec2f outgoing event is (0 0). The initial value of an MFVec2f outgoing event is [ ].

SFVec3f and MFVec3f

An SFVec3f field defines a vector in 3D space. An SFVec3f value consists of three floating point numbers separated by white space; such a value represents a vector going from the origin to the given point.

An MFVec3f field is a multiple-valued field containing any number of such 3D vectors. For example:

```
[ 0 0 0, 1.2 3.4 5.6, 98.6 -4e1 451 ]
```

The initial value of an SFVec3f outgoing event is (0 0 0). The initial value of an MFVec3f outgoing event is [ ].

Appendix A

Obsolete Nodes

Many of the nodes in VRML 2.0 have different names from those in VRML 1.0C (the corrected version of VRML 1.0). This appendix is provided for readers who encounter discussions of VRML 1.0 nodes and want to find out the VRML 2.0 equivalent.

Note that this appendix lists only those nodes whose names aren't used in VRML 2.0. The syntax for most nodes has changed at least a little from VRML 1.0 syntax, even for those nodes whose names have not changed. The Transform node, for instance, played a very different role in VRML 1.0 than it does in VRML 2.0. This appendix only points you to the new node equivalents; it doesn't explain the differences between 1.0 and 2.0 in detail.

If you have a VRML 1.0 file that you want to update, use the public domain utility Vrml1ToVrml2, available from

`http://vrml.sgi.com/tools`

Table A-1 lists the VRML 1.0C node names that are no longer valid, and where to look for information on the VRML 2.0 equivalents.

VRML 1.0C Node	VRML 2.0 Equivalent
AsciiText	use Text
Coordinate3	use Coordinate
Cube	use Box

Table A-1 Obsolete VRML 1.0C nodes and how to replace them

VRML 1.0C Node	VRML 2.0 Equivalent
Info	use WorldInfo
MaterialBinding	use fields in vertex-based geometry nodes
MatrixTransform	use Transform
NormalBinding	use fields in vertex-based geometry nodes
OrthographicCamera	use Viewpoint
PerspectiveCamera	use Viewpoint
Rotation	use Transform
Scale	use Transform
Separator	use Transform
ShapeHints	use fields in vertex-based geometry nodes
Texture2	use texturing nodes
Texture2Transform	use TextureTransform
TextureCoordinate2	use TextureCoordinate
TransformSeparator	use Transform
Translation	use Transform
WWWAnchor	use Anchor
WWWInline	use Inline

Table A-1 Obsolete VRML 1.0C nodes and how to replace them

Java Notes and Examples

This appendix provides general information on using Java in scripts, and Java versions of the scripting examples from Chapter 7, "Scripting." To use these examples with a VRML browser that understands Java, compile the Java source listings using your Java compiler, then save the resulting compiled files with the names given in the *url* fields of the Script nodes in Chapter 7. Few if any browsers can compile Java source code, so don't put the Java source directly into the Script node.

Except for the *url* field, the VRML files themselves don't change at all when you replace JavaScript scripts with Java scripts.

Note: At the time of this writing, the Java classes and methods for scripting are still being defined. This appendix is based on the most recent available information, but is not guaranteed to be accurate.

Java Notes

At the beginning of your Java source code, be sure to include these lines:

```
import vrml.*;
import vrml.field.*;
import vrml.node.*;
```

If you don't import the VRML package, you won't have access to any of the VRML field types or browser API functions. The Java package defines both a read-only (Const) class and a read/write class for each VRML field type; both kinds of classes define a **getValue()** method, and the read/write classes define a **setValue()** method as well. Each class for a field type that contains more than one number also provides methods for getting and setting individual numbers within the field value; for instance, the SFColor class provides **getRed()**, **getGreen()**, and **getBlue()** methods, and the MFInt32 class provides an **addValue()** method to add an SFInt32 value to the list.

Most of the **setValue()** methods can throw exceptions (generate errors); you may need to write exception handlers when you use those methods.

The VRML package also defines a Script class. Any class that you create to be called as a script from a Script node should extend the Script class. Your class definition must have the same name as the body of the filename.

Inside the class, usually in an **initialize()** method, you need to declare each field of the Script node (using the **getField()** method) and each outgoing event of the Script node (using the **getEventOut()** method).

When a Script receives a set of incoming events, it passes them to a Java method named **processEvents()**. The default behavior for that method is to pass each event individually to your defined event handler, which must be called **processEvent()**. You can redefine **processEvents()** if you want to, but most of the time you leave that method alone and redefine **processEvent()** to do your event handling.

The **processEvent()** method receives a single object of class Event. The Event class defines three methods: **getName()**, **getValue()**, and **getTimeStamp()**. The usual way to define **processEvent()** is as a series of **if** statements, each comparing the passed event name with the name of one of the incoming events in the Script node. Each **if** block consists of the code to handle the particular event.

You can use the standard Java mechanisms to start new threads. When the browser disposes of a Script node (as, for instance, when the current world is unloaded), it calls the **shutdown()** method for each currently active thread in the corresponding script, to give threads a chance to shut down gracefully.

If you want to keep static data in a script (that is, if you want to retain values from one invocation of the script to the next), you can use instance variables—local variables within the script, declared as private. However, you can't rely on the browser maintaining the values of such variables if the script is unloaded from the browser's memory. In general, static data should be kept in fields of the Script node.

Examples

This section provides a Java equivalent for each of the major scripting examples in Chapter 7.

Locate-Highlighting

The Highlighter prototype from the skull-highlighting example contains the URL of a compiled Java file called *HighlightOnTrue.class*. That file is compiled from the source code in another file, *HighlightOnTrue.java*:

```java
import vrml.*;
import vrml.field.*;
import vrml.node.*;

class HighlightOnTrue extends Script{

  // Declare fields
  private SFColor activeColor;
  private SFColor inactiveColor;

  // Declare eventOut
  private SFColor color;

  // Set up fields and eventOut
  public void initialize() {
    activeColor = (SFColor) getField("activeColor");
    inactiveColor = (SFColor) getField("inactiveColor");
    color = (SFColor) getEventOut("color");
  }

  // Handle events
  public void processEvent(Event event) {
    if (event.getName().equals("isActive")) {
      if (((ConstSFBool)event.getValue()) == true)
        color.setValue(activeColor);
      else color.setValue(inactiveColor);
    }
  }
}
```

Since there's only one incoming event in the Script node, the first **if** statement in this example isn't strictly necessary; if this script receives any event, it must be an *isActive* event. The event name test is included here for demonstration purposes.

Integer Interpolator

The SwitchInterpolator prototype from the eagle-animation example contains the URL of a compiled Java file called *Float2Int.class*. That file is compiled from the source code in another file, *Float2Int.java*:

```
import vrml.*;
import vrml.field.*;
import vrml.node.*;

class Float2Int extends Script {

  // Declare eventOut
  private SFInt32 value_changed;

  // Set up eventOut
  public void initialize() {
    value_changed = (SFInt32) getEventOut("value_changed");
  }

  // Handle events
  public void processEvent(Event event) {
    if (event.getName().equals("scalarValue")) {
      value_changed.setValue(
        ((ConstSFFloat)event.getValue()).intValue());
    }
  }
}
```

State Retention

The SPARK_TOGGLE script from the spark-animation two-state example contains the URL of a compiled Java file called *AnimationToggle.class*. That file is compiled from the source code in another file, *AnimationToggle.java*:

```
import vrml.*;
import vrml.field.*;
import vrml.node.*;

class AnimationToggle extends Script{

  // Declare field
  private SFBool isAnimating;
```

```
    // Declare eventOuts
    private SFTime startTime;
    private SFTime stopTime;
    private SFInt32 whichChoice;

    // Set up eventOut
    public void initialize() {
      isAnimating = (SFBool) getField("isAnimating");
      startTime = (SFTime) getEventOut("startTime");
      stopTime = (SFTime) getEventOut("stopTime");
      whichChoice = (SFInt32) getEventOut("whichChoice");
    }

    // Handle events
    public void processEvent(Event event) {
      if (event.getName().equals("touchTime")) {
        if (isAnimating.getValue() == false) {
          isAnimating.setValue(true);
          startTime.setValue((ConstSFTime)event.getValue());
          whichChoice.setValue(1);
        }
        else {
          isAnimating.setValue(false);
          stopTime.setValue((ConstSFTime)event.getValue());
          whichChoice.setValue(0);
        }
      }
    }
  }
}
```

Viewpoint Binding

The TourAnimator prototype from the viewpoint-binding example
contains the URL of a compiled Java file called *HandleTour.class*. That file is
compiled from the source code in another file, *HandleTour.java*:

```
import vrml.*;
import vrml.field.*;
import vrml.node.*;

class HandleTour extends Script{

  // Declare field
  private SFVec3f position;
  private SFRotation orientation;
  private SFBool inRange;
```

```
            private SFNode orientInterp;
            private SFNode posInterp;

            // Declare eventOuts
            private SFBool bind;
            private SFBool isBound;
            private SFTime startTime;
            private SFVec3f position_changed;
            private SFRotation orientation_changed;

            // Set up fields and eventOuts
            public void initialize() {
              position = (SFVec3f) getField("position");
              orientation = (SFRotation) getField("orientation");
              inRange = (SFBool) getField("inRange);
              orientInterp = (SFNode) getField("orientInterp");
              posInterp = (SFNode) getField("posInterp");
              bind = (SFBool) getEventOut("bind");
              isBound = (SFBool) getEventOut("isBound");
              startTime = (SFTime) getEventOut("startTime");
              position_changed = (SFVec3f)
                                  getEventOut("position_changed");
              orientation_changed = (SFRotation)
                                    getEventOut("orientation_changed");
            }

            // Handle events
            public void processEvent(Event event) {
              if (event.getName().equals("set_position")) {
                position.setValue((SFVec3f)event.getValue());
              }
              if (event.getName().equals("set_orientation")) {
                orientation.setValue((SFRotation)event.getValue());
              }
              if (event.getName().equals("touchTime")) {
                if (inRange.getValue() == true)
                {
                  position_changed.setValue(position);
                  orientation_changed.setValue(orientation);
                  isBound.setValue(true);
                  posInterp.keyValue[0].setValue(position);
                  orientInterp.keyValue[0].setValue(orientation);
                  startTime.setValue((SFTime)event.getValue());
                }
              }
```

```
    if (event.getName().equals("set_inRange")) {
      inRange.setValue((SFBool)event.getValue());
    }
    if (event.getName().equals("set_animating")) {
      if (((SFBool)event.getValue()) == false)
        isBound.setValue(false);
    }
  }
}
```

Glossary

API

Application Programming Interface. VRML 2.0 includes a set of browser API function calls that provide an interface for controlling viewpoints, backgrounds, and navigation information.

attenuate

To become less intense; to become fainter. The PointLight and SpotLight nodes have *attenuation* fields that allow you to specify how light drops off as distance from the light source increases. (Not all browsers support full lighting attenuation.)

authoring tool

A software application, such as Cosmo Create 3D, used by content creators to build VRML worlds. The application has a graphical user interface so that the scene designer does not, in most cases, need to work directly with the VRML file.

avatar

Geometry within the scene that represents the user. The location of the avatar corresponds to the user's viewing position.

backface culling

Process of eliminating the polygonal faces whose normals point away from the viewer. These faces don't need to be drawn because they aren't visible.

behaviors

A general term for the ability in VRML 2.0 to animate objects and to specify interactions among objects through output events, input events, routes, sensors, and scripts. Behaviors enable an author to specify how an object acts and reacts, not just how it looks.

billboard

The Billboard node, which usually contains a 2D surface that rotates around a specified axis so that it always faces the viewpoint. This node commonly uses 2D textures as a substitute for more complex 3D objects to improve performance. The Billboard node can also specify screen-aligned objects.

bind

To activate a Background, Viewpoint, or NavigationInfo node (referred to as *bindable* nodes). To specify a new bindable node, use the *bind* event with value TRUE. Only one bindable node of each type can be bound at a time. The browser maintains a stack for each type of bindable node.

bindings

A library of API function calls that use a particular programming language.

Boolean

A value that is either TRUE or FALSE.

bounding box

The smallest rectangular box that encloses a graphical object.

CGI

Common Gateway Interface. CGI is a method for communicating between a browser and a server for processing user input through a script and generating output that is sent back to the user. The script is usually placed in the *cgi-bin* directory on the server.

clamping

Limiting values to a certain range; in texture mapping, indicates that a texture should not be repeated. When a texture is clamped, the last row of pixels is repeated as much as necessary to fill the face of an object.

collision proxy

A simplified geometry used in place of the actual geometry to speed up collision testing.

coplanar

Existing in the same plane. A set of points is coplanar if a single plane passes through all of them.

crease angle

A tolerance angle, in radians, that determines whether edges should be faceted or smooth-shaded. If the angle between the normals for two adjacent faces is less than or equal to the specified value for the *creaseAngle* field of certain geometry nodes, the edge between the two faces is smooth-shaded. If the angle between the normals for two adjacent faces is greater than the specified *creaseAngle*, the edge between the two faces is faceted.

culling

Selecting objects to be ignored during rendering. Most browsers cull the view before they draw anything in the scene so that they don't waste time computing information about objects that aren't currently in view.

cumulative

Adding to the previous value. In VRML, transformations accumulate from parent to child (that is, they add to each other).

default

Built-in value used when you do not explicitly specify a value.

drag sensor

Sensor that generates events when a user moves a pointing device while holding down the device's button.

event

An indication that something has happened. Outgoing events send their values to incoming events, which receive values. The connection between two events is called a *route*.

field

A data element contained in a node. Each field has a name and a value of a particular type.

field of view

An angle, in radians, that together with the *orientation* and *position* of the viewpoint determines which parts of the scene are visible in the window at a given time.

firewall

A computer and a router that control the flow of traffic between the Internet and an internal network of computers. The firewall protects the internal network from access by outside sources.

flipbook animation

An animation created by displaying a series of texture maps onto a piece of geometry.

Gouraud shading

A method of interpolating colors for sophisticated shading of an object. The colors assigned to each vertex are interpolated linearly between the vertices and across each face of the polygon to achieve smooth gradations of color.

index

A number associated with an element in a list. Indexed lists in VRML start with 0. In an IndexedFaceSet, for example, each vertex has an associated index (the first point listed has index 0, the second point has index 1, and so on). The faces of the polygon are formed by connecting the indices in the order specified.

instances

Multiple references to the same node within a file. A name for the node is defined with DEF. Subsequent references to the node refer to it through the word USE plus the name of the node. Changes to the named node are reflected in all instances of that node.

instancing

Referring to the same node multiple times within a file. You first define a name for the node (with DEF). To reuse the node, specify USE and the name of the node. This creates a reference to the original node, not a copy of it.

interpolator

A node that uses a mathematical formula to "fill in" the values between two specified values, transitioning smoothly from one to the other. The values can be color, position, size, orientation, or normal values.

JPEG

Joint Photographic Experts Group. In this book, JPEG refers to a form of lossy image compression designed by this group. VRML 2.0 browsers must support JPEG image compression.

keyframes

Key poses at particular points in time, used to create an animation sequence. The animation defines the keyframes and then uses interpolators to create the in-between values to transition smoothly from one keyframe to the next.

light

A lighting node (a DirectionalLight, PointLight, or SpotLight node). In VRML, a lighting node describes how part of the scene should be lit, but it does not specify geometry for the light itself.

lighting equation

A formula for calculating how objects are shaded. This equation combines the colors of the object with the colors of the lights in the scene. It does not compute the shadows that would be cast by opaque objects between the light and the object being lit.

linear interpolation

Generating values mathematically by creating a smooth ramp of values from the first value to the second value.

linked

Also *hyperlinked*. In VRML, objects can be linked to other VRML worlds or to HTML documents using the Anchor node. The user clicks a specified piece of geometry to load the new VRML world or the HTML document. Sound and movie files can also be linked.

local coordinate system

The coordinate system defined by an object's Transform node (but before any of its parent Transform nodes are applied).

LOD

Level of Detail. An LOD node specifies alternate representations for an object in the scene, with varying levels of complexity, and is used to enhance performance.

lossy

Refers to image compression techniques where some information from the original image is lost during compression. Reconstructing an image that was processed using a lossy form of compression results in a file that is different from the original, uncompressed file. By contrast, with *lossless* compression techniques, there is an exact match between the original data and the data reconstructed from the compressed original.

marker

A screen-aligned icon that is linked to other documents.

MPEG

Motion Picture Experts Group. In this book, MPEG refers to the standard video format designed by this group. VRML 2.0 browsers must support the MPEG format for movies.

multiple-valued

A field that can contain more than one value of a particular type. Multiple-valued fields have names that begin with MF. SF indicates a single-valued field.

name

A character string assigned to a node with DEF. Naming a node allows you to refer to the same node multiple times in a file without re-creating the node itself.

nesting

Adding a node as the child of another node of the same type. For example, Transform nodes can be nested, in which case their transformations have a cumulative effect.

node

The basic unit of a VRML file. A node contains data for the scene in the form of *fields*. Some nodes also contain *events* (outgoing, incoming, or both).

normal vector

A directional line perpendicular to a surface, with a length of 1. A vector starts at the origin and passes through the given point.

origin

The point (0, 0, 0), where all simple geometry nodes are initially created.

panorama

Distant scenery, such as mountains and clouds, that does not translate or scale with respect to the viewer. The panorama is specified in the Background node.

performance LOD

An LOD node that does not specify explicit ranges for use of its *levels*. Instead, the browser chooses the appropriate level to maintain an acceptable interactive frame rate.

piecewise linear

Composed of straight-line segments (as opposed to being composed of actual curves). In the Extrusion node, the *crossSection* and *spine* paths are both piecewise linear.

planar

Indicates that all of a polygon's vertices are in the same plane.

PNG

Portable Network Graphics Specification. A standard format for lossless bitmapped image files. VRML 2.0 browsers must support the PNG format.

properties

Surface attributes of a shape, which include color, smoothness, shininess, and texture. Properties are defined in an Appearance node. Nodes commonly used to specify an object's appearance are Material, ImageTexture, MovieTexture, and PixelTexture.

prototype

A template for a new node type, which defines the fields and events that form the interface to the node. A prototype is defined as a combination of standard (previously defined) nodes.

proxy server

A computer that routes packets between an internal computer network and the outside world. The proxy server is a security measure, since it prevents direct interaction between the internal and external networks.

RGB

A color system that uses red, green, and blue color components to describe a color.

right-handed

Used to describe a coordinate system in which if the $+x$ axis points to the right, and the $+y$ axis points up, the $+z$ axis points toward the viewer (out of the screen).

route

Connection from an outgoing event to an incoming event of the same type.

scene

The collection of 3D objects defined in a VRML file; also referred to as a *world*, especially if it is large and immersive.

script

A program, written in a language such as VRMLScript, Java, or Perl, that is contained in the Script node. A script receives incoming events, processes them, and generates outgoing events. It is useful in controlling animations, binding viewpoints, backgrounds, and navigation information, and in manipulating the scene hierarchy.

sensor

A node that monitors a particular type of event, processes the input, and generates output events. Some sensors process user input from a pointing device such as a mouse, joystick, or trackball, and generate events. Other sensors respond to the passage of time (TimeSensor) and the location of the viewpoint in the scene (ProximitySensor).

server

A computer connected to the Internet and dedicated to providing data over the Web.

shape

The combination of geometry and appearance properties that describe a 3D object in a VRML scene.

siblings

Nodes that are children of the same parent node.

stack

A list of nodes, ordered from bottom to top, with the most recently added node on top. The usual analogy is to compare a stack to a nested collection of cafeteria trays in a spring-loaded container. When a tray is removed from the top of the stack, the springs at the bottom of the container *pop* the remaining trays up to fill the emptied space. When a tray is added to the top of the stack, the other trays are *pushed* down.

texture map

A 2D image that is applied to a surface. Also referred to as a *texture*. It can be in JPEG or PNG format.

transformations

Geometric changes that affect the coordinate system in which an object is drawn, by translating, rotating, and scaling the coordinates, as well as by changing the center of rotation and scaling for an object and changing the rotational orientation for scaling the object.

translating

Moving an object in any or all directions (x, y, z).

transparency

Degree to which light passes through an object. Transparency is specified in the Material node. Some textures also contain a transparency element.

UTF-8

The 8-bit character encoding scheme used by VRML 2.0. An acronym within an acronym: 8-bit UCS Transformation Format (UTF). UCS stands for Universal Coded Character Set. The ISO/IEC 10646 standard specifies the Universal Multiple-Octet Coded Character Set. This character set is used for the representation, transmission, interchange, processing, storage, input, and presentation of the written form of the languages of the world, as well as additional symbols.

vertex-based

Refers to shapes that are defined as a series of x, y, z coordinates, one for each vertex of the polygon. For example, the IndexedFace Set is a vertex-based node.

viewpoint

The position, orientation, and "lens angle" that define how the user sees the scene.

white space

Extra space between characters in the VRML file, created by tabs, spaces, and newlines. Commas are also treated as white space. White space adds to the readability of your files but makes them larger and thus require more transmission time. When you compress a file with *gzip*, unnecessary white space is automatically eliminated.

world coordinate system

The coordinate system for the entire scene, which is the accumulation of all transformations specified in the scene.

Index